Transdiagnostic
Emotion-Focused Therapy

Transdiagnostic
Emotion-Focused
Therapy

A Clinical Guide for Transforming Emotional Pain

Ladislav Timulak • Daragh Keogh

 AMERICAN PSYCHOLOGICAL ASSOCIATION

Published by
American Psychological Association
750 First Street, NE
Washington, DC 20002
https://www.apa.org

Order Department
https://www.apa.org/pubs/books
order@apa.org

In the U.K., Europe, Africa, and the Middle East, copies may be ordered from Eurospan
https://www.eurospanbookstore.com/apa
info@eurospangroup.com

Typeset in Charter and Interstate by Circle Graphics, Inc., Reisterstown, MD

Printer: Gasch Printing, Odenton, MD
Cover Designer: Anthony Paular Design, Newbury Park, CA

Library of Congress Cataloging-in-Publication Data

Names: Timulak, Ladislav, author. | Keogh, Daragh, author.
Title: Transdiagnostic emotion-focused therapy : a clinical guide for transforming emotional pain / by Ladislav Timulak and Daragh Keogh.
Description: Washington : American Psychological Association, 2022. | Includes bibliographical references and index.
Identifiers: LCCN 2021010648 (print) | LCCN 2021010649 (ebook) | ISBN 9781433836633 (paperback) | ISBN 9781433838057 (ebook)
Subjects: LCSH: Emotion-focused therapy. | Emotions. | Mental health.
Classification: LCC RC489.F62 T56 2022 (print) | LCC RC489.F62 (ebook) | DDC 616.89/14—dc23
LC record available at https://lccn.loc.gov/2021010648
LC ebook record available at https://lccn.loc.gov/2021010649

https://doi.org/10.1037/0000253-000

Printed in the United States of America

10 9 8 7 6 5 4 3 2 1

Dedicated to my parents and to Katka, Adam, Dominika, and Natalia.

—LT

Dedicated to Owen, Evelyn, Marian, and Holly.

—DK

Contents

Foreword

In this book, Timulak and Keogh present a valuable and cogent trans-diagnostic view of treatment that focuses on the transformation of core emotional vulnerability rather than on the treatment of symptoms. They contrast emotion-focused therapy (EFT) with more cognitive behavioral approaches to transdiagnostic treatment and show how EFT differs from a cognitive behavior approach.

The authors explain the EFT proposition that emotion dysfunction occurs not only when symptomatic secondary emotions are dysregulated but also when underlying primary emotions are disclaimed. In EFT, it is not the avoidance of symptomatic secondary emotion—like fear, anxiety, hopeless-ness, or shame—nor dysregulation of symptomatic emotion—like panic, fear, shame, and anger—that is treated by exposure or coping skills to reduce arousal. Rather, a more layered view of emotion discriminates between symp-tomatic secondary and primary emotions, both adaptive and maladaptive, and change is seen as occurring by having new emotional experiences replace old ones. A transdiagnostic EFT also stresses the importance of the dyadic regulation of affect by means of an empathically attuned relationship and the cocreation of new narratives regardless of diagnosis. The change process in EFT involves arriving at emotion by approaching, becoming aware of, allowing, tolerating, regulating, symbolizing, and accepting emotion, as well as transforming maladaptive thoughts with alternate emotional action tenden-cies and constructing new narratives informed by new emotions.

The key transdiagnostic element of EFT—core emotional vulnerability and its various expressions that transcend diagnosis—is clearly illuminated. The authors demonstrate how mental health problems are based on emotional suffering, and this is the main treatment target. EFT postulates that, despite diagnosis, addressing and transforming core painful feelings will lead to symptom alleviation and improved mental health. Furthermore, EFT asserts that emotional transformation happens in therapy through the generation of new adaptive emotional responses (e.g., self-compassion, healthy boundary-setting anger) to change old maladaptive emotions. In this view, transformation is not the mere reduction of negative affect nor the reduction of secondary, symptomatic affect by exposure, extinction, or habituation; rather, transformation is an enhancement of the experience and expression of primary emotion. Change occurs not by cognitive reappraisal but by acceptance: making sense of and transforming core painful emotions by activating adaptive emotion.

The authors' transdiagnostic approach demonstrates how patients can not only cope with symptomatic emotions but also transform underlying painful emotions of which they often were not initially aware. The necessary first step in changing emotion with emotion is to *increase* the dreaded painful underlying emotion rather than *reduce* the presenting symptomatic emotion. The aim, then, is not the extinction of the activated underlying emotion but, instead, its transformation with new experience. EFT is not based on exposure (as it is sometimes misconstrued); it focuses on memory change rather than on the inhibition of old memories. Changing emotion with emotion involves procedural learning in which old memories are changed by new experience in the psychotherapy session. Transformation involves implicit psychological processes of change through the synthesis of old elements of experience, which have been stored as emotion schematic memories, with new experiences in the session (Greenberg, 2015). This transformation works as the brain makes new implicit linkages; unlike other therapeutic approaches, EFT does not involve making the client conscious of previously denied feelings, helping them achieve new insights, or engaging in cognitive reappraisals or counterlearnings.

EFT sees people as complex, dynamic systems and is based on theories of development (J. Pascual-Leone, 1991; Piaget, 1954) rather than on learning theory. This view of functioning is more compatible with a transdiagnostic view than other approaches. In complex, self-organizing systems, emotions are not viewed as stimulus driven, nor are they explained in stimulus–organism–response (S-O-R) terms. Rather, they stem from automatic, goal-directed processes that produce action tendencies designed to reduce discrepancy between present and desired states. They are better depicted as R–O^{NGV1} systems in which responses (R) are generated to meet at least one need/goal value (NGV1) and possibly many. Although some approaches view human experience as being derived from some form of associative learning, EFT sees the human brain as having added higher level learning and meaning construction processes to the basic form of associative learning. People are not simply passive reactors to stimuli or their appraisals but are agents whose responses are determined by implicit needs and goals as well as by the anticipated effect that their responses will have. People operate by forward-modeling processes that anticipate which responses will produce which outcomes. And they are dynamic self-organizing systems that are constantly updating what they feel and do to adapt to their ever-changing environment. Seeing people as complex, holistic, meaning-making agents offers a different view of functioning than a disease model in which differential diagnosis leads to different treatments for different disorders.

Because people are multilevel learners operating at schematic and conceptual as well as associative levels of learning, integrative and transdiagnostic approaches need to tackle the whole person's self-organizing functioning and address core levels of functioning—not just symptomatic levels. This book takes important steps in offering a transdiagnostic approach to not only reduce symptomatic emotions but also transform underlying painful emotions—frequently those not initially in awareness or expressed—that are the underlying determinants of presenting problems.

—Leslie S. Greenberg, PhD
Distinguished Research Professor Emeritus
York University, Toronto, Ontario, Canada
January 2021

Acknowledgments

This book summarizes our learning over the past decade of adapting emotion-focused therapy (EFT) for various client presentations. It would not have been possible without the generous contribution of many people around us. The ideas in this book stand on the shoulders of those who have preceded us. First, we acknowledge Les Greenberg's landmark contribution to the field of emotions in psychotherapy. The book solidly stands on the learning opportunities afforded us by the generous support of Les Greenberg and Robert Elliott, who trained the first author (LT) in EFT and whose training magic also was experienced by the second author (DK). We are indebted to many other EFT scholars as well, particularly Jeanne Watson, Rhonda Goldman, Sandra Paivio, and Antonio Pascual-Leone, all of whom have shaped our thinking about EFT.

We thank all the clients and research collaborators who contributed to our learning and to the ideas presented in this book. The book is also based on projects sponsored by the Irish Health Research Board (H01388-HRA POR/2010/7 and HRA-POR-2015-1052).

A large number of research projects investigating the process of emotion transformation contributed directly to the ideas outlined in this book. Many of my (LT's) students—now colleagues—are among those contributors: thanks to Ciara Keogh, Casey O'Brien, Siobhan McNally, Andrew Dillon, Katie O'Brien, Niall Crowley, Sam Hughes, Jen Murphy, Lucy Rowell, Anne McQuaid, Richard Meacham, Peter Clare, Elena Chepukova, Nora O'Keeffe, Rosie O'Flynn, Aoife Durcan, Hannah Cullen, Rochelle Toolan, Megan Devereux, Bridget Lucey,

Anne Golden, James Brosnan, Laurena Nally, Sinead Lynch, Suyi Qiu, Jessica Daily, Aaron Jackson, Julie Anne O'Connell Kent, Joana Hissa, Eva Reinhofer, Aman Kwatra, James McElvaney, and Allison Connolly. We also thank our colleagues James McElvaney, Natalie Hession, Ciaran Jennings, Sonja Schmitt, Katarina Timulakova, and Eva Reinhofer for working with us specifically on the transdiagnostic project.

I (LT) thank those students and colleagues with whom I continue to collaborate on other related EFT research projects (see our EFT research group website, https://emotionfocusedtherapygroup.ie). I hope that these studies will lead to new publications in the near future. I also thank my colleagues in the counseling psychology program at Trinity College Dublin for continuing their support of my research and for creating an excellent working environment.

We thank the American Psychological Association team, including Ida Audeh, Susan Reynolds, Joe Albrecht, and Laurel Vincenty.

I (LT) thank my family, my parents, my sister, and especially my wife, Katka, for all the support they have given me over the years. I thank my children, Adam, Dominika, and Natalia, for the many stimulating debates that have contributed to my thinking as presented in this book. In addition, I am grateful to my daughter Natalia for proofreading Chapter 10.

I (DK) thank my coauthor for extending the invitation to collaborate on this project. I also thank my parents, Owen and Evelyn, as well as my brother, Fiachra, and my sister, Róisín, for their unquestioning support. I thank my wife, Marian, for her patience regarding the many early mornings and late evenings. I also thank the many, many individuals—from Dublin to Glasgow, Toronto to Oslo—who have shared this EFT journey. Finally, I thank my clients for trusting me in your world and teaching me what we are capable of.

Transdiagnostic
Emotion-Focused
Therapy

INTRODUCTION
The Rationale for Transdiagnostic Emotion-Focused Therapy

This book is the fruit of our clinical experience and of a decade-long research program. Our experience of adapting emotion-focused therapy (EFT) for generalized anxiety (e.g., Timulak & McElvaney, 2016, 2018) in the context of high comorbidity (e.g., Timulak et al., 2017, 2018), together with our research on the transformation of core chronic painful emotions (e.g., Dillon et al., 2018; McNally et al., 2014; Timulak, 2015) and on symptomatic presentations (e.g., Murphy et al., 2017; Toolan et al., 2019), shaped our thinking about the various diagnostic groups we were encountering. In our conceptualizations, we started to differentiate between symptom-level work and work that sought to transform deeper, underlying emotional vulnerability, and we began to study both dimensions in an explicit manner. This is what we refer to as *transdiagnostic emotion-focused therapy* (EFT-T; Timulak & Keogh, 2020; Timulak et al., 2020). In this book, we seek to systematically articulate these two dimensions of working both in the context of traditional, marker-guided EFT writing (e.g., Elliott et al., 2004; Greenberg et al., 1993; see also Chapter 2, this volume) and in the context of diagnostic classification systems. In particular, we focus on the diagnostic cluster most typically addressed by transdiagnostic treatments: depression, anxiety, and related

https://doi.org/10.1037/0000253-001
Transdiagnostic Emotion-Focused Therapy: A Clinical Guide for Transforming Emotional Pain, by L. Timulak and D. Keogh

disorders, such as posttraumatic stress disorder (PTSD) and obsessive-compulsive disorder (OCD).

Although transdiagnostic EFT addresses both symptom-level presentation and core underlying vulnerability, we argue that the central work of therapy happens on the level of underlying core emotional vulnerability (e.g., Greenberg, 2017). Hence, we draw on the transformation model of working with and transforming core maladaptive painful emotion developed by A. Pascual-Leone and colleagues (A. Pascual-Leone & Greenberg, 2007a; Timulak, 2015; Timulak & Pascual-Leone, 2015).

THE CONCEPT OF TRANSDIAGNOSTIC APPROACHES TO PSYCHOTHERAPY

Psychotherapy was originally developed as a universal treatment that was more or less independent of specific diagnostic categories but, instead, tailored to the individual client by way of an idiosyncratic case conceptualization (Roy-Byrne, 2017). The advent of cognitive behavior therapy (CBT) in the 1970s and 1980s resulted in the development of therapy protocols that were diagnosis specific. This development was then further strengthened with the advent of the empirically validated (and, later, empirically supported) therapies movement that, as part of its formulation of the criteria by which therapies could be evaluated as evidence based, required therapies to be tested for specific diagnostic groups (Chambless & Hollon, 1998). This requirement naturally led to the development of single-disorder treatments (e.g., CBT for social anxiety). However, given the high comorbidity of mental health difficulties, difficulties with differential diagnosis, empirical findings about the shared etiology of mental health conditions, as well as shared psychopathology-maintaining mechanisms (Kennedy & Barlow, 2018), a reversal of this trend is starting to be seen, and we are now looking at a field in which more and more transdiagnostic treatments have started to appear.

The trend in developing transdiagnostic treatments is related to developments in our understanding of psychopathology, which suggest that discreet psychiatric disorders may have more in common than has traditionally been assumed (e.g., Caspi et al., 2014; for more about the rationale for transdiagnostic treatment, see Chapter 1, this volume). The developers of transdiagnostic therapies argue that, in contrast to traditional generic (in particular, psychodynamic and humanistic) psychotherapies, current transdiagnostic therapies either use a modular approach targeting clusters of symptoms irrespective of diagnosis or target underlying psychopathological mechanisms shared by several diagnostic groups (Sauer-Zavala et al., 2017), and thus still differ from more traditional formulations. Essentially the claim is that even though the new breed of transdiagnostic treatment formulations cut across diagnoses, these therapies are still formulated in the context of existing classification systems and engage with those systems directly by explicating the relationship between particular diagnoses and the underlying difficulties that give rise to those diagnoses.

Transdiagnostic formulations have emerged primarily within the CBT paradigm, the psychotherapeutic paradigm most closely associated with the development of disorder-specific treatments. In particular, transdiagnostic formulations have been developed in the area of treating depression and anxiety disorders in which the problem of comorbidity is particularly pronounced (e.g., Brown, Campbell, et al., 2001). For example, transdiagnostic models targeting the shared mechanism of depression and varied anxiety disorders have been created as treatments for individuals by Barlow and colleagues (Unified Protocol for Transdiagnostic Treatment of Emotional Disorders; Barlow, Farchione, Sauer-Zavala, et al., 2017) and group treatments by Norton (2012). Similar developments have been made in the area of eating disorders in which a transdiagnostic treatment has been developed to simultaneously target several types of eating disorders (Fairburn et al., 2008). Some transdiagnostic CBT formulations have moved further from the psychiatric diagnostic classification system, and although they still refer to that system, they focus instead on targeting certain psychopathological characteristics, such as perfectionism, present in several disorders (Riley et al., 2007).

These developments have led to the creation of transdiagnostic therapeutic manuals that have the potential to gradually replace protocols for single-diagnosis treatments. An important argument here is that it may be preferable to train therapists to deliver a single intervention effective at treating many disorders rather than to train them to deliver multiple single-disorder protocols. The movement toward the development of transdiagnostic treatments has also received a boost from initial evidence suggesting that transdiagnostic therapies appear to be equally effective as single-diagnosis therapies, particularly in the area of anxiety disorders and depression (Barlow, Farchione, Bullis, et al., 2017; Newby et al., 2015; Pearl & Norton, 2017).

TRANSDIAGNOSTIC EMOTION-FOCUSED THERAPY

Non-CBT therapies, such as EFT (Greenberg, 2015, 2017; Greenberg et al., 1993), were traditionally developed as generic therapies whereby the therapist met the client wherever their difficulties lay and without explicit reference to psychiatric diagnostic categories. EFT was developed in the context of the rich tradition of humanistic therapies, such as client-centered therapy (Rogers, 1951) and Gestalt therapy (Perls et al., 1994/1951). Although these classic therapies were subsequently assessed for efficacy in the context of various diagnostic groups (see Elliott et al., 2013, 2021), they did not traditionally emphasize diagnostic categorization. However, once the main features of the EFT approach were outlined in the late 1980s and early 1990s, further developments followed.

The mainstream trend (mentioned earlier) of developing therapies for specific diagnostic groups led EFT developers to adapt the therapy for a variety of presentations, such as depression (Greenberg & Watson, 2006), complex trauma (Paivio & Pascual-Leone, 2010), generalized anxiety (Timulak & McElvaney, 2018; Watson & Greenberg, 2017), and social anxiety (Elliott & Shahar, 2017). Early work has also been undertaken in adapting EFT for other diagnostic groups (for an overview of the clinical adaptations of EFT, see the edited handbook by Greenberg & Goldman, 2019). All of this work has built on efficacy research on EFT for these diagnostic groups (e.g., Goldman et al., 2006; Greenberg & Watson, 1998; Paivio & Nieuwenhuis, 2001; Shahar et al., 2017; Timulak et al., 2017; Watson et al., 2003).

In this book (see also Timulak & Keogh, 2020), we conceptualize and systematize EFT in the context of current transdiagnostic formulations (Sauer-Zavala et al., 2017) using elements of a modular transdiagnostic approach that target clusters of symptoms (i.e., primary diagnoses or presentations) while simultaneously and primarily focusing on the underlying vulnerability (i.e., chronic emotional vulnerability) shared by these varied diagnostic groups. As we (e.g., O'Brien et al., 2017; Timulak, 2015; Timulak & Pascual-Leone, 2015) and other EFT writers (e.g., Greenberg, 2017) have already outlined, and as we elaborate on within this book, this shared emotional vulnerability appears to be centered on chronic painful emotions of sadness/loneliness, shame, and fear/terror.

OVERVIEW OF THE BOOK

Part I of the book presents the theoretical underpinnings of EFT-T. Chapter 1 provides a rationale for transdiagnostic treatments in general and then specifically for emotion-focused transdiagnostic treatment. This rationale is offered particularly with regard to the nature of client difficulties (e.g., comorbidity, shared etiology) but also with reference to practical reasons, such as good treatment outcomes for both primary and comorbid diagnoses, and pragmatic factors, such as the benefits of training therapists in one rather than multiple approaches. In Chapter 2, we present an introduction to EFT as traditionally conceptualized. We introduce the reader to a number of core theoretical developments within this approach in terms of our understanding of the nature of emotion-based psychopathology but also regarding the nature of therapeutic work.

Chapter 3 presents a comprehensive outline of our thinking in terms of understanding the shared emotional vulnerability at the core of psychological difficulties, such as depression, anxiety and related disorders. We also present our understanding regarding the nature of symptom-level difficulties that clients present with and that are responsible for clients' meeting diagnostic criteria for various diagnoses. We present our understanding of the interplay between underlying emotional vulnerability and symptom-level presentations as well as discuss the implications this interplay has for our treatment approach. As already stated, this approach focuses primarily on targeting an underlying vulnerability that is not defining of symptom-level presentation while also targeting those diagnosis-relevant symptoms that are the expression of this vulnerability. The chapter, thus, is decisive in outlining our model of EFT-T.

Part II essentially presents a manual for how to conduct EFT-T. The ordering of subsequent chapters follows a logic whereby we first establish foundations and then address symptom-level distress before moving on to the core work of transforming underlying emotional vulnerability. Specifically, we begin in Chapter 4 by presenting our view of the role of the therapeutic relationship in EFT-T. We propose that the relationship must create a sense of safety for clients to be able to access and explore their most vulnerable feelings. The relationship facilitates client engagement in therapeutic tasks, and it can also be a place for corrective emotional experiences, including those that result from the repair of relational ruptures. We also discuss therapist reflections on client interpersonal interactions and their interplay with client emotional processing.

Chapter 5 looks at the use of case conceptualization and its application to various types of primary difficulties (e.g., depression, social anxiety, generalized anxiety, panic disorder, PTSD, OCD). Chapter 6 focuses on working with clients who become emotionally overwhelmed. We discuss the roles of empathic holding, grounding, and instructions for self-regulating as well as experiential tasks, such as clearing a space and self-soothing. Chapter 7 describes the nature of work with the opposite problem: when clients are emotionally restricted, thus interrupting their feelings or the expression of feelings in a manner that leads to psychological difficulties. This chapter also presents an overview of the use of two-chair tasks for situational, chronic, or behavioral self-interruption.

Chapter 8 highlights the major features of working with various symptoms. It elaborates on our modular transdiagnostic approach that assumes that, although common underlying difficulties are shared by depression, anxiety, and related disorders, clusters of symptoms also may need to be addressed in a targeted way. This chapter presents several experiential tasks that target clusters of symptoms, including two-chair dialogue for self-worrying, for self-rumination, and for obsessions, self-worrying, and compulsions; and the retelling of traumatic memories. Chapter 9 introduces the two major experiential tasks that target underlying core emotional vulnerability: the two-chair dialogue for problematic self-treatment and the empty-chair dialogue for an interpersonal emotional injury. We focus on the transdiagnostic aspects of those tasks.

Chapter 10, the final chapter, considers the practicalities of delivering EFT-T. We discuss various formats of EFT-T, such as short-term, brief, and long-term therapy. We also discuss a range of practical issues, including the use of medication, life events interfering with therapy, cultural and gender considerations, the use of homework, and group and self-help formats. We provide an overview of the therapeutic process and summarize key points made in the previous chapters.

Throughout the book, we use many clinical vignettes and case examples. In some instances, they are fictional or composite examples. In other instances, we present illustrative cases or session segments based on real transcripts. In all instances in which we base our illustrations and excerpts on real clients, we have sought consent from clients for such use. Transcripts have been altered and edited both for didactic purposes and to disguise client identify, thus preserving client confidentiality.

THE INTENDED AUDIENCE

The intended audience for this book includes clinical and counseling psychologists, psychotherapists, counselors, and graduate students in those disciplines. It also includes those interested in humanistic psychotherapies or those working with typical outpatient presentations, such as depression, generalized anxiety, social anxiety, panic disorder, specific phobias, OCD, and PTSD.

The approach presented in the book is transdiagnostic. Thus, we explain therapeutic processes applicable across the aforementioned diagnoses (i.e., we focus on commonalities) and describe interventions that target specific clusters of symptoms more typical for particular diagnostic groups. The book can serve as a basis for training in EFT internationally, particularly through the network of trainings provided by the institutes organized through the International Society for Emotion Focused Therapy (see http://www.iseft.org).

I THEORETICAL
UNDERPINNINGS

1

EMOTIONAL VULNERABILITY
The Focus of Transdiagnostic Therapy

In the Introduction, we highlighted several reasons for the advent of transdiagnostic treatments. Some of these reasons are pragmatic—for example, the argument that it is logistically preferable to train practitioners in a single approach having the potential to be effective as a treatment for multiple diagnostic groups. In this chapter, we outline trends in current psychopathology research suggesting that varied psychological difficulties share common features. We briefly introduce trends among transdiagnostic therapies addressing these postulated common features. We then situate a transdiagnostic emotion-focused therapy approach (EFT-T) in the context of transdiagnostic thinking. We present the concept of emotional vulnerability as a common process at the core of various psychological difficulties. We also elaborate on the constituent elements of emotional vulnerability: chronically painful and self-defining emotional experiences of loneliness/sadness, shame, and fear.

https://doi.org/10.1037/0000253-002
Transdiagnostic Emotion-Focused Therapy: A Clinical Guide for Transforming Emotional Pain, by L. Timulak and D. Keogh

THE TRANSDIAGNOSTIC VIEW OF PSYCHOPATHOLOGY

Although there are pragmatic reasons to consider a transdiagnostic approach, the main reasons are more scientific. Principal among these are difficulties with comorbid diagnoses and a research literature increasingly pointing to the idea that shared etiological factors underpin a broad range of psychological difficulties common to many diagnostic groups. With regard to the issue of high comorbidity, it has been our experience while running several outcome trials in the context of primary care psychology services and using standard assessment instruments, such as the Structured Clinical Interview for *DSM-5* (First et al., 2015), that single-diagnosis clients are the exception rather than the rule. Using the Anxiety Disorder Schedule for the fourth edition of the *Diagnostic and Statistical Manual of Mental Disorders* (*DSM-IV*; American Psychiatric Association, 1994; DiNardo et al., 1994), an interview schedule that assesses for the main (although not all) diagnostic groups, Brown, Campbell, et al. (2001) examined the comorbidity of more than 1,000 clients visiting their outpatient research clinic. They found an 81% lifetime prevalence of comorbid conditions. Somewhat lower but still high percentages have been reported in epidemiological studies on the 12 months and lifetime prevalence of comorbidity (45% and 59%, respectively; Kessler, Berglund, et al., 2005; Kessler, Chiu, et al., 2005). These prevalence rates become further compounded when personality disorders are included (Lenzenweger et al., 2007).

Furthermore, at least with some diagnostic categories, there are potential problems in terms of reliability (e.g., Brown, Di Nardo, et al., 2001; Regier et al., 2013). For instance, comparing generalized anxiety disorder diagnoses derived from use of the two main internationally applied diagnostic systems, the *International Statistical Classification of Diseases and Related Health Problems* (*ICD*) and the *Diagnostic and Statistical Manual of Mental Disorders* (*DSM*), Slade and Andrews (2001) concluded that although both systems reported similar generalized anxiety disorder prevalence rates, the two systems were diagnosing differing groups of people.

Taken together, the aforementioned findings suggest that despite overlapping and perhaps also transient (e.g., sequential) differences in symptomatology, common factors might underlie the expression of psychopathological symptoms. Moreover, symptoms may rather be understood as phenotypical expressions of underlying psychological processes rather than indicative of disorders in their own right.

Indeed, there is now solid evidence, based on cross-sectional as well as longitudinal studies, that mental disorders as classified by the major diagnostic systems (e.g., the *DSM* and *ICD*) can, to a great extent, be explained by a general p factor conceptualized as a single dimension that elucidates the majority of psychiatric symptoms captured broadly by externalizing, internalizing, and cognitive domains (Caspi et al., 2014; Caspi & Moffitt, 2018). This p factor can explain shared risk factors, biomarkers, and response to the same therapies (Caspi & Moffitt, 2018). It is also increasingly clear that this general p factor is not simply a methodological artifact (Lahey et al., 2012, 2017). Corresponding shared mechanisms/processes are, for instance, present in structural as well as functional brain imaging studies (Lahey et al., 2017). This does not automatically mean that every single disorder is explainable purely by one factor; rather, Caspi et al. (2014) spoke in terms of dimension and compared p to a common g factor known from the conceptualization of intelligence. The evidence does suggest that mental health disorders are influenced broadly by significant shared genetic factors (e.g., Middeldorp et al., 2005; Smoller et al., 2015) and shared environmental factors (Bond et al., 2001; Caspi et al., 2014; Côté et al., 2009; McMahon et al., 2003). Environmental factors include common developmental risk factors, such as childhood maltreatment and abuse, bullying experiences, negative peer experiences, parental distress and family dysfunction, experiences of social exclusion, experiences of prejudice and stereotypically oppressive practices, socioeconomic factors, and current stressors (e.g., work-related stressors; S. B. Harvey et al., 2017).

In addition, apart from shared genetic and environmental factors, mental health disorders, clusters of disorders, and symptoms (as currently conceptualized) are also influenced by specific environmental and genetic factors that may result in a unique disorder or cluster of symptoms (Lahey et al., 2017). For instance, Shanahan et al. (2008) demonstrated that in addition to nonspecific influence of developmental/environmental factors in a longitudinal study of children between 9 and 16 years old, they could identify specific predictors for specific disorders (e.g., neglect was more common in cases of oppositional disorder) or for clusters of related disorders (e.g., a dangerous environment was more common in cases of anxiety disorders). Similar findings have been reported when disorders are paired against each other for comparison, offering evidence for both shared factors but also some more unique predictors (e.g., Moffitt et al., 2007). Furthermore, mental health difficulties are also affected by an interplay of factors—for example, the interplay of genetic and developmental environmental influences on brain integrity (Caspi et al., 2014). The problem with etiological studies, however, is that they often are studied for a particular disorder without necessarily examining the effect on other disorders in parallel.

Lahey et al. (2017) saw a parallel to their thinking about the shared and unique etiology of mental disorders in the National Institute of Mental Health Research Domain Criteria, which proposes studying constructs responsible for the presentation of psychopathology more broadly rather than simply within specific diagnoses. This broad examination of influences has the potential to lead to an understanding that could help reconceptualize our classification of mental disorders. (Caspi & Moffitt, 2018, countered that their conceptualization of a p dimension does not require changing the existing classification systems.) Lahey et al. (2017) argued for studying constructs (both genetic and developmental/environmental) that have an impact on psychopathological presentations across the currently existing diagnostic groups—with the possibility that such research may lead to a reclassifying of diagnostic systems such that these systems better match the accumulated evidence. Their dimensional approach (similar to the approach of other authors—e.g., Brown & Barlow, 2009) means that psychopathology-influencing or -explaining factors or constructs are understood as present on a continuum from norm to psychopathological and that it is the unique interplay of such factors that influence a particular psychopathological presentation at a given time.

TRANSDIAGNOSTIC PSYCHOLOGICAL THERAPIES

Lahey et al. (2017) recommended that etiological factors be studied in the context of overall psychopathology (all disorders/symptoms) because of their pleiotropic nature (i.e., one factor influences more than one disorder). They did, however, note that clusters of similar disorders/symptoms (e.g., internalized disorders) may share more in terms of etiology compared to disorders/symptoms that appear to have a qualitatively different presentation (e.g., externalized disorders). Therefore, when discussing the implications of their findings for the development of transdiagnostic treatments, they advised in favor of efforts to develop transdiagnostic treatments for groupings of "similar" disorders. One example of such an endeavor is the work of Barlow (Barlow, Farchione, Sauer-Zavala, et al., 2017) on developing a transdiagnostic treatment for emotional disorders (in particular, mood, anxiety, and related disorders) characterized by (a) intense negative emotions, (b) aversive reaction to them, and (c) an effort to avoid them or dampen them (Bullis et al., 2019).

Barlow, Farchione, Sauer-Zavala, et al. (2017) developed a transdiagnostic model that targets shared mechanisms pivotal for psychopathology as present in emotional disorders. Practically speaking, their model was developed primarily to target depression; anxiety disorders (e.g., social anxiety, general anxiety, specific phobias, panic disorder); and related disorders, such as posttraumatic stress disorder and obsessive-compulsive disorder, although broader applications are now being tested (see Barlow & Farchione, 2018). In many ways, Barlow, Farchione, Sauer-Zavala et al.'s approach was an inspiration for our own work; thus, what the reader will find in this book particularly pertains to this class of disorders (i.e., depression, anxiety, and related disorders).

Barlow, Farchione, Sauer-Zavala, et al.'s (2017) approach, firmly embedded in the cognitive behavior therapy (CBT) tradition, targets the shared mechanisms of what they defined as *emotional disorders*: negative emotionality (neuroticism), negative appraisal of emotions, and avoidance or dampening of unwelcomed emotions (Bullis et al., 2019; Kennedy & Barlow, 2018). Kennedy and Barlow (2018) particularly focused on the underlying shared factor of neuroticism because it has an extensive empirical literature behind it and is firmly anchored in the behavioral tradition. Barlow and colleagues (Kennedy & Barlow, 2018; Rosellini et al., 2015) discussed neuroticism in the context of overlapping constructs, such as negative affect and trait anxiety. In their view, neuroticism is the major emotional vulnerability that, coupled with negative attitude toward (negative) emotions and efforts to avoid or dampen those emotions, leads to the development of emotional disorders. Their transdiagnostic treatment thus targets these three interacting processes by seeking to increase experiential tolerance of negative emotions by cultivating a more flexible appraisal of such emotions and by promoting behavior that engages with, rather than seeks to avoid or dampen, negative emotions (Barlow, Farchione, Sauer-Zavala, et al., 2017). The approach we present in this book also focuses on emotional vulnerability; however, our understanding of emotional vulnerability and our strategies for working with emotional vulnerability substantially differ from the understanding and approaches proposed in the Unified Protocol for Transdiagnostic Treatment of Emotional Disorders (Unified Protocol; Barlow, Farchione, Sauer-Zavala, et al., 2017) framework (see the next section on transdiagnostic conceptualization and EFT).

Barlow and colleagues (Kennedy & Barlow, 2018; Rosellini et al., 2015) discussed their conceptualization in the context of corresponding constructs, such as experiential avoidance, emotion suppression, and anxiety sensitivity. Each of these constructs has yielded original research that can help with shaping the understanding of emotional difficulties and that can be informative in terms of treatment. These authors also advocated for a multidimensional assessment of clinically relevant constructs that may inform case conceptualization in practice (Boettcher & Conklin, 2018; Rosellini et al., 2015). In addition to neuroticism and avoidance, this multidimensional assessment considers overlapping constructs, such as depressed mood, autonomic arousal, somatic anxiety, social evaluation concerns, intrusive cognitions, traumatic reexperiencing and dissociation, and positive temperament—which is viewed as a buffer to the others. These dimensions are further considered in their transdiagnostic treatment planning.

While Barlow, Farchione, Sauer-Zavala, et al. (2017) focused their conceptualization on negative emotions (emotionality), their negative appraisal, and their avoidance, others, such as scholars in the United Kingdom (e.g., A. Harvey et al., 2004; Mansell et al., 2008), have looked at common cognitive and behavioral processes that cut across Axis I (as conceptualized in the *DSM-IV*; American Psychiatric Association, 1994) disorders. They have highlighted problems with attention (e.g., selective attention, attentional avoidance), memory (e.g., selective, overgeneral), reasoning (e.g., biases, emotion-based), thinking (e.g., ruminations, problematic beliefs), and behavior (e.g., avoidance, safety-focused) that are shared by many disorders. Targeting those problematic processes should then, according to them, be the focus of transdiagnostic treatments. So, for example, these transdiagnostic approaches focus on higher order constructs, such as the perfectionism that is present in depression, anxiety disorders, and eating disorders, on the hypothesis that a treatment focused on this construct should lead to improvements in these disorders (e.g., Egan et al., 2011, 2014). Given the overlap (e.g., Shafran et al., 2002) between the concepts of perfectionism and of self-criticism, and that self-criticism is targeted by emotion-focused therapy (EFT; e.g., Shahar et al., 2012), the transdiagnostic concept of perfectionism is of interest to us (see Chapter 9, this volume).

TRANSDIAGNOSTIC CONCEPTUALIZATION AND EFT: BRIDGING THE GAP

These transdiagnostic treatment conceptualizations emanating from within the CBT paradigm (e.g., Unified Protocol of Barlow, Farchione, Sauer-Zavala, et al., 2017; perfectionism-focused treatment discussed in Egan et al., 2014) focus on theoretically important constructs (e.g., negative emotionality and its avoidance, perfectionism), the addressing of which is intended to bring about a broad-spectrum improvement in symptomatic presentation—in other words, a reduction in depression and anxiety. The constructs targeted in these cognitive behavior transdiagnostic approaches are theoretically rich and are supported by empirical evidence establishing their relevance to mental health. They also readily inform therapeutic strategies. They are what we would refer to as midlevel constructs because the etiology leading to their manifestation at problematic levels (on a dimension from normal to psychopathological) is multifactored. They constitute what Sauer-Zavala et al. (2017) referred to as shared mechanism variables that need to be targeted by transdiagnostic treatments.

Looking at these constructs from an emotion-focused perspective, we see their relevance. For instance, from an EFT perspective, negative emotionality can be understood in terms of *primary maladaptive emotions* (Greenberg, 2017; Greenberg & Safran, 1989), that is, the chronic self-defining emotions (and emotional vulnerabilities) postulated by EFT as being at the core of psychopathology. Perfectionism, as mentioned earlier, overlaps with self-criticism that from an EFT perspective is understood as a form of self-relating that generates particularly chronic experiences of shame (e.g., Greenberg, 2015; Shahar et al., 2012; Timulak, 2015).

Working with negative emotionality, its negative appraisal, and its experiential avoidance is relevant for CBT interventions that seek to build tolerance of negative emotions, more flexible appraisal of emotion, and a more proactive behavioral engagement that would counteract emotional avoidance. However, from an EFT perspective, the concept of negative emotionality does not have much explanatory utility. Indeed, the term "negative" is not even used in EFT theory, because we see all types of emotions as potentially adaptive or maladaptive depending on a particular context rather than as negative per se (Greenberg, 2017). In EFT-T, we also seek to work with midlevel constructs that are central to psychopathology and that underlie symptomatic presentation. We focus our attention on, and are particularly interested in, the construct of emotional vulnerability and particular expressions of emotional vulnerability. Specifically, we are interested in those chronic emotions and emotion schemes that are idiosyncratic to and defining for each client (e.g., chronically feeling alone) and that indicate what (emotional) needs (e.g., for connection) are not being met for the client in important relationships or life projects.

Originally, in EFT conceptualizations, these were referred to as primary maladaptive emotions (Greenberg et al., 1993; Greenberg & Safran, 1989) or, somewhat more poetically, as core emotional pain (Greenberg & Goldman, 2007). Historically, given that EFT is a process-focused approach (i.e., interested more in how people process their experience rather than what particular content is being processed), there was a reluctance to specify which emotions might be at the core of clients' vulnerability. Greenberg and other authors typically offered examples of chronic painful emotions but hesitated to offer anything resembling a definitive list of them. More recently, our own empirical work and the work of other authors has suggested that chronic emotional experiences (also conceptualized as problematic emotion schemes; Greenberg, 2017; Greenberg et al., 1993; see also Chapter 2, this volume) produced in interaction with the environment take the form of idiosyncratic variations and mixtures of loneliness/sadness (e.g., "I am alone"), shame (e.g., "I am worthless"), or fear (e.g., "I am scared"; e.g., Dillon et al., 2018; Hissa et al., 2020; McNally et al., 2014; O'Brien et al., 2019; A. Pascual-Leone & Greenberg, 2007a).

EMOTIONAL VULNERABILITY (CORE EMOTIONAL PAIN) AS THE FOCUS OF EFT-T

The chronic painful emotions of loneliness/sadness, shame, and fear, as well as their corresponding unmet needs (e.g., to be connected, to be valued, to be safe), are postulated by us as being the primary focus of EFT-T. We want to transform these specific emotional vulnerabilities as idiosyncratically present in clients with depression, anxiety, and related disorders. We postulate that addressing and transforming these chronic feelings through EFT interventions will lead to symptom alleviation and improved mental health. This emotional transformation happens in therapy through the generation of adaptive emotional responses (e.g., self-compassion, healthy boundary-setting anger) to the unmet emotional needs embedded in these chronic painful emotions and as a consequence of the ensuing restructuring of problematic emotion schemes (see Chapter 2). The process is sequential, moving from building a capacity to access and tolerate painful emotions (similar to overcoming emotional avoidance in the Unified Protocol; Barlow, Farchione, Sauer-Zavala, et al., 2017) to focusing on the self–other and self–self processes at the center of problematic emotion schemes, accessing chronic primary maladaptive emotions, articulating the unmet needs embedded in those emotions, and ultimately transforming those emotions through the generation of adaptive healthy emotional responses.

EFT-T also addresses problematic symptom presentations (e.g., depression, anxiety) that are conceptualized as phenotypical presentations of more fundamental, chronic emotional vulnerabilities. The core of the work in EFT, however, is focused on transforming the underlying chronic emotional vulnerabilities (i.e., chronic loneliness/sadness, shame, and fear, as well as their idiosyncratic constellations). Because all emotions can also be experienced in an adaptive form (e.g., it is adaptive to feel some shame when one transgresses against one's own values), when referring to chronic painful loneliness/ sadness, shame, and fear, we specifically talk about maladaptive manifestations of these emotions. Let us inspect those chronic problematic emotions in the context of existing empirical literature.

Loneliness/Sadness

Loneliness can be an adaptive emotional experience. Loneliness, sadness, or loss informs us that we have needs for connection and its variations (e.g., love, closeness, community). When an emotional experience of loneliness or sadness leads to us eliciting contact or restoring connection, it prompts us to function in an adaptive way to fulfill our needs for interaction and belonging with others. These types of healthy and adaptive experiences, however, are not typically the reason why somebody develops psychological difficulties. What gets focused on in therapy, rather, are maladaptive forms of loneliness/sadness that do not inform adaptive action but instead lead to resignation (e.g., depression) or anxiety about forthcoming experiences of sadness, loneliness, or loss.

Emotional experiencing and expression of loneliness and sadness can take various forms. During therapy sessions, when clients are at their most vulnerable, we have observed feelings of loneliness/sadness expressed with phrases such as "I feel lonely," "I feel alone," "I feel not loved," "I feel on my own," "I feel empty," "I have nobody to turn to," "I do not have anybody," "I miss my [close person]," "I never had [her/his] love [again, a close person]," and "I feel sad" (e.g., O'Brien et al., 2019). Client expressions of sadness and loneliness can also be combined with feelings of shame (e.g., "I was rejected, so I feel alone") or fear (e.g., "I am alone and unprotected").

The basic psychological research on loneliness, loss, and experiences of exclusion suggests that in its chronic and nonadaptive forms, loneliness has a detrimental effect on overall health, including psychopathological symptoms (Cacioppo & Patrick, 2008). The negative impact of loneliness may include difficulties with the cardiovascular system (Hawkley et al., 2003), immune system functioning (Pressman et al., 2005), high levels of stress hormones, and difficulties with sleep (Cacioppo & Patrick, 2008). Many chronic health difficulties may be further exacerbated by experiences of increased loneliness and isolation resulting from the chronic illness (Petitte et al., 2015). People with a chronic sense of loneliness are also more likely to engage in problematic behavior, such as unhealthy food and alcohol consumption as well as lack of exercise (Cacioppo & Patrick, 2008).

Neuroscientific research (see Eisenberger, 2011, 2015) suggests that experiences of loss, exclusion, and rejection share neural regions with physical pain. (While exclusion points to a sense of loneliness, rejection implies a combination of loneliness and shame—e.g., the shame of not being of value; this is a thin line that we discuss in other parts of this book.) Physical and emotional pain in the form of exclusion have also been shown to interact in an interesting way; for instance, the mild experience of emotional pain (e.g., exclusion by strangers) has been shown to increase physical pain sensitivity (lowering the threshold for tolerance of physical intrusion), whereas a more drastic experimental manipulation (e.g., suggesting that you will end up alone in life) can result in an overall sense of resignation, including physical resignation in a form of analgesia (Chen & Williams, 2011; DeWall & Baumeister, 2006; Eisenberger, 2011).

Animal and human studies (see the review in Way & Taylor, 2011) suggest that there may also be differences in genetic predispositions that color how people experience the presence of others and how susceptible we are to the optimal presence of others, particularly caring others. These studies also show the impact the caring presence of others has on biological predispositions when processing social interactions much later in life (e.g., the absence of a caring presence negatively affects levels of oxytocin, which, in turn, increases the likelihood of irritability later in life; see Way & Taylor, 2011). Theoretically, we are particularly interested in pivotal experiences that may lead to the development of a sense of loneliness, loss, and sadness. For instance, there are suggestions that early experiences of parental loss may have psychological but also long-term physiological effects (Luecken, 1998, 2008; Nicolson, 2004). Overall, the caring and loving presence of a stable caregiver has an important affect-regulating impact (Tronick, 2005).

Early life experiences of loneliness in peer relationships are also influential (Asher & Paquette, 2003). Such experiences are not only subjectively experienced as highly unpleasant and upsetting, but they also shape future experiences and appear to have the potential to exert a long-term impact (Parker et al., 2006). Indeed, every developmental stage brings unique risks (Qualter et al., 2015). However, as mentioned earlier, we are particularly interested in pivotal periods that we hypothesize become quite defining of the experience of loneliness and also defining of perceptions of the self, others, and the world.

The broader societal or community context may contribute to painful experiences of loneliness (e.g., Fox et al., 2020), too. Being a part of a minority or marginalized group (e.g., culturally or through being different from the "norm") can bring experiences of exclusion and not belonging that can leave a lasting scar. Part of the power of these experiences of exclusion may result from instances of exclusion that constitute part of a wider societal norm—for example, whereby a larger segment of society legitimizes practices of excluding and forgetting people belonging to a marginalized group. Cultural context also affects one's relationship with one's own emotional vulnerability, thus influencing internal attitudes toward vulnerability and its expression as well as ways of connecting with others and seeking support.

Pivotal experiences shape future orientation and future emotional processing of similar situations, particularly interactions with others. From an EFT perspective, they are seen as shaping the development of problematic emotion schemes (Greenberg, 2017), a concept we fully present in the next chapter. Indeed, there are empirical suggestions that people who experience chronic loneliness can sense that loneliness even in the presence of other people (Cacioppo & Patrick, 2008). Thus, their perception and experience of interaction is not sufficient to fulfill their need for connection. We hypothesize that when current triggers resemble those historically significant situations that gave rise to problematic feelings of aloneness in the past, individuals experience a similarly intense experience in the here and now. From an EFT perspective, we conceptualize the memory-based ways we process new interactions in terms of emotion schemes. Problematic emotional schematic processing can occur whereby the individual develops a proneness to emotionally process current situations in a way that triggers a chronic sense of loneliness, loss, or sadness. This processing may be coupled with a tendency to interrupt or avoid feelings as well as a tendency to avoid those situations that could trigger such feelings. Thus, an individual might become avoidant of social contact, and that avoidance then further solidifies a vicious circle of experienced loneliness.

New experiences of loneliness, sadness, and loss activate and are experienced in the context of past painful experiences of loneliness, sadness, or loss, further frustrating and aggravating the pain of the unmet needs for closeness, contact, love, or care embedded in these feelings. These needs thus remain chronically unmet, and the individual may become either apprehensive about having these needs frustrated again (e.g., social anxiety) or resigned to the pointlessness of trying to have them fulfilled (e.g., depression, resignation). Instead of experiencing fresh sadness and longing, the individual feels apprehension and anxiety or resignation and depression, or a mixture of the two. We refer to this level of distress (i.e., the symptoms of anxiety and depression) as *symptomatic distress*.

Within the domain of behavior, according to a comprehensive account by Cacioppo and Patrick (2008), people with a chronic sense of loneliness can be less skilled at eliciting cooperation with others or at seeking support. They may be less trusting that others are interested in their presence and may expect abandonment (Jones et al., 1981). Indeed, low expectations for closeness and intimacy may increase the likelihood that individuals miss signs of the potential for intimacy (MacDonald et al., 2011).

A variation on loneliness/sadness is the experience of loss, which may present in various forms. Most typical is the loss of a person (Stroebe et al., 2008). When that person is someone (e.g., parent, carer, partner, sibling) who, either developmentally or currently, constituted a primary source of emotional support for the individual (i.e., the bond has had an important emotion regulatory function), the loss may pose a huge upset. The loss of someone in your care (e.g., a child) also may be particularly difficult. Typical are losses linked to bodily or life role/project changes resulting from chronic illnesses, such as cancer (Connolly-Zubot et al., 2020). Losses can also be linked to different developmental stages (e.g., aging). In these circumstances, the pain of the current loss is typically experienced in combination with pain related to previous losses both of people important to the individual and of aspects of life important to the individual's sense of self. Losses in developmentally sensitive periods may contribute to the formation of problematic emotion schemes such that further losses or potential losses become emotionally unbearable.

In therapy, we try to restructure these problematic emotion schemes through the generation of vivid experiences of connection, care, and compassion. Typically, this happens in the form of imaginary chair dialogues that we use to foster vivid emotional experience (see Part II of this book), and through the corrective, caring, and compassionate emotional presence of the therapist. Outside therapy, caring and connecting experiences in close relationships may serve as important buffers to mitigate emotional vulnerabilities related to loneliness, sadness, and loss. These experiences may occur between family members, or among friends, but are particularly powerful in the context of close intimate relationships, one of the functions of which is to provide emotional support, thus facilitating emotional regulation (Greenberg & Goldman, 2008; Greenberg & Johnson, 1988; Johnson, 2004). This is a domain in which EFT offers not only a comprehensive theory but also an applied contribution (e.g., couples therapy, couples retreats).

Indeed, ample evidence shows that the presence of a caring partner or spouse has a calming effect—even to the point of increasing the physical pain threshold (e.g., the famous hand-holding experiments; Coan et al., 2006; Master et al., 2009). This pertains to loneliness but even more so to fear and tolerance of trauma (see the later section on fear). Indeed, the effect of caring for and loving another person in one's life appears to have implications for many aspects of life, including one's own physical health (e.g., Holt-Lunstad et al., 2008; Kiecolt-Glaser & Newton, 2001), whereas difficulties within a couple's relationship have been shown to have a detrimental impact across many domains of functioning (Umberson et al., 2006). Theoretically (e.g., Greenberg & Goldman, 2008), many conflicts within relationships can be understood as linked to underlying vulnerabilities among which loneliness often plays a significant part.

Shame

As with experiences of loneliness/sadness/loss, experiences of shame may be adaptive. Shame can inform us that we have transgressed against our own values (or external values that we respect) and that we may want to make amends for that transgression. Shame that informs adaptive actions (e.g., making amends) typically is unrelated to the emotional vulnerability at the center of psychological difficulties. Therefore, when we talk about shame-based problematic emotion schemes, we again refer not to these experiences but to those shameful emotional experiences defining of the self that do not lead to adaptive action but, instead, impede healthy functioning.

Experiences of chronic shame may overlap with experiences of loneliness/ sadness because the experience of the self as shameful, defective, or unworthy may include the experience of the self as unworthy of the acceptance and company of others. In reality, many experiences of shame are intertwined with experiences of social/interpersonal rejection, although they also may be a result of self-judgment linked to particular interpersonal and social contexts. MacDonald et al. (2011) summarized a series of experiments illustrating how rejection (social threat) has an additive and independent effect when compared with noninclusion alone. Within the therapy session, our and other EFT studies (e.g., Dillon et al., 2018; Hissa et al., 2020; McNally et al., 2014; O'Brien et al., 2019; A. Pascual-Leone & Greenberg, 2007a) have shown that shame can take the form of client expressions, such as "I feel ashamed," "I feel embarrassed," "I feel worthless," "I feel humiliated," "I feel unlovable," "I feel inadequate," "I feel like a failure," "I feel flawed," "I feel guilty," "I am broken," "I can't handle things," "I feel/am stupid," "I am incompetent," "I am awkward/weird," "I feel small/like a child," "I am immature," and "I am weak."

Psychologically, experiences of rejection have the potential to not only evoke feelings of shameful unworthiness but also trigger shutdown, avoidance, and withdrawal (DeWall & Bushman, 2011; MacDonald et al., 2011) or the opposite: irritability and aggression (DeWall & Bushman, 2011; DeWall et al., 2011; Leary et al., 2006). In EFT, we view both withdrawal and avoidance (i.e., internalizing symptoms commonly associated with both depression and anxiety) and irritability and hostility (i.e., externalizing, problematic anger-based symptoms) as secondary symptomatic expressions of underlying shame-associated vulnerable emotional experiences (see Chapter 3). The actual form symptom-level expression takes is likely a result of an interaction between genetic (e.g., Caspi et al., 2002; Way & Taylor, 2011) and social/developmental/environmental (Davidson & Demaray, 2007; Reitz et al., 2006) factors. Problematic symptoms then further compound difficulties in interaction with others (e.g., socially anxious individuals may come across as awkward in social interactions), thus further aggravating the individual's experience of rejection and shame (MacDonald et al., 2011).

As we highlighted earlier in our discussion about loneliness, experiences of rejection bring an immediate but also a potentially delayed physiological impact. Neuroscientific studies suggest that experiences of pain resulting from rejection share neural circuitry with experiences of physical pain (Eisenberger, 2011, 2015). Chronic negative evaluation and rejection have a debilitating effect on the cardiovascular, neuroendocrine, and immune systems (Dickerson, 2011). The detrimental effect of social/interpersonal rejection can be demonstrated, for instance, by higher levels of stress hormones, such as cortisol in acute but also in long-term (perhaps through the mechanism of rumination) responses to the rejection (Dickerson & Zoccola, 2013). This can happen early on in life—for example, among preschool-age children rejected by peers—because their production of stress hormone can increase (Gunnar et al., 2003). Early experiences of rejection also can have a particularly significant impact on the developing brain (Cohen et al., 2006; De Bellis et al., 1999).

From the perspective of psychotherapy, we are particularly interested in pivotal, often developmentally significant, experiences of rejection and judgment as well as less obvious but nonetheless impactful experiences whereby an individual did not receive the attention, recognition, validation, or emotional support they needed. Such interpersonal interactions and situations can evoke experiences of shame, diminished worth and esteem, or a sense of the self as inadequate or falling short. Such pivotal and defining interactions as well as the emotional experiences they evoke shape the individual and can be metaphorically seen as forming a lens through which future interactions are experienced and processed. Thus, the probability is increased that future experiences will also give rise to similar emotional experiences of shame and inadequacy, leaving the person's needs for recognition, approval, and acceptance chronically unfulfilled. These shame and related experiences are thus seen within EFT as forming the basis of emotion schemes (Greenberg, 2017) that produce chronic experiences of shame and its variations in assorted situational contexts.

The pivotal experiences we are talking about typically involve interactions with significant others, such as caregivers whose criticism, disappointment, or disinterest evoke feelings of rejection and inadequacy. Clients may, early on in life, internalize diminishing messages, explicit judgments, or expressed disappointments by parents or other significant people in their world (McCranie & Bass, 1984). Or they may take the significant other's lack of interest or unavailability and attribute it to the self with the hope that self-improvement (e.g., driven by perfectionism or self-criticism) will elicit the desired response from the other. Attributing responsibility for the non-responsiveness or problematic responsiveness of the other to the self may be adaptive in particular circumstances. It may bring the person a sense of having some control over what is painful in their life—that changing their own self may win over and get the desired response from the salient significant other—for example, "If I succeed, I will get the attention and esteem I yearn for" (for more on problematic self-treatment in the context of problematic behavior of the other, see Chapter 3).

The other key important type of interaction to consider here are developmentally significant interactions with peers. Experiences of rejection by peers, in particular, bullying (which may take the form of shaming), have long-lasting effects (Arseneault et al., 2010). Again, these experiences become encoded in problematic emotion schemes and shape perceptual-emotional processing prospectively. Later in life, the individual may encounter situations that further compound such early developed vulnerabilities or, as a consequence of which, new vulnerabilities are developed. Particularly significant experiences in later life are those that take place in the workplace (S. B. Harvey et al., 2017) or in the context of a close romantic relationship (Romero-Canyas et al., 2010). Belonging to a minority group can also be a potential lifelong factor (e.g., Navarrete & Jenkins, 2011). Broader communal or societal perspectives on what is unacceptable and deserving of condemnation can have a powerful emotional impact. This impact can be particularly cruel if it is based on prejudice and the rejection of difference (Kite & Whitley, 2016).

Experiences of shame and their variants (e.g., embarrassment, humiliation, excessive guilt) point to unmet needs embedded in these feelings. These include needs for acceptance, recognition, and validation. We, therefore, endeavor to generate these needs in therapy through a validating client–therapist relationship, whereby the validating presence of the therapist constitutes a corrective emotional experience, but also through the vivid self-to-self imaginary dialogues that we engage clients in. Experiences of pride and accomplishment are an antidote to shame, so these are experiences that we seek to facilitate in therapy. Rather than doing so by way of examining the evidence about one's self (as in CBT), we endeavor instead to facilitate such feelings by generating humane responses to the self's experiences of rejection and mistreatment (Timulak, 2015); that is, by helping the individual witness the pain of their mistreatment, we can facilitate their experiencing caring compassion from the self or facilitate their experiencing healthy boundary-setting anger.

Fear

As with loneliness/sadness and shame, emotional experiences of fear may be highly adaptive. Fear informs us about danger and our need for safety. Experiences of fear that lead to adaptive action (e.g., seeking protection, mobilizing resources to extenuate threat), again, are not typically central to psychological difficulties. Thus, when we talk about problematic fear-based emotional experiences, we are not referring to those experiences of fear that inform adaptive action. Rather, we are referring to those experiences in which the feelings of fear are unbearable and lead to the development of chronic fear-based emotional processing and to psychological difficulties that prevent the person's healthy functioning.

The experience of chronic fear may overlap with experiences of loneliness and shame because loneliness or rejection may also leave an individual unprotected. Experiences of fear, however, may also be directly linked to traumatic experiences in which one's health or life was or is in danger. Similarly, experiences of physical pain can evoke the fearful experience of being intruded on in an uncontrollable and painful manner. Research into client expressions of fear in EFT (e.g., Dillon et al., 2018; Hissa et al., 2020; McNally et al., 2014; O'Brien et al., 2019; A. Pascual-Leone & Greenberg, 2007a) show that at their most vulnerable moments, clients express fear with phrases such as "I am afraid," "I am scared," "I am terrified," "I am unsafe," "I am overwhelmed/falling apart," "I am unprotected," "I have been invaded/intruded," "I have been terrorized," or "I feel dread."

It is critical that experiences of primary fear are distinguished from and understood as different from secondary apprehensive anxiety. To distinguish between the two, we offer an example from Timulak (2015): When flying on an airplane, we may experience an apprehensive (secondary) anxiety that the plane could fall from the sky (i.e., something traumatic might happen); however, we most likely will feel primary fear should the plane actually begin to fall (i.e., the trauma is actually happening). We see apprehensive anxiety as a secondary emotion that is linked to the anticipation of core painful emotions, such as loneliness/sadness, shame, or primary fear. Apprehensive anxiety of triggers that could evoke emotional pain coupled with avoidance of the emotional pain these triggers would evoke is a symptom-level presentation. The specific pain that those triggers would evoke (e.g., "I feel alone," "I feel flawed," "I feel scared") is the underlying primary emotion. If this emotion is too painful and unbearable (maladaptive), it becomes chronic, and we refer to it as an "underlying core painful emotion" or "core pain."

In some cases, that underlying painful emotion can be fear; it also can be loneliness/sadness, shame, or unique mixtures of loneliness/sadness, shame, and fear. In our transdiagnostic approach, the primary focus of treatment is not the treatment of fear or anxiety that is secondary to the chronic core pain but, rather, the treatment of the chronic core pain itself. While we do address symptomatic-level anxiety, there are important differences in the way we work with primary fear and secondary anxiety. We discuss this distinction at many points in the book, but, in general, it can be understood as one example of the central distinction we make between symptomatic-level work and core pain-related work.

Chronic fear-based problematic emotion schemes develop as a result of past situations in which the individual experienced unbearable primary fear. For example, primary fear (or terror) can be evoked in the context of traumatic experiences of intrusion or violation over which the individual has no control. The word *trauma* is used to describe both the triggering event (e.g., intrusion/violation) and the individual's psychological and physiological reaction to that trigger (Courtois & Ford, 2009). The experience of fear may include any of a wide variety of highly distressful aspects, including panic, emotional and bodily upset, a sense of uncontrollability, self-disintegration, or an inability to self-regulate accompanied by physical physiological pain or the immediate threat of pain. The fear experience typically involves a sense of danger, a lack of safety, and the sense of immediate threat to physical health or life. It can also involve dissociation. Often, a sense of uncontrollability or the inability (or possibility of inability) to defend oneself is central to the experience. Chronic maladaptive fear-based emotion schemes may result from once-off past experiences of trauma or from repeated traumatic experiences (e.g., physical beating).

Experiences of fear, panic, or terror have an immediate impact concurrent with the trauma but can also often have a posttraumatic impact. In the case of posttraumatic effects, the individual may experience flashbacks (as if the traumatic experience is reoccurring) or experience the fear anew in situations or interactions that resemble the original traumatic situation.

The immediacy of fear and its shear unpleasantness often preclude full aware-ness of, engagement with, or psychological processing of the experience, and the resulting tendencies toward avoidance—whether emotional (numbing of the emotions) or behavioral (avoiding situations resembling the traumatic event or reminding one of it)—can be particularly strong. Avoidance of the felt experience or behavior that could bring that experience is thus a highly characteristic feature of fear-based chronic problematic emotion schemes.

The power of fear is demonstrated in how quickly we get conditioned to fear-provoking stimuli (Öhman & Rück, 2007). Obviously, danger to life or health will take precedence over the majority of other situations that we are likely to encounter in our interactions with the environment. The speed at which we get conditioned may be compounded by the fact that some people appear to be more reactive or predisposed to fear-provoking stimuli than others. For instance, the strength of emotional reaction to masked fear objects varies among people; some are more reactive than others (Öhman & Soares, 1994). Emotional experiences of fear override our other attentional foci. Fear directs our attention to engage with the perceived threat (the exception to this is if we dissociate), potentially increasing the level of expe-rienced fear even further (Öhman & Rück, 2007). For instance, if we hear a dangerous sound, we focus on its potential source. Thus, we concentrate on details of the scary situation, and doing so makes the experience even more unpleasant and terrifying. Particularly problematic are repeated and chronic fear experiences whose physiological impact can lead to irreversible changes in brain functioning (Quirk, 2007).

Abusive and traumatic experiences during developmentally sensitive times (e.g., childhood, early adolescence) can be especially problematic. During these times, we typically do not have enough independence or access to resources to mitigate against any potential traumatic or abusive experiences. Indeed, the experience of helplessness—that is, the inability to protect the self in the face of mistreatment—can be part of what makes such adverse experiences traumatic. Problematic, fear-based emotion schemes formed in such developmental contexts are likely to be especially ingrained and powerful, and restructuring them in therapy is a challenging task. Early abusive experiences, moderated by genetic influences, may have a profound functional and structural effect on the brain and thus also on overall health and mental health functioning (Nemeroff, 2016; Syed & Nemeroff, 2017).

Traumatic experiences are not limited to experiences in childhood or adolescents. They can be encountered at any point in life (e.g., being assaulted, involvement in a life-threatening accident, physical injury, inhumane treat-ment in the context of war or criminal activity). Experience of life-threatening illness, for example, can give rise to experiences of fear that can have a long-lasting and chronic impact (Hissa et al., 2020). Even when traumatic experiences do not take place during developmentally sensitive periods in life, they can still be a source of problematic fear-based emotion schemes. While we are still learning a lot about how trauma affects us, it is generally hypothesized that it is the intensity of the traumatic triggers or the intensity of our emotional reactions to those triggers (shaped by an interaction of biological predispositions, early life experience, and the availability of mitigating resources, such as the validating support of significant others)—or both—that most likely influences the impact of any traumatic experiences on the development of psychological difficulties.

The evolutionary function of fear (i.e., to inform us of direct threat to our survival) means that fear-based schemes are perhaps more difficult to shift then other problematic emotion schemes. For instance (see the overview in Hermans et al., 2006), fear is highly contextually dependent, so overcoming the fear in an environment not matching the dangerous situation (e.g., therapy room vs. home if that is where the traumatic event occurred) may have limited generalization. The same applies to specificity of triggers that are particularly powerful. For instance, breathing air that smells similar to the air breathed during a trauma (e.g., the smell of the air in a country where a soldier was deployed and experienced trauma) can trigger a fear reaction. Similarly, a new traumatization (e.g., being assaulted a second time) can easily reestablish a previously "extinguished" connection between triggers and an emotional experience. Thus, new traumatic experiences may reestablish previously restructured problematic emotion schemes, thus quickly undoing therapeutic progress.

Most of the aforementioned research has been conducted within a behavioral paradigm in which it is referred to as "extinction research." The focus in EFT is on restructuring problematic emotion schemes (chronic fear-based schemes) through the articulation of unmet needs in the fear experiences and through the generation of responses to those needs. The unmet needs present in experiences of fear are needs for safety and protection. The responses to these needs that we want to generate in therapy are a calming and soothing protective presence (from the self or from the imagined other, or both—e.g., "You are safe," "I calm you," "I protect you") and a determined, boundary-setting, healthy protective anger directed toward the threat (e.g., "I won't allow you to scare me"). The EFT paradigm for treatment is thus quite different from the exposure and extinction paradigm present in behavior therapy. There is some overlap, and in the following chapters, we elaborate on how we guide clients to engage with the feared triggers/stimuli to bring into awareness of how such triggers are linked to the fear and also to reclaim personal control and power over the feared triggers. However, although some elements of our therapeutic strategy may be considered to involve exposure, we outline in the forthcoming chapters how EFT's approach to the treatment of problematic fear goes beyond behavioral therapeutic principles of exposure and habituation.

CONCLUSION

In this chapter, we aimed to lay out the rationale for an emotion-focused transdiagnostic approach. Overwhelming evidence shows that psychological difficulties (at least those categorized in related diagnostic groups, such as depression, anxiety, and related disorders—i.e., the so-called internalized disorders) tap into similar or shared underlying processes. Therefore, there is good reason to believe that a deeper understanding of these common processes may help explicate the seemingly varied symptomatology associated with these diagnoses. Clear evidence indicates a shared etiology (whether genetic/biological, environmental, or their interplay) among many psychological/psychiatric disorders and especially for disorders characterized by similar clusters of difficulties (e.g., internalized disorders).

Currently, several transdiagnostic approaches to treatment exist; they typically emanate from within the CBT paradigm. These transdiagnostic treatments have predominantly been developed to treat depression, anxiety, and related disorders, and some of these treatments see emotional vulnerability (e.g., neuroticism) and emotional processing difficulties (e.g., an aversive response to emotions and attempts to avoid emotional reaction) as targets for treatment. We propose a non-CBT alternative built on the tradition of humanistic psychotherapy, generally, and EFT, specifically.

In the following pages, we outline how emotional vulnerability centers on specific chronic emotional experiences of loneliness/sadness, shame, and fear that have developed in the course of one's life into problematic maladaptive emotion schemes. We discuss how those chronic painful emotions and the unmet needs in them (e.g., for connection, acceptance, and safety) can be responded to in therapy by the generation of healthy emotions, such as compassion and healthy boundary-setting anger. We also outline how, apart from healing the underlying vulnerability that is at the center of one's difficulties, we can also address specific ingrained symptoms that, although stemming from the underlying vulnerability, have become problematic to the individual's functioning, independent of the underlying emotional vulnerability of which they are an expression.

2

EMOTION-FOCUSED THERAPY
A Brief Overview of Theory and Practice

In this chapter, we provide an overview of emotion-focused therapy (EFT). We start by situating EFT in the psychotherapy field. We then provide the historical context in which this therapy developed. Next, we outline its major theoretical tenets and review important constructs, particularly those most relevant to our transdiagnostic conceptualization. We introduce the theory of change and refer to typical therapeutic practices that define EFT. We also situate our transdiagnostic contribution (which is fully fleshed out in the remaining chapters of this book) in the context of theoretical developments within the EFT body of work.

CONTEXT

EFT (Greenberg, 2017; Greenberg et al., 1993) is an empirically supported psychotherapeutic treatment rooted in the humanistic–existential traditions of client-centered, gestalt and experiential psychotherapy (Gendlin, 1981, 1996; Perls et al., 1994/1951; Rogers, 1951). EFT focuses on working

https://doi.org/10.1037/0000253-003
Transdiagnostic Emotion-Focused Therapy: A Clinical Guide for Transforming Emotional Pain, by L. Timulak and D. Keogh

experientially with client emotional processes in the session with the aim of enhancing client capacity to adaptively process emotional experiences, thus facilitating adaptive action in the world outside of therapy. While in essence the approach can be understood as building on client-centered, experiential, and gestalt psychotherapy, its development has also been influenced by contemporary cognitive, systems, and emotion theory. EFT exists as a treatment modality for both individuals and couples. However, the focus in this chapter (and this book) is on EFT as a treatment for individuals, and we refer readers interested in couples work to the main texts in that area (i.e., Greenberg & Goldman, 2008; Greenberg & Johnson, 1988; Johnson, 2004).

Initially called process–experiential psychotherapy (Greenberg et al., 1993), EFT developed in the context of a systematic program of process research investigating in-session change processes in psychotherapy (Rice & Greenberg, 1984). Innovative methods, such as task analysis (Greenberg, 2007b), were used to conceptually map out and investigate how particular therapeutic interventions facilitated specific in-session therapeutic processes. In turn, these processes facilitated the in-session resolution of particular tasks, the resolution of which were understood as making a difference to therapeutic gains across therapy. In this manner, the following were developed: (a) systematic evocative unfolding as a therapeutic task to facilitate the client's working through of problematic emotional reactions (Rice & Saperia, 1984), (b) two-chair dialogue for a self-evaluative conflict split as a therapeutic task to work with client self-criticism (e.g., Greenberg, 1979, 1980, 1983), and (c) empty-chair dialogue for unfinished business as a task for working with lingering bad feelings in relation to a significant other (e.g., Greenberg & Foerster, 1996).

Combined with research into the role of emotion in psychotherapy (Greenberg & Safran, 1987, 1989) and influenced by Rogerian perspectives on the transformative effects of the therapeutic relationship itself (Rogers, 1957), these developments led to the evolution of EFT as a marker-driven, task-focused experiential psychotherapy whereby clearly defined in-session client presentations prompt the therapist to initiate specific research-informed therapeutic tasks with the aim of facilitating specific in-session emotional processes—all within the context of a facilitative therapeutic relationship. From early on in its development, EFT also focused on how chronic maladaptive emotions can be transformed in therapy by the generation of adaptive emotions (Greenberg, 2015, 2017).

Although EFT was initially developed as a treatment using universally applicable principles, it has been developed and studied in the context of specific diagnostic presentations. In particular, it has been studied as a treatment for major depression (Goldman et al., 2006; Greenberg & Watson, 1998;

Watson et al., 2003). It also has been studied as a treatment for complex trauma (e.g., Paivio & Nieuwenhuis, 2001) and, more recently, as a treatment for social anxiety (Shahar et al., 2017) and generalized anxiety (O'Connell Kent et al., 2021; Timulak et al., 2017). In all these cases, the clinical adaptations of EFT have been presented in the form of treatment manuals—for example, for depression (Greenberg & Watson, 2006), for complex trauma (Paivio & Pascual-Leone, 2010), for generalized anxiety (Timulak & McElvaney, 2018; Watson & Greenberg, 2017), and for early work on social anxiety (see Elliott & Shahar, 2017).

These developments, together with our clinical experience with comorbid presentations in research projects (e.g., Timulak et al., 2017, 2018), led us to reconceptualize and systematize these clinical applications and experiences into a systematic transdiagnostic approach as well as to examine this systematic transdiagnostic approach in the context of a trial (Timulak et al., 2020). For a broad overview of the research evidence on EFT, see Elliott et al. (2021). A summary of qualitative and case study research can be found in Timulak et al. (2019). In addition, although beyond the purview of this book, a summary of the research into EFT for couples can be found in Wiebe and Johnson (2016) and Woldarsky Meneses and McKinnon (2019).

BASIC ASSUMPTIONS

EFT has roots in humanistic–experiential approaches to therapy. Individuals are seen as having resources and as being capable of awareness and choice, as well as having potential for agency and creativity (Greenberg, 2017, p. 13). Individuals are viewed as dynamic self-organizing systems in constant interchange with the environment with which they engage in self-regulating or other-regulating ways (Greenberg, 2017, p. 35). They are also seen as possessing an innate tendency toward self-development, growth, and mastery (see Rogers, 1959), and the human emotion system is viewed as being at the heart of this capacity for growth and adaptability (Greenberg, 2017; Greenberg et al., 1993). Through our emotional system, we experience the world, and emotions are thus a source of important information about the world. Emotional processes facilitate the rapid, automatic appraisal of complex situations, telling us whether our interaction with the environment is good for us or is potentially detrimental to our well-being (Greenberg, 2017, p. 31). Emotions tell us whether our needs are being met (e.g., Greenberg, 2011, 2017; Timulak, 2015), and they set in motion appropriate action tendencies related to those needs (e.g., to run from danger). Emotions are also a fast and effective way of communicating with others (e.g., if you see a tear in my eye, you sense I am sad, and you may be more likely to comfort me), and have an effect on others in such a way that others are likely to respond to our needs (e.g., expressed pain evoking a compassionate response from the other).

Emotional processing is thus a rapid way of assessing our environment, setting goals, and engaging in tasks for more deliberate conceptual processing (Greenberg, 2017). However, while awareness of emotions and their experience informs us how we are in the world, emotional processing is more than simply an information processing system. Our emotional experience is an embodied experience with emotion being an important part of the direct referent of how we are in the world. The manner in which emotional processing interacts with a reflective meaning-making process not only tells us about ourselves, others, and the world but essentially constitutes our experience of self, others, and the world (e.g., Greenberg, 2017).

Several characteristics of emotions have a direct relevance for psychotherapy. For instance, emotional awareness, differentiation of emotions, and articulation of emotional experience in symbolization/language—emotion researcher Feldman Barrett used the term *emotional granularity* to capture these processes (Barrett et al., 2014)—not only gives us clarity that guides our more deliberate actions but also has a regulatory function (Lieberman et al., 2007). This is important for psychotherapy because psychotherapy by its very nature contributes to an increased awareness of emotional experiences. Emotions also tend to influence our cognitive and conceptual processes (e.g., Baumeister et al., 2002; Forgas, 1995; Mayer & Hanson, 1995). If I see something that looks like a snake, I first act (by jumping aside) and only then analyze whether it actually is a snake or not. Emotions also linger—for example, if I am affected by a sad movie, I am more likely to see neutral information in a mood-compatible way. Again, these qualities of emotions have direct implications for psychotherapy because a dialectical interaction between emotional experience and conceptual reflection is at the core of the psychotherapeutic process.

Another point here—and one that is central from an EFT perspective—is that while certain emotional experiences can become chronically maladaptive, which is the case in difficulties, such as depression, anxiety disorders, and related disorders, these chronically difficult emotions can be changed by the generation of adaptive emotional experiences (A. Pascual-Leone, 2018). A primary goal in EFT therefore is to transform maladaptive emotional schematic processing, which gives rise to chronically painful emotions (Lane et al., 2015) by activating those painful feelings (e.g., by experientially recalling formative painful experiences) and by facilitating adaptive emotional responses to that pain (i.e., in the context of those recalled emotion-laden formative experiences).

Emotion Schemes and Self-Organizations

The concept of emotion schemes (Greenberg, 2017; Greenberg et al., 1993) is central to EFT's theory of dysfunction and how dysfunction is addressed in therapy. Greenberg (2017) described *emotion schemes* as "internal emotion memory structures that synthesize affective, motivational, cognitive and behavioral elements into internal organizations that are activated rapidly, out of awareness, by relevant cues" (pp. 39–40). Thus, emotional responses in the moment are mediated by emotional schematic processing, meaning that what we experience in the moment is not just related to stimuli in the here and now but is also influenced by our previous experiences of similar situations. Past experiences are thus implicitly present in current experiences, and current emotional experiences are generated through schemes formed in the past. Thus, despite its inherently adaptive nature (e.g., facilitating the rapid appraisal of complex situational information), emotional processing based on the building blocks of emotion schemes can also lead to the generation of maladaptive emotional responses. For example, an individual who repeatedly experienced shaming in social situations may process relatively benign situations as filling them with feelings of shame. When emotion schemes have become problematic, rigid, and maladaptive (see the next section on theory of dysfunction), they can be difficult to transform into schemes that are more tentative, more accommodating of the complexity of new situations, and thus more facilitative of processing interactions with the environment in a more adaptive way.

Emotion schemes provide a scaffolding for how we experience and process our interactions with the environment. They are also building blocks of our *self-organizations*, the ways we understand who we are and how we experience ourselves in our relationships and in the world (Greenberg, 2011, 2017). From an EFT perspective, the self is seen as an ever-emerging phenomenon, a process rather than a structure. Humans are viewed as dynamic, self-organizing systems, constantly synthesizing experiences from different levels of processing, such as sensorimotor, emotional, and conceptual processing (Greenberg, 2017). The coherence of those levels of processing is crucial for healthy functioning (Greenberg, 2017). When self-organization is dominated by problematic emotion schemes (which serve as attractors [Greenberg, 2019] for particular pathways of processing), we can, in turn, become defined by particular problematic self-organizations. From a therapeutic perspective, there are also opportunities here for change. A "self" comprising multiple self-organizations allows for a shift in terms of both dominant problematic emotion schemes and the self-organizations based on them. The person may thus move from a dominant self-organization of feeling flawed to a fluidity that oscillates between feeling flawed in one moment and proud of the self at another. This all has implications for therapy.

THEORY OF DYSFUNCTION: A GENERIC FRAMEWORK

Originally in EFT, psychological dysfunction was seen as stemming from (a) a lack of awareness of the richness of emotional experiencing and (b) chronic problematic emotion schemes that gave rise to problematic experiences and problematic self-organizations (Greenberg et al., 1993). The first of these is, in a way, similar to Rogers's (1959) conceptualization, assuming as it does that symbolization of experience may not capture the depth and intricacies of the totality of emotional experiencing. When an individual has a reduced ability to symbolize bodily felt experience in awareness, they are deprived of valuable information and are therefore limited in their capacity to recognize their own needs and respond adaptively to situations (Greenberg, 2011; Greenberg & Watson, 2006). For instance, not being aware of feeling offended in an interaction with a bully does not allow for mobilization of healthy boundary-setting anger. In the context of this book, we also want to state that increasing awareness of one's emotional experiences is also an important transdiagnostic concept. However, it is not only lack of awareness that may be a problem but also difficulties in emotion expression because emotion expression both changes our interaction with the environment and "forms the self in the act of expression" (Greenberg, 2019, p. 49).

Although a lack of awareness of emotions can be a problem for some clients, other clients are painfully aware of what they are feeling. The second type of dysfunction thus assumes that established pathways of emotional processing—that is, emotion schemes—exist that may be rigid, therefore generating chronically painful experience that does not inform adaptive actions. These emotion schemes can be defining of the self in problematic ways (e.g., "I often experience myself as inadequate"). These problematic emotion schemes are typically formed in developmentally pivotal contexts that gave rise to painful experiences in which important needs (e.g., for connection, acknowledgment, safety) were not met. These schemes then play a role in the emotional processing of new interactions, increasing the likelihood that these new interactions will be processed in a way that evokes chronically difficult feelings. For example, the experience of ostracization from peers may leave a person feeling somehow weird and shameful, which is how the person may then experience similar interpersonal and social situations.

As we highlighted in the previous chapter and do throughout this book, it is problematic emotion schemes—the established pathways though which the client processes their interaction with the environment—that constitute the emotional vulnerability that we want to target through transdiagnostic EFT. Such problematic emotion schemes, which give rise to chronic painful experiences of loneliness/sadness, shame, and fear/terror as well as dominate the individual's self-organizations, need to be accessed and restructured in therapy.

Later EFT literature has captured other difficulties that may give rise to psychological dysfunction. These include difficulties in emotion regulation and problems with meaning making (Greenberg, 2011, 2017; Greenberg & Watson, 2006). In terms of emotion regulation, many difficulties in psychological functioning are the result of having too much or too little emotion (Greenberg, 2011, 2017). Indeed, emotional underregulation or overregulation may, at times, be more of an issue than the actual emotions experienced. Appropriate emotion regulation is an important part of healthy emotional processing. From a transdiagnostic perspective, it is important to highlight that many symptomatic presentations can be conceptualized as unsuccessful and costly attempts to regulate underlying, core, chronically painful emotions. In the upcoming chapters, we look at how to target those varied clusters of symptoms.

Plenty of evidence indicates that the quality of pivotal relationships (e.g., attachment relationships with caregivers) plays a central role in the development of emotion regulation capacity (see the review in Greenberg, 2017). This has implications for the nature of the therapeutic relationship, which can fulfill a relational regulation function that might then be internalized by the client. Greenberg (2017) talked about an implicit regulation and self-soothing that can supplement the relational regulation of a soothing caring other. The perspective on emotion regulation in EFT differs from other mainstream formulations in that EFT does not propose to control emotions but, rather, to befriend and attune to them. The regulation of emotions in EFT is seen as something to be achieved by a modulation of emotional experiencing (e.g., awareness of emotions, balancing emotions with emotions) that becomes automatic and is linked to the generation of emotions themselves rather than via variations of forced self-control (i.e., deliberate regulation).

A coherent and differentiated self-narrative, as well as meaning making that accounts for the complexity of our experiences, is central to healthy psychological functioning, and deficits in this coherence or elaboration have the potential to give rise to psychological dysfunction (Angus & Greenberg, 2011). Rigid narratives not matching the totality of our experiences cannot give rise to adaptive actions. Also, narratives that do not give rise to hope or are devoid of the personal meaning that would propel us in life cannot harness the potential that we are perhaps built for. EFT, as is the case with many other therapies, is thus also an area for important meaning making that can offer the client encouraging perspectives on their growth and development— even in the face of adversity that they may have encountered. This is the case irrespective of the client's diagnosis or presenting issues.

Particularly in the context of couples and family therapy, EFT also looks at interactional dysfunction (Greenberg, 2019). Problematic rigid interactional stances that serve self-protective functions but in interactionally maladaptive ways tend to give rise to ongoing interpersonal conflicts. If these interactional stances develop into chronic maladaptive cycles of interaction that further perpetuate the conflict, we can see full blown *interactional dysfunction* (Greenberg & Goldman, 2008; Greenberg & Johnson, 1988; Johnson, 2004). We focus on this type of dysfunction in Chapter 5.

THEORY OF CHANGE

Therapeutic change in EFT is achieved primarily via two processes (Greenberg et al., 1993). The first major process is represented by a systematic effort to increase coherence in the client's emotional and conceptual processing, which can be shown in increased emotional awareness, optimal emotion modulation, emotion expression, and a coherent hopeful and adaptive outlook that promotes a narrative anchored in emotional experiencing. The second major process includes activation of problematic emotion schemes and their transformation. Greenberg (2004, 2006, 2011, 2017) offered a perspective on these major processes, recognizing six principles of change: (a) awareness of emotion (this involves "feeling the feeling" rather than simply talking about feelings), (b) expression of emotion, (c) regulation of emotion, (d) reflection on emotion, (e) transformation of emotion, and (f) the experience of a corrective emotional experience. Although many of these processes involve intrapsychological dimensions, they are facilitated in the context of a therapeutic relationship that can also thus be recognized as a vehicle of change. The relational context and the therapist can be a vehicle for change either via being facilitative of optimal client intrapersonal emotional and conceptual processes or via the therapist's directly contributing interpersonally to new transformative corrective experiences (Greenberg & Elliott, 2012).

Emotion transformation is particularly pivotal in understanding the theory of change in EFT (Greenberg, 2002, 2004, 2006; A. Pascual-Leone & Greenberg, 2007a). We restructure problematic emotion schemes by generating adaptive emotional experiences in the context of previously maladaptive ones. In other words, *emotional transformation* refers to the process of changing emotion with emotion (Greenberg, 2011, 2017). For example, where maladaptive shame was, we may seek to facilitate an experience of adaptive pride; where maladaptive fear was, adaptive courage; and where maladaptive loneliness was, an adaptive sense of connection.

While the concept of transforming maladaptive emotions by accessing adaptive emotions has been central to EFT from its inception, recent years have seen extensive research (see the review in A. Pascual-Leone, 2018) into how this process of emotional transformation actually takes place in psychotherapy—both within individual sessions (A. Pascual-Leone, 2009; A. Pascual-Leone & Greenberg, 2007a) and across the course of therapy (Dillon et al., 2018; McNally et al., 2014; A. Pascual-Leone et al., 2019). In a pivotal study, A. Pascual-Leone and Greenberg (2007a) analyzed observable moment-by-moment steps in emotional processing as they occurred within productive sessions of experiential therapy. On the basis of their findings, they proposed a sequential model of the optimal therapeutic processing of core emotional pain. In brief, the model proposed that successful clients moved in their moment-by-moment emotional processing from an initial state of global distress (e.g., poorly differentiated hopelessness) through maladaptive emotions (fear or shame); to negative self-evaluations; and, eventually, though the articulation of need; to the activation of adaptive emotional processes, such as assertive anger, self-soothing, and adaptive grieving; and, ultimately, to a position of acceptance and enhanced agency. An alternate pathway whereby some clients moved from global distress to adaptive emotional states via the expression of rejecting anger (other directed, reactive, and typically highly aroused anger) was also identified. A. Pascual-Leone (2009) observed that clients did not necessarily move through the entire model smoothly (i.e., attain successful emotional processing) but, rather, that this often occurred in a "two steps forward, one step back" fashion (p. 124). He also showed that although progression though the model was often complicated by setbacks, collapses to earlier stages of the model typically became shorter in productive sessions. Similar processes have also been observed across sessions (e.g., Dillon et al., 2018).

The framework just described, as well as subsequent research showing that adaptations of the A. Pascual-Leone and Greenberg (2007a) model could meaningfully describe the across-therapy process of emotional transformation, has formed the basis for the therapeutic model and strategies described in this book and first formulated in previous books by the first author (Timulak, 2015; Timulak & McElvaney, 2018). Here, in this book, we expand on this formulation to develop a transdiagnostic framework within which we extrapolate on the relationship between underlying core painful emotions (core emotional vulnerability) and various symptomatic presentations. We present the framework, of which some features can be seen already in the previous chapter, fully in the next chapter and then thereafter throughout the rest of the book.

OTHER RELEVANT EFT CONSTRUCTS

Researchers from within the EFT tradition have developed other constructs that have subsequently been researched and that inform the practice of EFT. The work of Les Greenberg and his students—later, colleagues—has been particularly pivotal here. Similarly, in the area of individual therapy that this book focuses on, original contributions have been made by many other researchers, including Robert Elliott, Jeanne Watson, Rhonda Goldman, and Sandra Paivio, as well as a newer generation of EFT researchers, such as Antonio Pascual-Leone, Ben Shahar, Shigeru Iwakabe, Serine Warwar, Alberta Pos, João Salgado, Carla Cunha, Lars Auszra, Imke Herrmann, Ueli Kramer, and many more (see the edited volume by Greenberg & Goldman, 2019). We look at some of those constructs here.

One also has to be aware that these concepts build on the rich tradition of research into humanistic therapies (Angus et al., 2015). Clinically relevant constructs developed in the broader humanistic tradition, such as depth of experiencing (Klein et al., 1969) or client vocal quality (Rice et al., 1979), have been incorporated into EFT programs of research and have stayed relevant to the practice of EFT. For a nice integration of all this tradition into a single volume, we refer the reader to Goldman and Greenberg (2015).

TYPES OF EMOTIONS

One of the first clinically useful constructs in EFT was the classification of emotions into four distinct categories: primary adaptive, primary maladaptive, secondary, and instrumental (Greenberg & Safran, 1987, 1989).

The classification served early on as a heuristic tool that could guide the therapist's clinical actions in therapy. It has subsequently given rise to useful research (e.g., Herrmann & Auszra, 2019). While EFT focuses on emotion in therapy, it does not focus on all emotions and all kinds of emotional processes equally. The aim instead is to focus on those emotional processes that facilitate productive in-session emotional work. In brief, we want to focus in therapy on primary emotions, transforming primary maladaptive emotions via the generation of primary adaptive emotions. Secondary emotions and instrumental emotions are to be acknowledged but are not necessarily seen as central. To understand these premises, we need to explicate these different types of emotions.

Primary Adaptive Emotions

Primary adaptive emotions are immediate responses to the situation the person is in and that help the person take appropriate action (Greenberg, 2017; Greenberg & Safran, 1987, 1989). They can be seen as healthy emotional responses, fulfilling the adaptive function of emotion to rapidly process situations and provide information to prepare the person to take effective action. In this way, fear experienced in the context of danger is a primary adaptive emotional response, alerting the individual to the danger and mobilizing the individual to take appropriate action. Similarly, sadness in the context of loss or anger in the context of mistreatment can be seen as a primary adaptive emotional response, prompting comfort-seeking and support in the first instance and self-assertive protection and distancing in the second. In therapy, we seek to attend to and work with primary adaptive emotions because they represent the client's immediate response to a situation, because they contain adaptive information, and because the action tendencies inherent in such emotional experiences tend to be constructive responses to the situation the client finds themselves in. Much of the work in EFT is about facilitating and nurturing adaptive emotional responses within the session.

We illustrate each of the four types of emotional responses with a fictional example. We begin with the example and return to and elaborate on it in the sections that follow:

> If I come home after a difficult day and seek connection and soothing support from my partner, but she is not mentally available to me because she is instead paying attention to work on her laptop, her unavailability might evoke in me the sadness of missing connection. If this sadness is adaptive, it leads me to seek closeness in a way that can be seen as a nondemanding bid for connection. I approach my partner and gently share my need for connection in a way

that is inviting, thus increasing the likelihood of her responding. In this context, primary adaptive sadness informs my actions in such a way that my need for connection and support is met.

Primary Maladaptive Emotions

Primary maladaptive emotions are also immediate responses to a situation, but, unlike primary adaptive responses, they do not allow the person to respond adaptively to that situation but, instead, interfere with functioning (Greenberg, 2017; Greenberg & Safran, 1987, 1989). Primary maladaptive emotional responses involve activation of emotion schemes based on past situations that left the person with painful, upsetting, overwhelming, or otherwise problematic experience. While, at one point, the emotional response may have constituted an adaptive attempt to respond to a traumatic, abusive, or otherwise difficult situation, maladaptive emotional schematic processing means that even benign situations are processed as if they had the potential to be traumatic or otherwise difficult. For instance, critical feedback in a work context might be processed through the lens of constant humiliation and criticism experienced in developmentally pivotal times when growing up. Often, clients report a sense of being stuck in such feelings, describing them as uncomfortably familiar. Research suggests that primary maladaptive emotions presented by clients in therapy are typically related to chronic senses of shame, sadness/loneliness, or fear (Greenberg, 2017; Timulak, 2015). The work of therapy in EFT is predominantly to access such chronic painful states to facilitate the client's enhanced capacity to accept, tolerate, and ultimately transform them via the generation of primary adaptive experiences (Greenberg, 2017; A. Pascual-Leone & Greenberg, 2007a).

Returning to our example, in some ways, maladaptive sadness might look and feel similar to adaptive sadness. However, in a number of critical ways, it is different:

> The sadness evoked by the immediate context would be experienced in the context of all the abandonments I experienced previously in life. As such, the nonattendance of my partner might be impossible to tolerate. The sadness might be experienced as all-encompassing and as defining of me. I might be left feeling not just that my partner is not there for me in this moment but that she never will be there for me—and that nobody will ever be there for me. Rather than reaching out to my partner for closeness and comfort, the action tendency in such maladaptive primary sadness might be to withdraw.

Secondary Emotions

Secondary emotions are responses to primary emotional processes or responses to internal cognitive processes linked to primary emotions (Greenberg, 2017;

Greenberg & Safran, 1987, 1989). For example, an individual experiencing shame (primary emotion) in response to rejection, may become angry (secondary emotion) either toward themselves or the individual rejecting them. Secondary emotions are regarded as unproductive because by obfuscating primary emotions, they prevent the processing of those primary emotional experiences, restrict access to adaptive information, and, instead, lead to actions that may not be congruent with or helpful to the current situation. The most typical secondary emotions that we find in transdiagnostic therapy for depression, anxiety, and related disorders are those corresponding to symptom clusters, such as hopelessness and helplessness (in depression), irritability (depression), anxiety (anxiety disorders), and undifferentiated emotional upset (a variety of disorders). In therapy, we acknowledge secondary emotions, but we do not focus on them, instead directing our focus to primary emotion. *Secondary emotions* are thus empathically responded to so that we can explore the underlying primary emotions from which they stem.

In our example, secondary emotion might follow from primary maladaptive sadness:

> I have a sense that my partner is not there and that she never will be (primary maladaptive sadness), which leads me to withdraw and resign. I retreat to the bedroom, lie down in my bed, and start to feel hopeless (secondary emotion)—that my life will never be different and that I will always feel alone. This resignation and hopelessness can persist and can become the defining or dominant aspect of my experience. It may develop into a lingering hopelessness (a symptom-level secondary emotion) that may eventually lead me to seek treatment for depression.

Instrumental Emotions

Instrumental emotions are emotions expressed with the intention of influencing others to respond in a particular way (Greenberg, 2017; Greenberg & Safran, 1987, 1989). The individual may or may not be aware that they are using emotion in this way. Examples include anger expressed to control others, "crocodile tears" expressed to evoke sympathy, or shame expressed to appear more socially acceptable. In each of these instances, the expressed emotion serves a function that relates to the underlying primary emotions in the person's primary emotional response to the situation. In therapy, the therapist does not focus on these processes; instead, the therapist acknowledges them and the needs they might serve but primarily directs attention to underlying or related primary emotions. Particularly problematic instrumental emotions may correspond with presentations commonly conceptualized as personality disorders, but instrumental emotions are universal and present in all types of clients, including those presenting with depression, anxiety, and related disorders.

An example of instrumental emotion in the example we are using might be this:

> After feeling the all-encompassing maladaptive sadness of my partner's not being there when I seek closeness, I do not collapse into secondary hopelessness. Instead, I go to the kitchen and, in a rage, start destroying dishes (instrumental emotion) so that my partner will notice (the function of instrumental emotion) that I am upset. In this instance, the instrumental rage is linked to the primary (maladaptive) sadness.

EMOTIONAL AROUSAL AND EMOTIONAL PRODUCTIVITY

Two EFT constructs with immense clinical utility are the concepts of emotional arousal and emotional productivity, both of which have been developed in the context of process research (Greenberg, 2017; Herrmann & Auszra, 2019; Warwar & Greenberg, 1999). The relationship between level of emotional arousal and therapeutic outcome is complicated; for instance, it is mediated by what type of emotions are aroused, in what context, and in what sequence (see the summary in Herrmann & Auszra, 2019). However, the client's level of emotional arousal is a useful indicator of the extent to which they are engaging with that experience. A useful tool for assessing level of arousal in therapy is the Client Emotional Arousal Scale–III (CEAS-III; Warwar & Greenberg, 1999), a 7-point scale ranging from 1 (e.g., *Client does not express any feelings. Voice gestures or verbal content do not disclose any arousal*) to 7 (e.g., *Arousal is full and intense. No sense of restriction. The person is focused, freely expressing, with voice, words, or physical movement an intense state of arousal*). This scale assesses voice quality (disruption), bodily arousal, the presence of constriction in expression, and more. Importantly, research has shown that individuals vary in their baseline level of arousal so that what constitutes a significantly elevated level of arousal for one individual might constitute a normal level of arousal for another. When using the CEAS-III, it is therefore important to calibrate it for an individual participant. Another important learning is that observed level of arousal is a more reliable predictor of fruitful therapeutic processes than self-reported levels of arousal (Warwar & Greenberg, 1999).

A certain level of emotional arousal is necessary to have access to emotional experience containing valuable information for conceptual processing (e.g., around midpoint on the CEAS-III [Warwar & Greenberg, 1999]—

moderate arousal in voice and body, disruption in ordinary speech patterns, freedom from control and restraints, emotional expression still somewhat restricted). Activation of emotions in an aroused manner is also crucial for transformation of problematic emotion schemes. Only those schemes that are activated in session can be transformed through the generation of other emotions; only then we can rework, reshape, and modulate them. Emotional overregulation (low levels of arousal as measured by the CEAS-III) does not allow access to adaptive information in the emotional experience (e.g., what is needed) and constrains the full activation of problematic schemes; these lower levels of emotional arousal inhibit potential transformation of these problematic schemes. On the other hand, with too much arousal, clients can become overwhelmed and are unable to benefit from information contained in the emotion. Where there is too much emotional arousal, the restructuring of activated emotion schemes is also less feasible because activated emotion schemes become disorganizing, thus leaving the client confused, dysregulated, and out of control. Therefore, it is typically moderate levels of arousal that are productive in therapy (Carryer & Greenberg, 2010).

Research into the complex relationship between in-session emotional experience and therapeutic outcomes has led to the articulation of the construct of *emotional productivity,* a concept that aims to describe what constitutes productive emotional experiences from the perspective of therapeutic change (Greenberg et al., 2007). This clinically useful construct was expounded on in the Client Emotional Productivity Scale–Revised (Auszra et al., 2010). For in-session emotion to be considered therapeutically productive, the emotion has to be activated (i.e., present in an aroused manner), has to be primary, and has to be processed in an aware manner (Auszra & Greenberg, 2007; Greenberg et al., 2007). This third point requires that the emotion is attended to rather than avoided, that it is symbolized in words, that symbolization and emotional expression are congruent, that the client is not overwhelmed and can accept the emotion as well as ownership of the emotion, and that the client can differentiate various aspects of the emotional experiencing (Auszra & Greenberg, 2007; Greenberg et al., 2007). If emotions are not present, or if the experienced emotions are secondary, the process is considered not emotionally productive. Maladaptive primary emotions are considered productive if the client is able to stay with them, is not overwhelmed by them, or is not running away from them. The meeting of these criteria signals the possibility that such emotions (emotion schemes) may be amenable to transformation.

THEORY OF THERAPEUTIC WORK IN EFT

Therapeutic work in EFT consists of several pillars (see a recent overview in Greenberg & Goldman, 2019). Here, we divide them into three. The first pillar is that EFT is a relational therapy. It seeks to offer an authentic caring, therapeutic relationship that provides safety for the clients to explore their vulnerable feelings while it also constitutes a corrective compassionate and validating interpersonal experience. The second pillar represents therapist thinking about therapeutic process that informs the therapist's actions—that is, the therapist's case conceptualization. The third pillar is the therapist's use of experiential tasks at in-session presentations that indicate the client is having a particular difficulty in emotional processing, and this difficulty is sufficiently salient to be focused on in the session. These particular presentations are what is known in EFT as *markers*.

The Relationship

EFT developed within the humanistic tradition, and as such, the therapist's nonjudgmental, empathic, and authentic presence has always been recognized as fundamental (Rogers, 1957). While EFT is a marker-driven, task-focused, experiential psychotherapy in which defined in-session client presentations prompt the therapist to initiate specific therapeutic tasks with the aim of facilitating specific in-session emotional processes, all this therapeutic work takes place within the context of a caring therapeutic relationship. Providing, then establishing, a relationship characterized by empathic exploration and understanding is the EFT therapist's default primary in-session goal (see Chapter 4).

Importantly, the concept of empathic presence and the repertoire of therapist empathic interventions are somewhat broader in EFT compared to in client-centered therapy. The EFT therapist is especially focused on empathic attunement to client affect, and the therapist uses a broad repertoire of empathic interventions that have various functions in different moments of therapy. In one of the pivotal EFT books dedicated to trainees learning this approach, Elliott et al. (2004) outlined the variety of these empathic responses, ranging from those that can be seen as forms of empathic exploration (e.g., exploratory reflections, evocative reflections, empathic exploratory questions, checking or fit questions, client process observations, empathic conjectures [guesses], and empathic refocusing in which the therapist refocuses the client on some aspect of the client's experience) to those seen as forms of communicating empathic understanding (e.g., empathic reflections, empathic following that provides acknowledgment of the client's experience, empathic affirmation).

The therapist's gentleness, warmth, and soothing manner invites the client to experience their vulnerability, thus enabling clients to become aware of and symbolize painful aspects of their experience. In addition, transformation of emotional pain in EFT is typically facilitated via the use of experiential tasks, such as chair dialogues (see the Experiential Tasks section), and therapist attunement to client affect is critical both in terms of optimizing client emotional processing during such tasks and because a strong therapeutic alliance facilitates client engagement with the often emotionally challenging work of engaging with such tasks. The quality of the therapist's empathic presence is also important because it helps clients regulate a painful emotional experience (Watson et al., 1998). Furthermore, the therapist's compassionate and validating presence at moments of heightened vulnerability and pain can be seen as providing a corrective interpersonal emotional experience (e.g., Greenberg & Elliott, 2012). We discuss our perspective on the nature of the therapeutic relationship in EFT and in the context of transdiagnostic treatment in detail in Chapter 4.

Case Conceptualization

In line with a humanistic tradition in psychotherapy that was skeptical about the idea of the therapist being an expert on the client (e.g., Rogers, 1951), EFT theorists have been reluctant to engage in developing a systematic case conceptualization framework. Rather, EFT has evolved as a marker-driven, process-oriented psychotherapy whereby moment-to-moment therapist interventions are informed by moment-to-moment process assessments of client presentation, in-session markers, and within-task microprocess markers. It was through an engagement with other approaches that case conceptualization eventually started to be developed more formally in EFT (Greenberg & Goldman, 2007). In recent years, case conceptualization has been seen as a useful therapeutic tool (although "case conceptualization," which is our preferred term, and "case formulation," which is the term more often used [e.g., Goldman & Greenberg, 2015], can, at times, be taken to mean different things; broadly speaking, they refer to the same concept). For instance, although it continues to be assumed that case conceptualization is not a static process but, rather, is ever evolving and fluid, there has been a recognition that it is possible to formulate and apply therapeutic principles beyond in-session presentation and the presence of a marker.

Over the years, a number of contributions to case conceptualization framework have been made by EFT writers (e.g., Goldman & Greenberg, 2015;

Greenberg & Goldman, 2007; Timulak & Pascual-Leone, 2015; Watson, 2010). While there are different takes on conceptualization, all approaches are informed by at least the following: a close assessment of the client's emotional processing style; level of emotional arousal; emotional productivity; primary, secondary, or instrumental emotions; maladaptive emotion schemes (i.e., underlying core painful emotions); unmet needs; and identity- and attachment-related presenting issues. EFT therapists also conceptualize therapeutic work in terms of a *pain compass* (Greenberg & Goldman, 2007) in which where they empathically follow what is most painful in the client's experiencing, thus opening up the possibility of transforming that core pain (core emotional vulnerability) in therapy. We present our own thinking in the area of case conceptualization in Chapters 3 and 5, doing so in the context of a variety of diagnostic presentations as well in the context of a transdiagnostic formulation.

Experiential Tasks

A distinct feature of EFT is that it developed as a marker-guided therapy (Greenberg et al., 1993). *Markers* in this context refer to client in-session presentations typical of some sort of problematic processing. When such markers arise in session, they are noted by the therapist, who may then introduce specific experiential therapeutic tasks, each of which has been developed to optimally facilitate therapeutic work with the relevant type of in-session problematic processing. Markers as defined in EFT inform the therapist not just that a particular emotional processing difficulty exists and that a particular therapeutic task is indicated, but also that it is timely to introduce that task—that is, the marker also indicates client readiness to work on the underlying problem. Markers are thus strategic opportunities for therapists to apply particular therapeutic tasks at opportune moments. The therapist then uses experiential tasks (specific therapeutic processes, e.g., imaginary dialogues using chairs) to facilitate optimal emotional processing or transformation of maladaptive emotional experiences typically through the generation of more adaptive experiences.

Examples of markers include an interruption of emotional experience or expression, harsh self-criticism, a puzzling emotional reaction to a specific situation, or "unfinished business" (referring to a lingering emotional injury in relation to a significant other). Each marker is then associated with a corresponding task (described shortly)—for example: for self-interruption, two-chair enactment dialogue; for self-criticism, two-chair dialogue for a self-evaluative conflict split; for a puzzling emotional reaction, systematic evocative unfolding; and for unfinished business, empty-chair dialogue. Many of these tasks were developed in the context of systematic programmatic process research studying fruitful processes in client-centered and gestalt therapy (Rice & Greenberg, 1984). Almost all tasks in EFT have direct empirical backing and were developed by observing clinically successful in-session processes. We cite many of these studies in the book when discussing individual tasks. This area is a particular strength of EFT. It is what makes EFT a truly research-informed therapy.

Elliott et al. (2004), building on an earlier outline in Greenberg et al. (1993), offered an overview of the various EFT tasks (although true to the researched-informed nature of EFT, these tasks have further evolved, and both new tasks and variants of already established tasks continue to be developed, as we illustrate in the later chapters of this book). Tasks (descriptions to follow), presented by Elliott et al. (2004), range from general therapeutic processes, such as empathic exploration and alliance formation, to more specific experiential enactments, such as empty-chair and two-chair dialogues. Empathic exploration is the default task in EFT, continuing across the course of therapy. Through a variety of empathic responses, the therapist facilitates an exploration of the client's experiencing. The therapist responds empathically to all aspects of the client's experience but is particularly attuned to affect, thus facilitating exploration of the most painful, primary, and problematic aspects of the clients emotional experiencing. Empathic exploration seeks to facilitate differentiation, awareness, understanding, and owning of emotional experiences while additionally eliciting markers for other therapeutic tasks.

Intense client vulnerability is a marker for *empathic affirmation*, whereby the therapist is fully present, accepting, and validating of the client's vulnerability as it is at that moment (Elliott et al., 2004; Greenberg et al., 1993). When the client is in such an intensely vulnerable state (e.g., incredibly fragile, feeling intense shame, depleted, helpless/hopeless), the therapist attunes to this vulnerability, seeking to compassionately and nonintrusively convey affirmation and acceptance. *Alliance formation*, an important task particularly in the early sessions of therapy (Elliott et al., 2004), is when the therapist seeks to collaboratively establish a focus for therapy, to agree on goals, and to agree on the ways the client and therapist will work together to achieve those goals. Difficulties or ruptures in the therapeutic alliance are markers for a *dialogue aimed at repairing the rupture* in which the therapist seeks to engage the client in a dialogue, genuinely and openly exploring with the client what happened and nondefensively acknowledging and validating client concerns.

The *clearing a space* task is indicated when clients are so overwhelmed that they cannot focus on the work of therapy (Elliott et al., 2004). The therapist invites the client to focus their attention inwardly on the bodily felt sense of their concerns to link aspects of that felt sense to situational cues, to name these aspects, and to visualize putting these aspects aside in their imagination. An unclear felt sense whereby the client reports feeling something but is confused or unclear as to what they are feeling is a marker for *experiential focusing* (based on the work of Gendlin, 1981, 1996; for the EFT adaptation, see Elliott et al., 2004, and Greenberg et al., 1993). In this task, the therapist invites the client to focus inwardly, attend to embodied aspects of their experience with curiosity and openness, and to symbolize aspects of that embodied experience in language or images.

The *trauma retelling* task facilitates the unfolding of an intense emotional reaction to a traumatic life event about which the client experiences a strong need to process (Elliott et al., 2004). In trauma retelling, the client is guided to tell the story of the trauma and to reexperience key elements of the experience while being emotionally supported by the therapist. *Meaning protest*, whereby a client expresses distress or confusion at the manner in which a life event threatens a "cherished belief," is a marker for *meaning creation* work (Clarke, 1989; see also Elliott et al., 2004). In that work, clients are facilitated to specify the challenged belief, to explore emotional reactions to the life event, and to consider and review the tenability of the hitherto held belief. A marker for *systematic evocative unfolding* is the already described problematic emotional reaction as manifest in client puzzlement or confusion in response to a particular situation (Greenberg et al., 1993; Rice & Saperia, 1984). In *systematic evocative unfolding*, the client is guided to recall the situation leading to the reaction as vividly as possible. Describing their experiences in a step-by-step manner, they are facilitated to attend to both situational cues and internal experiences. This slowed-down, evocative process promotes a reexperiencing of the situation and facilitates the emergence of a meaning bridge between particular aspects of the situation and the client's emotional reaction and broader self-functioning.

A *self-evaluative conflict split* occurs when the client criticizes, attacks, or denigrates themselves. Such a split is a marker for a *two-chair dialogue for self-evaluation* (Elliott et al., 2004; Greenberg et al., 1993) whereby the problematic self-treatment is enacted, core maladaptive emotion schemes activated, need identified, and adaptive transformative responses to that need facilitated typically via compassionate softening toward the self or self-protective anger in the face of the critic's mistreatment. *Two-chair enactment dialogue* for self-interruption is implemented when there is a marker for self-interruption of emotional experience or expression (see Elliott et al., 2004, and Greenberg et al., 1993). In this task, the client is facilitated by the therapist to enact in one chair the interrupter—that part of the self that interrupts emotional experiencing or expression—and to experience in the other chair the impact of this interruption on the self. In doing so, the client becomes aware of their own agency in the process, experiences the cost of this self-interruption, and is facilitated to overcome the interruption typically via a stepping down of the self-interrupter or via increased determination on behalf of the experiencing self to stand up to that interruption, and to feel and express emotions more freely.

Empty-chair dialogue for a marker of unfinished business is used in the context of lingering, unresolved emotional hurt or injury related to an emotionally significant other (Elliott et al., 2004; Greenberg et al., 1993). In the empty-chair task, the client is guided through an imaginary dialogue with the other within which underlying core pain is activated. Emotional transformation is facilitated via activation of adaptive emotional responses to that pain and to the needs implicit in the pain. Although the significant other is obviously not actually present, clients often experience a sense of resolution in empty-chair work, letting go of unresolved feelings either through a process of forgiveness (which can result from a changed view of the other) or by assertively standing up to the other and holding them accountable for the emotional mistreatment.

A number of general points may be made about the previously described tasks. Tasks range from general therapeutic processes, such as empathic exploration and alliance formation, to more specific experiential enactments, such as empty-chair and two-chair dialogues. All of these tasks have evolved as a result of decades of programmatic process research, and many have been empirically investigated (the latest overview can be found in Greenberg & Goldman, 2019), leading to empirically validated models (e.g., empty-chair dialogue for unfinished business or two-chair dialogue for self-evaluative conflict splits). Therapists thus initiate tasks based on in-session markers indicating that specific client emotional processing difficulties are present and amenable to being worked with. Within tasks, the therapist also empathically attends to client processing *micromarkers*, specific in-task client presentations that prompt the therapist to guide the process in specific ways shown by research to optimize productive emotional processing (Goldman & Greenberg, 2015, pp. 120–122). These within-session, in-task micromarkers are at the heart of EFT, informing therapist interventions intended to access or regulate emotion, activate core primary maladaptive emotions, or transform such emotions by activating adaptive emotion responses. During tasks, therapist interventions are a combination of empathic responses and process guidance. In Chapters 6 through 9, we present variants of these tasks as well as newly developed or adapted tasks in the context of transdiagnostic treatment.

TRANSDIAGNOSTIC PERSPECTIVE

EFT was developed as a generic form of treatment that is applicable to a variety of presentations (Greenberg et al., 1993). The theoretical constructs presented at the beginning of this chapter were intended to encompass universal (or generic) processes involved in the development of psychological difficulties as well as universal processes that need to be followed (i.e., theory of change and theory of treatment) to address those difficulties. The original outline of the therapy itself (Elliott et al., 2004; Greenberg et al., 1993) was also universal and intended for working with a variety of presentations. In comparison to what we present in this book, original EFT formulations did not distinguish between symptom-level work and underlying vulnerability work. It, however, targeted primarily what we refer to here as the underlying vulnerability work.

It was only later, when the wider field of psychotherapy moved focus to "single-disorder"–focused therapies that EFT started to be articulated for specific presentations. The generic EFT model was then fleshed out in the context of specific presentations, and books on depression (Greenberg & Watson, 2006), complex trauma (Paivio & Pascual-Leone, 2010), and generalized anxiety (Timulak & McElvaney, 2018; Watson & Greenberg, 2017) appeared. Such specific presentation-focused EFT (typically referred to in the mainstream psychotherapy literature as "single-disorder"; in the EFT community, we do not particularly like the word "disorder") applied the principles of generic EFT—for example, a generic/universal description of dysfunction and theory of change as well as therapeutic procedures—to a specific presentation/"disorder" (e.g., depression).

Transdiagnostic EFT (EFT-T), as presented in this book, is simply a logical next step that seeks to systematically build a bridge between the generic work targeting underlying emotional vulnerability and the symptom-level work common to working with clusters of similar presentations (e.g., shared symptoms of anxiety disorders). EFT-T offers a systematic conceptualization of client difficulties through the lenses of emotional vulnerability and its symptomatic expression. It explicitly and systematically differentiates between underlying vulnerability work and symptom-level work. In addition, it specifies that symptom-level work may not be single "disorder" specific but, rather, may describe work with clusters of symptoms shared by a variety of "disorders."

EFT-T builds on the generic theoretical EFT constructs presented in this chapter. The relevance of these constructs to a transdiagnostic framework are apparent in the next chapter in which we articulate the main features of EFT-T. EFT-T sees emotional experiences as central to our processing of interactions with our (particularly social) environment. The nature of these emotional experiences is influenced by our biological makeup but is also developmentally and sequentially shaped by our life experiences. Experiences shape future experiences through the formation of emotion schemes with experiences that do not lead to productive and adaptive interactions/experiences, thus potentially giving rise to problematic emotion schemes. These problematic emotion schemes can be seen as constituting an emotional vulnerability to certain kinds of experiences/interactions that finds expression in the form of various symptoms.

Because emotion schemes are involved in the processing of our moment-to-moment interaction with the environment, this emotional vulnerability (rooted in past problematic interactions/experiences) increases the likelihood of new problematic interactions/experiences, which, in turn, further compounds and shapes emotional vulnerability. Dominant problematic emotion schemes can thus shape dominant self-organizations, leaving the person with a chronically painful sense of themselves as well as with a susceptibility to feel feelings that do not inform adaptive actions. Varied symptom-level presentations (e.g., depression, social anxiety, panic attacks, engagement in rituals) are expressions of this underlying vulnerability (e.g., chronic loneliness, shame, fear).

In EFT-T, we therefore systematically combine generic EFT features that seek to transform problematic emotion schemes, on an underlying core (primary maladaptive) emotions level, with a secondary symptom-level focus. In the next chapter, we provide a theoretical account of the interplay between the underlying emotional vulnerability and its symptomatic presentation. In the remaining chapters, we then provide a systematic road map that allows therapists to move between the symptom-level work and the underlying emotional vulnerability (core pain) work. The underlying work here relies on transforming primary maladaptive emotions (core painful emotions, e.g., loneliness/sadness, shame, fear) through the generation of primary adaptive emotions (e.g., compassion, love, protective anger, pride). The symptom-level work addresses symptoms (e.g., worry, rumination) through increasing client awareness of their own agency and through an experiential mobilization of the self (e.g., setting boundaries, letting go) to counter the experiential toll of the symptoms. In the next chapter, we start with an outline that details an emotion-focused transdiagnostic approach.

CONCLUSION

In this chapter, we provided a brief overview of EFT theory and practice. We discussed its roots in a humanistic tradition that fundamentally sees humans as capable of adaptive growth and action and explained how EFT has evolved as a result of decades of programmatic research into productive processes in psychotherapy. We presented basic assumptions made in EFT about the nature of emotion, the self, psychopathology, and treatment as well as described core concepts, such as the differentiation among primary, secondary, and instrumental emotions and the role of emotion schemes in emotional processing.

In addition, we described the various mechanisms of change by which EFT therapists seek to facilitate change in therapy. Specifically, we elaborated on the concept of transforming chronic painful emotions by accessing adaptive emotional processes. We discussed the marker-driven nature of interventions and the role of case conceptualization, and then we briefly outlined the main tasks therapists draw on within therapy. Finally, we emphasized the multi-faceted role of the therapeutic relationship. Next, in Chapter 3, we turn our attention to elaborating on the role of the relationship in more detail.

3 TRANSDIAGNOSTIC EMOTION-FOCUSED CONCEPTUALIZATION

In Chapter 1, we presented a rationale for, and some very basic tenets of, our transdiagnostic emotion-focused formulation. Here, we provide a more detailed outline of how we think about cases (case conceptualization) and the processes of emotion transformation in the course of transdiagnostic emotion-focused therapy (EFT-T). We use a framework that we have developed based on the work of A. Pascual-Leone and Greenberg (2007a; A. Pascual-Leone, 2009, 2018). This framework is one that I (LT) and my colleagues have presented in previous work, some of it transdiagnostic in nature (e.g., Timulak, 2015; Timulak & Keogh, 2020; Timulak & Pascual-Leone, 2015), and some specific to single disorders (e.g., generalized anxiety disorder [GAD]; Timulak & McElvaney, 2018). The framework has also served as a basis for empirical work that has contributed to the development of the EFT-T model presented in this book (e.g., Connolly-Zubot et al., 2020; Dillon et al., 2018; McNally et al., 2014; O'Brien et al., 2019; Timulak et al., 2017, 2018, 2020). We provided an early outline of this conceptualization in Timulak and Keogh (2020), and, in this chapter, we provide an expanded articulation of that early formulation.

https://doi.org/10.1037/0000253-004
Transdiagnostic Emotion-Focused Therapy: A Clinical Guide for Transforming Emotional Pain, by L. Timulak and D. Keogh

The transdiagnostic case conceptualization (Timulak & Keogh, 2020; see Figure 3.1) assumes that there are particular, painful *triggers*—situations or perceptions—in the client's life that are difficult for them to process emotionally. These triggers are embedded in the client's personal history and typically are linked to past painful experiences (e.g., experiences of ostracization, rejection, trauma, invalidation). They activate the client's emotional vulnerability, a vulnerability that is idiosyncratic to each particular client. While this vulnerability constitutes the essence of the experienced emotional pain, it can potentially also be expressed, on a symptomatic level, in a form recognizable as belonging to diagnostic clusters, such as depression, anxiety, or related disorders. The client can become afraid of these triggers and of the painful emotional experiences they bring (e.g., a sense of being abandoned, rejected, intruded on), and they can attempt to avoid the triggers (behaviorally or emotionally), to somehow manage themselves in the context of these triggers (e.g., through self-criticism—a form of problematic self-treatment, which is discussed later in the chapter), or to somehow prepare themselves for these triggers (e.g., through worrying about them in advance). Although these strategies are often understandable in the context of the client's history and may have been somewhat effective at helping the client cope with past painful experiences, they are also problematic and can become counterproductive over time.

These largely unsuccessful attempts to cope with painful feelings can leave the client experiencing an undifferentiated state of global distress combined with anxiety and avoidance. Global distress (e.g., hopelessness, helplessness, irritability, generalized upset) and apprehensive anxiety are considered symptom-level, secondary emotional experiences, and the particular form these experiences take can define the specific diagnostic group the client may fit into (e.g., depression, social anxiety, GAD, panic disorder). The specific constellations of symptom-level presentations are informed by a multitude of interacting factors, some of which we address later. However, irrespective of the particular symptomatic presentation, the underlying core emotional vulnerability typically characterized by intolerable painful feelings of loneliness/sadness, shame, or primary fear is obscured, and unmet needs linked to those core painful experiences are unarticulated.

Seen in this light, the work of therapy consists of a number of interwoven processes (see Figure 3.1). The triggers of emotional pain and problematic self-treatment need to be acknowledged and recognized (e.g., "When I am rejected, it hurts, and I tend to blame myself for this rejection and hurt"). The avoidance of emotional pain has to be overcome (e.g., the fear of being in touch with own sense of shame and defectiveness). Secondary undifferentiated distress (e.g., "I feel down") needs to be acknowledged but essentially

FIGURE 3.1. Case Conceptualization Framework for Transdiagnostic Emotion-Focused Therapy

Triggers
Historical and current situations bringing emotional pain

Behavioral Avoidance

Global Distress/Secondary Emotions
Hopelessness, helplessness, irritability, anxiety, hypervigilance, agitation

Emotional Avoidance

Problematic Self-Treatment
Self-criticism, self-worrying, self-scaring, self-managing, self-interrupting

Anxiety/ Apprehension

Core Pain
Loneliness/sadness
Shame
Fear/terror

Unmet Needs
To be loved (connected)
To be accepted
To be safe

Compassion

Protective Anger

Grieving and Letting Go

Relief

Agency and Empowerment

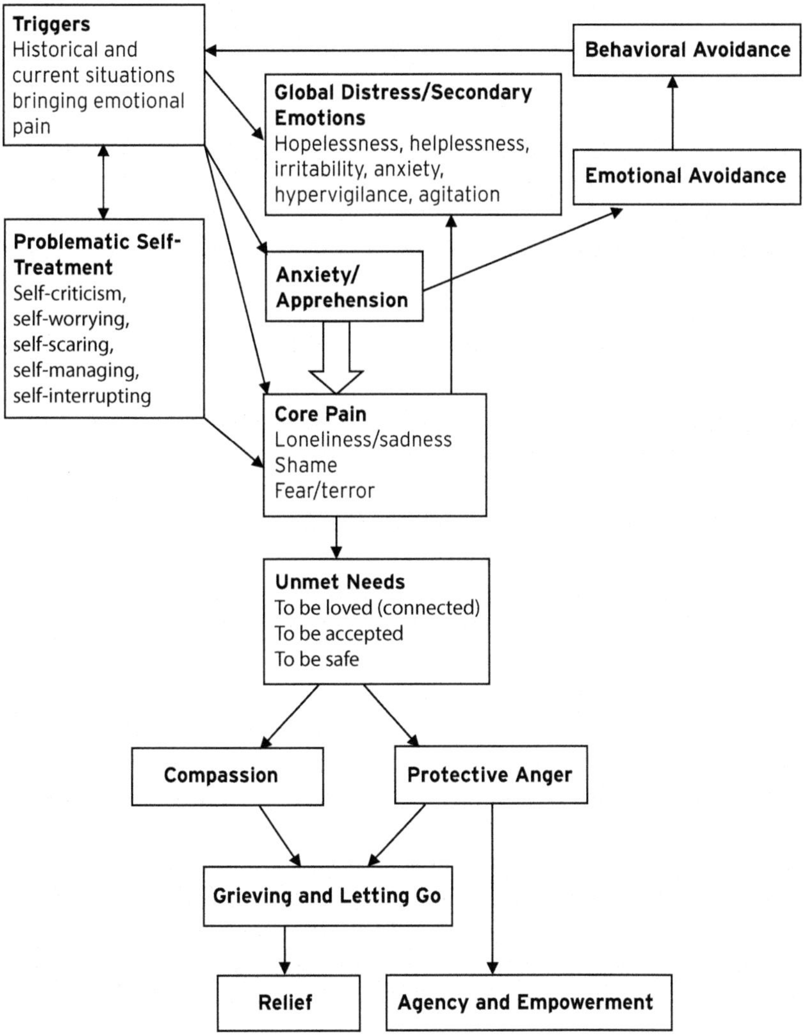

Note. From "Transforming Emotion Schemes in Emotion Focused Therapy: A Case Study Investigation," by S. McNally, L. Timulak, and L. S. Greenberg, 2014, *Person-Centered & Experiential Psychotherapies, 13*(2), pp. 136, 142 (https://doi.org/10.1080/14779757.2013.871573). Copyright 2014 by Taylor and Francis. Adapted with permission; and "Emotion-Focused Therapy: A Transdiagnostic Formulation," by L. Timulak and D. Keogh, 2020, *Journal of Contemporary Psychotherapy, 50*, p. 3 (https://doi.org/10.1007/s10879-019-09426-7). Copyright 2020 by Springer. Adapted with permission.

bypassed so that core painful feelings (e.g., the shame of feeling defective) can be accessed, and the client has to be facilitated to develop a capacity to tolerate these chronic painful feelings. Unmet needs embedded in chronic painful emotions (e.g., "I want to be seen as being okay") have to be articulated and responded to through the facilitation of adaptive emotional responses, such as compassion (e.g., "I care for and I see your value") and healthy protective anger (e.g., "I have a value and deserve to be seen"). Where this occurs, a process of grieving typically ensues whereby the client experiences and expresses grief in relation to those past emotional injuries that contributed to the development of emotional vulnerability (e.g., "All the rejections of the past, particularly from those people who mattered most to me"). This grieving process often is accompanied by novel experiences of empowerment in the face of current pain-inducing triggers (e.g., "I am determined to overcome setbacks/rejections in my life"). Concurrent with, and as a consequence of, the emergence of these more adaptive emotional processes, a decrease is seen in experiences of global distress, emotional avoidance, apprehensive anxiety, and problematic self-treatment.

We now look at this model in more detail. We also provide illustrations of how this transdiagnostic model pertains to the various diagnostic groups discussed in this book: depression, social anxiety, GAD, panic disorder, specific phobias, obsessive-compulsive disorder (OCD), and posttraumatic stress disorder (PTSD). The case conceptualization framework that we present here does not fully account for, nor is it intended to account for, the development of psychological difficulties. For this reason, although we occasionally may comment on personal or historical factors that have potentially shaped particular dynamics, we do not go into much detail as to why specific symptom presentations are likely to have developed. As we outlined in Chapter 1, we do recognize that genetic and biological factors in interaction with developmental and other environmental factors most likely contributed to the dynamics that we are going to comment on. From time to time here, we make clinical observations pertaining to therapeutic strategy; however, it is in the following chapters that we turn our attention to offering greater detail about the clinical implications of the conceptualization framework presented in this chapter.

TRIGGERS OF EMOTIONAL PAIN

Most of our learning about the triggers of emotional pain comes from our clinical and research work. Our experience of listening to hundreds of clients in therapy, in supervision, and on therapy tapes that we and our colleagues have analyzed has led us to map some of the typical triggers behind the emotional pain that clients bring to therapy (e.g., O'Brien et al., 2019). Triggers of emotional pain are, in essence, the clients' presenting issues or their context. Clients often present with either historical or current distressing interpersonal interactions (e.g., experiences of exclusion, rejection, intrusion), but they can also present with nonpersonal distresses (e.g., an illness, a particularly upsetting life event like loss of a job) that can be a context for problematic self-treatment (e.g., not getting a promotion, which gives rise to harsh self-criticism). In other instances, the presenting issue(s) can be a mixture of social, interpersonal, and impersonal events. What all instances have in common, however, is that clients report triggering experiences that are emotionally difficult to cope with. In essence, we can think of these triggers as a perceptual field that the client's internal experiencing interacts with. The issues in question become psychologically problematic insofar as the client's emotional processing of them becomes problematic.

We differentiate between historical and current triggers of emotional pain. *Historical triggers* are those events or circumstances that brought pain in the past and were pivotal in shaping how the clients' vulnerability (to particular triggers) developed. They usually involved pivotal interpersonal interactions with developmentally important people that brought painful emotions for which, in the developmental context in question (e.g., childhood), the individual did not have enough resources to cope with. These events, typically involving parents, caregivers, siblings, and peers (and, later on, romantic relationships) but also individuals in authority (e.g., teachers), as well as broader community forces (e.g., a prejudicial or threatening environment), were important in shaping who the client is as a person, what most distresses them, and how they respond to that distress. While such events may consist of experiences of mistreatment or invalidation, they can equally consist of absences, omissions, or neglect. They can be pervasive and persistent, but, equally, they can consist of isolated events or be sudden in nature (e.g., the loss of a parent).

The nature of triggers may perhaps contribute to a particular symptomatic presentation. For instance, we have noticed a higher prevalence of unforeseen losses or other traumatic experiences of a sudden nature in our clients with GAD (see also Borkovec et al., 2004). Similarly, clients presenting with trauma are often, and understandably, particularly triggered by specific types of events and situations similar to those that brought on the trauma. However, although we have observed that certain types of triggers might more likely be present in specific diagnostic presentations (we offer examples in Table 3.1), we assume that the link between specific triggers and particular

TABLE 3.1. Examples of Historical Events Potentially Linked to a Specific Symptom Presentation

Diagnostic groups with common symptomatic presentation	Possible historical triggers
Depression	Rejection, exclusion, helplessness/hopelessness about getting supportive/validating response from important others
Generalized anxiety	Unpredictable, often sudden, adverse events (often of interpersonal nature, although not necessarily)
Social anxiety	Powerful social/interpersonal rejections repeated across important as well as less important relationships
Obsessive-compulsive presentation	Experiences of being unsupported in frightening and anxiety-provoking situations
Posttraumatic stress	Traumatic events involving people (e.g., assault) or not (e.g., accident)

symptomatic presentations (or diagnostic categories) is not necessarily direct and is often nonspecific. Generally, we see triggers as corresponding more to the type of emotional pain at the core of an individual client's vulnerability. So, for example, triggers are typically linked to experiences of loneliness/ loss (e.g., exclusion, loss of a loved one), shame (e.g., interpersonal rejection), or fear (e.g., a traumatic event).

Historical triggers contribute to the development of emotional vulnerability. *Current triggers*, then, interact with that emotional vulnerability, giving rise to the current crisis—the current experience of emotional pain that leads clients to seek help for their emotional difficulties. Given that our emotional processing operates through schemes (Greenberg, 2017; see also Chapter 2, this volume), it is the perceptual interplay of current triggers with original historical triggers that activates processing pathways oscillating around problematic schemes and emotional vulnerabilities, and that leads to experiences of chronically problematic and painful feelings (core emotional pain). Thus, current problematic interpersonal interactions (e.g., rejection) trigger a processing pathway that was shaped through the nonoptimal processing of past pivotal problematic triggers (e.g., pivotal experiences of rejection). A similar process occurs with nonpersonal problematic triggers—for example, the scary illness is processed through pathways shaped by previous scary experiences.

Many anxiety presentations (e.g., social anxiety, GAD) are also characterized by client fears that specific triggering situations might happen. For instance, clients may be afraid to risk developing closeness in a relationship out of fear that they might be rejected. Clients also can engage in prolonged observation and analysis of particular contexts in anticipation of potential painful triggering incidents. They may study the behavior of others in relational situations and then either skeptically interpret the other's behavior or predict how the other will behave. In the case of anxiety presentations, we can therefore also talk about potential triggers of emotional pain (Timulak & McElvaney, 2018).

Historical and current triggers are both explored in therapy through empathic exploration and through the use of the experiential tasks that are a defining feature of emotion-focused therapy (EFT). For instance, to help unfold triggers, the client may, in an imaginary dialogue, be asked to enact a significant other in an empty chair and to articulate and enact the message given by that significant other. In such an instance, the therapist might instruct the client: "Now be your mother. What is she really saying to you?" (for more about imaginary dialogues with significant others, see Chapter 9). The enactment of triggers in experiential tasks often has a freshness that helps bring clarity as to what it was about those triggers that elicits such pain for the client. Tasks thus not only facilitate an experiential process for the client but, through their vivid experiential quality, also help the therapist get a proper sense of what the specific issues or triggers are for a particular client.

In general, it has been our experience that when therapists use this framework (see Figure 3.1) postsession to make note of what triggers arose in session, or when client in-session presentations are mapped during research work conducted by trained observers (O'Brien et al., 2019), specific overlapping triggers emerge as sources of the client's emotional pain. Links also emerge between historical and current triggers. It is possible to share these observations either in psychoeducation ("hot teaching") directly with the client (see Chapter 5) or when communicating about the client with other professionals (e.g., in supervision).

PROBLEMATIC SELF-TREATMENT

Self-awareness regarding our actions and interactions in the world can prompt us to adjust or moderate how we act as well as how we seek to act or interact in similar situations in the future. If I am aware that my behavior is perceived by others in a particular way, I may adjust my behavior accordingly. So, for example, if I perceive that somebody experiences my jokes as hurtful, I may refrain from making similar jokes the next time we encounter each other. In general, this process of self-aware self-adjustment to our environment can be seen as central to human functioning, the facilitation of survival, and the achievement of goals. For instance, it is an aspect of human motivation that we motivate ourselves—for example, we *make* ourselves study because we know that by doing so, we will achieve goals that are important to us.

In our conceptualization, we refer to this process of self-aware self-adjustment as *self-treatment,* and contend that although it is a deeply human and adaptive process, it also is one that has the potential to become problematic. In part, this is because it has the potential to develop from efforts to self-adjust in particular contexts to problematic attitudes held toward the self more generally. We may be happy with ourselves or we may not; we may feel confident in our abilities or doubtful about our skills. We have outlined examples of the development of problematic self-treatment in our previous work (e.g., Timulak, 2015; Timulak & McElvaney, 2018; Timulak & Pascual-Leone, 2015). For instance, if a child cannot get recognition from a parent, they endeavor to get that recognition by behaving in a particular way aimed at impressing the parent. However, if nothing the child tries is successful at getting that recognition, they may attribute the difficulty to the self (e.g., "I am not talented," "I am not smart enough"). In this developmental context, such self-treatment may be seen as quite functional: The child can only change themselves and not the parent. Over time, this harsh attitude toward the self may be seen by the child as a driving force for self-improvement and thus may even be considered by the child as helpful.

As the example with the child illustrates, problematic self-treatment typically develops in the context of other triggers: "The other person does not see me [trigger]; therefore, I am responsible for it and am to be blamed [problematic self-treatment]." In therapy, either through empathic exploration or the use of experiential tasks, such as chair dialogues, we can elucidate both triggers and the problematic self-treatment often present in the context of those triggers. For instance, in the famous Les Greenberg video with client Dion (Greenberg & Carlson, 2007), it emerges that the client is self-critical in the context of her child's distress and blames herself for her child's suffering. A self-critical process (and variants, e.g., self-judgment, self-contempt), is indeed the most typical example of problematic self-treatment. It is also the process that is most well-known and often described in the EFT literature (e.g., Greenberg et al., 1993; Whelton & Greenberg, 2005). The therapeutic processes involved in experientially addressing and transforming self-criticism are also well described and studied, and this writing and research constitute an important contribution by EFT to the psychotherapy literature (Greenberg, 1979; Greenberg & Dompierre, 1981; Greenberg & Higgins, 1980; see also Chapter 9, this volume).

Problematic self-criticism is characterized by negative judgments of the self (e.g., "I am not smart enough"), expressions of self-contempt (e.g., the client might smirk in reference to self), self-critical beliefs (e.g., "To take pride or pleasure in one's own accomplishments is not good"), and, at times, also beliefs about self-criticism (e.g., "It is good to be self-critical"). It is also typically present in the form of a characterological judgment of the self (e.g., "I am lazy") that is defining of the self (e.g., "This is who I am"). In EFT, the self-critical process is typically addressed through chair dialogues in which the client is guided to experientially enact their own self-critical process, articulating the self-criticism from the position or perspective of the part of the self that is critical ("the critic"). The critic is guided to criticize the self as if talking with another person (e.g., "You are lazy," "You are stupid"). As the client does so, the experiential quality of the self-criticism comes to the fore. The therapist, who may notice that the client is self-contemptuous, harsh, or unforgiving in their attitude toward the self, can bring these qualities to the client's awareness. Through experiential work, the therapist may help the client to become aware of the function of this self-criticism (e.g., "I am attacking myself in order that I improve so that those close to me do not suffer again"). Indeed, experiential work is a good way to distill the nature of problematic self-criticism both in terms of its function and its impact, which is usually intense emotional pain and often some variation of shame.

Self-criticism is a self-defining problematic self-treatment, the effect of which (either in the context of problematic triggers or together with those triggers) may elicit core emotional vulnerability (core chronic painful feelings). It is an aspect of the problematic emotion scheme that brings client experiences of chronic emotional pain and vulnerability (e.g., a sense of inadequacy, weakness). Its variants and idiosyncratic expressions are therefore a focus of transdiagnostic transformational work in EFT-T. We want to capture the self-critical process, make the client aware of it, and ultimately transform this process and the feelings it elicits in the client.

We have observed that problematic self-treatment in the form of some variation of self-criticism is a process shared by clients who meet criteria for various diagnostic groups (see Table 3.2). For instance, in both depression (e.g., "I am unworthy") and social anxiety (e.g., "I am unworthy; therefore, I will be rejected"), it is clearly a defining process. Similarly, clients diagnosed with GAD can be self-critical in a variety of ways (e.g., "I am incapable, so I may cause a lot of problems"; "Something will happen to my children, and it will be my fault"; see Toolan et al., 2019), whereas clients presenting with PTSD often blame themselves for the trauma (e.g., "It is my fault that it happened") or, in case of OCD, for intrusive thoughts/images they

TABLE 3.2. Examples of Variations of Self-Criticism as May Pertain to Various Primary Diagnostic Groups

Diagnostic groups with common symptomatic presentation	Possible more specific variant of self-criticism
Depression	"I am not worthy."
Generalized anxiety	"Something bad will happen, and I will be responsible because I am defective."
Social anxiety	"Others can see how defective I am."
Obsessive-compulsive presentation	"I have these images/thoughts; I am a bad person."
Posttraumatic stress	"It is my fault that it happened."
Panic and agoraphobia	"I am a defective person given that I have these strong physiological reactions."

experience (e.g., "I am a bad person for having these thoughts"). Overall, then, self-criticism is a transdiagnostic process characterized by some form of judgment or nonacceptance of the self and by a harsh self-treatment that brings chronic painful feelings. In Chapter 9, we look in detail at how this transdiagnostic process is addressed and transformed in therapy.

Across diagnostic groups, we also find self-blame related to the client's own symptoms (i.e., criticism of the self for being depressed/anxious; e.g., "I shouldn't be depressed"). Les Greenberg (2017) traditionally referred to this type of criticism as coming from the "coach" critic. In general, although we see this type of self-criticism as a more superficial process, it is still fundamentally an expression of some sort of nonacceptance of the self and can therefore have more substantial correlates (e.g., "I am weak").

In addition to self-blame related to symptoms, it is possible to identify a whole range of symptom-level, problematic self-treatments (see Table 3.3), which, in their various forms, are closely linked to specific diagnostic categories. For instance, excessive worrying can be considered a problematic form of self-treatment whereby the client worries the self (self-worrying) in anticipation of triggers that could bring painful feelings (e.g., "Something bad is going to happen to my son"). Worrying is a defining feature of anxiety and related disorders—for example, in social anxiety, clients worry about social judgment and subsequent shame; in generalized anxiety, about various idiosyncratic triggers that could evoke underlying pain; in panic disorder, about having a panic attack; in OCD, about various intrusive thoughts or images; and in PTSD, about further traumatization. The function of worry is to prevent or prepare oneself for any potential threat (trigger) that would evoke underlying pain. Paradoxically, worrying engages the clients with that

TABLE 3.3. Examples of More Diagnosis-Specific, Symptom-Level, Problematic Self-Treatment as May Pertain to Primary Diagnostic Groups

Diagnostic groups with common symptomatic presentation	Example of a more diagnosis-specific, symptom-level, problematic self-treatment
Depression	Ruminating about past failures
Generalized anxiety	Worrying about potential situations that might bring unbearable painful feelings
Social anxiety	Worrying about potential social/interpersonal situations that might bring unbearable painful feelings of shame
Obsessive-compulsive presentation	Worrying/obsessing about intrusive thoughts/images; engaging in compulsive rituals to neutralize images/ thoughts and the feelings they bring
Posttraumatic stress	Worrying about further traumatization
Panic and agoraphobia	Worrying about physiological reactions and the situations in which they may occur

potential threat and thus brings distress in the form of some sort of anxiety. Furthermore, worrying also serves an avoidance function ("The more I worry, the less time I have to engage with other uncomfortable feelings I may feel") and may lead to avoidant behavior (e.g., "I'm constantly checking in on my children"). The known evil (the anxiety the worrying brings) replaces a potentially unpredictable evil (the feelings I may have to deal with if I allow myself attend to, acknowledge, or express them; see Newman & Llera, 2011).

Rumination (self-rumination) is a similar form of problematic self-treatment. In contrast with worrying in which the client engages with a potential threat in the future, *rumination* involves going over and over a past troubling event. For instance, a client may go over and over an embarrassing situation with the hope of figuring out what went wrong. Ostensibly, the function here is that if I figure out what went wrong, I may come up with some reassuring understanding or increase my control in the future should similar situations arise. However, the reality may be that I simply dwell on, and reexperience, the uncomfortable feelings I felt in the situation. Again, spending time in rumination is more predictable than living more openly and thus has some, albeit not fully satisfying, benefits. It can bring a temporary calming through reassurance while also keeping me so preoccupied that I do not focus attention on issues that may be difficult in my life.

Another common form of problematic self-treatment that has already been captured in the EFT literature (e.g., Greenberg et al., 1993) is emotional self-interruption, a process that can either be conscious or occur outside of full awareness. *Emotional self-interruption* is a process of dampening either emotional experience itself or the expression of that emotional experience (e.g., self-messages like "Don't feel or don't express what you feel"). It can also take a behavioral form when it orients the individual not to engage in situations that could bring painful feelings (e.g., "Don't get close to somebody so you will not get hurt"). The function here is to protect oneself from painful feelings by avoiding feeling, by avoiding expression of feelings, or by avoiding getting into situations in which painful feelings could arise. The cost is usually a sense of physiological obstruction or a sense of being cut off from the self or others (see Chapter 7). Dissociation can also be seen as a form of self-interruption (emotional avoidance), although the self-agency in it may be difficult to recognize.

Engagement in compulsive rituals (self-compulsion) can also be seen as a form of emotional self-interruption. Here, the client wants to neutralize or mitigate the unwanted thoughts/images and the unpleasant feelings they bring. For instance, the client may have an intrusive image (e.g., seeing themselves engaging in a violent act) and seeks to neutralize it by performing a ritual (e.g., counting). The function is to dampen the distressing feelings (often fear or shame) that the thoughts/images bring; the cost is dependence on the rituals and the impairment such dependence brings (e.g., time consuming, exhausting). Furthermore, engagement in obsessive thoughts and rituals distracts the client from other issues that may be happening in their life. We cover the process of working with symptom-level, problematic self-treatment in Chapters 7 and 8 as well as the process of working with core vulnerability–level, problematic self-treatment in Chapter 9.

GLOBAL DISTRESS AND SECONDARY EMOTIONS

"Global distress" as a term was introduced by Antonio Pascual-Leone and Les Greenberg (2007a) in their article reporting on the sequential model of emotional processing, the model that serves as the basis for the formulation we present is this book. Broadly speaking, *global distress* refers to an emotional state characterized by *secondary emotions* (Greenberg & Safran, 1989), the term more traditionally used in EFT literature and, as such, typically corresponds with a symptom-level presentation. It is most typically an undifferentiated distress that is generalized, nonspecific (hence, "global"), and not directly attributable to a specific trigger. In the example used in Chapter 2 in which a hypothetical person comes home to an unresponsive partner, feels sad (primary emotion) at not being responded to, and then falls into a sense of hopelessness (secondary emotion) that life is bleak and that nobody will ever be there for them to meet their need for closeness, it is this hopelessness that constitutes global distress. Often, the original triggers (in that instance, the unresponsiveness of the partner) are buried under layers of more generalized distress—for example, the hopelessness of it all and subsequent resignation. Indeed, it is hopelessness coupled with helplessness that characterizes prototypical examples of global distress.

Hopelessness and helplessness are indicative of an inability to find responses to underlying needs embedded in chronic painful feelings (e.g., needs to be seen, responded to, appreciated, cared for, protected) and a resignation to the idea that those needs will never be responded to. It is the chronic nonfulfillment of those needs that brings distinct core painful feelings. However, the resignation, hopelessness and helplessness typically cover and obfuscate this core pain. Hopelessness, helplessness, and general resignation thus constitute a surface-level aspect to emotional pain, the core of which can be differentiated into distinct, idiosyncratic emotions.

Hopelessness and helplessness are prototypical depressive symptoms. Another example of a primarily depressive symptom is diffuse irritability. In EFT terms, we view such irritability as most likely an expression of secondary anger. In the preceding example, when the client is not responded to by their partner, underlying sadness about lack of connection may be covered not only by hopelessness and resignation but also by an anger directed first to the partner (e.g., "You are not here again") and then perhaps manifesting as a more generalized irritability. The work of A. Pascual-Leone and Greenberg (2007a) observed that reactive, rejecting anger could be present in the early phases of emotional processing. So, such anger may not simply constitute global irritability but, rather, may constitute a distinct secondary emotional reaction covering underlying vulnerability. For instance, in Chapter 1, we mentioned examples of angry reaction to rejection in which the underlying primary feeling is shame (DeWall & Bushman, 2011; DeWall et al., 2011; Leary et al., 2006).

Secondary anger is typically characterized by high reactivity and high arousal (e.g., "You bastard! How could you do this to me?"). The person is often "in the other's face," irritated by the presence of the other, or preoccupied with the specific behavior of the other. By comparison, healthy boundary-setting anger (see Figure 3.1) is lower in arousal and more self-affirmatory (self-empowering, offering an inner sense of confidence and strength) as if saying, "I am strong enough; you cannot hurt me." In reality, it is often the case that the line between secondary anger, covering underlying vulnerability, and boundary-setting, self-affirming anger is quite thin. It has been our research and clinical experience that distinguishing between the two in any given context requires an understanding of the individual case as a whole, and that, even then, it is largely a heuristic decision.

Another typical form of global distress is anxiety, which may be either generalized or situationally specific. For instance, in GAD, there can be quite a wide range of experiences of anxiety, from anxiety that is clearly linked to specific idiosyncratic potential triggers (e.g., "I don't want my children to suffer as I did") to anxiety that is more displaced. In the instance of more displaced anxiety, the associative nature of emotions might mean that anxiety about specific idiosyncratic potential triggers leads inexorably to anxiety about distant variants of those personally relevant triggers (e.g., "I don't want anybody to suffer like I did—not only those close to me").

Secondary anxiety or more general anxiety is characteristic of anxiety disorders. Indeed, the form secondary anxiety takes can be indicative of a diagnostic group as currently conceptualized. For instance, anxiety linked to situations that might bring social or interpersonal judgment is typical of social anxiety, whereas anxiety linked to intrusive thoughts or images is typical of OCD (here, the primary underlying vulnerability may be fear or shame linked to the thoughts or images). Anxiety is linked to efforts to avoid the pain that may arise were the client to engage with the triggers that would bring about that pain. Regardless of the individual's efforts (which may be in or out of awareness) to avoid the pain or those triggers that would trigger the pain, avoidance is not fully successful, and some anxiety seeps through to the felt experience. This may also be a reason why anxiety is often present in a more diffuse form rather than being clearly trigger specific.

Another aspect of global distress is the presence of various physical symptoms linked to psychological suffering. Examples include the physiological manifestations and impacts of anxiety (e.g., tension, physiological arousal, hypervigilance; subsequent tiredness, tightness, lightheadedness, nausea); longer term consequences of anxiety, such as muscle stiffness and aches; and other physiological feelings, such as the tiredness and heaviness that can come with resignation or numbness. These various physical symptoms are often the result of strong aroused emotions and the constriction stemming from attempts to avoid those same emotions. The result is typically a plethora of unpleasant feelings that gives rise to a lot of suffering.

Overall, then, we see the majority of symptoms of depression, anxiety, and related disorders as secondary emotions characteristic of global distress. We see them as a sign that there is some more core, underlying vulnerability that is an idiosyncratic expression of problematic emotion schemes shaped through adverse events/experiences and unsuccessful attempts to process them. In a way, we see depression, anxiety, and the symptoms associated with those disorders as analogous to fever in the context of a physical illness; whereas the fever may need treatment in its own right, it is also indicative of something deeper and more problematic going on (e.g., a bacterial infection). Similarly, although we may need to attend to "surface"-level symptoms, particularly in those cases in which symptoms give rise to significant impairment and distress, as well as taking on a life of their own independent of the developmental processes that gave rise to them, our primary goal is to address the underlying vulnerability that gives rise to those symptoms—not just to treat the symptoms themselves.

APPREHENSIVE ANXIETY, EMOTIONAL AND BEHAVIORAL AVOIDANCE

The potential for triggers to evoke distressingly painful feelings means that, in some cases, even the possibility of triggers becoming activated is a source of apprehensive anxiety. *Apprehensive anxiety* is thus a fear that particular triggers, or variants of those triggers, could be activated, thereby triggering in the person dreaded, chronic painful feelings. This apprehensive anxiety is not only felt (see our description in the preceding section on global distress) but also leads to emotional avoidance and behavioral avoidance. For example, clients afraid of potential judgment by others (social anxiety) may try to avoid feelings of primary shame and secondary anxiety (emotional avoidance), in part, by avoiding social situations that might trigger that shame and anxiety (behavioral avoidance). In many instances, this anxiety will be vividly and distressingly present in the client's experience and awareness. At other times, however, avoidant behavior (e.g., placating others) driven by that anxiety may successfully ensure that no physical distress characteristic of that same anxiety is actually felt. Often, clients experience/engage in a mixture of the two. They feel some anxiety while also engaging in emotional and behavioral avoidance that mitigates the full extent of possible anxiety they would otherwise feel. As is the case with core painful feelings and efforts to avoid potential triggers of that pain, when clients often oscillate between successful and less successful avoidance, client also oscillate between successful and less successful efforts to not feel apprehensive anxiety.

Clients engage in various strategies that are an expression of such apprehensive anxiety, some of which we already covered in the earlier section titled Problematic Self-Treatment. For instance, clients may worry about potential triggers and act accordingly. So, for example, I can worry about my children on a school trip (which is a form of emotional avoidance), but I can also repeatedly call them on the telephone, thus trying to control them (which is a form of behavioral avoidance). Such worry may serve an avoidance function because by worrying about my children, my mind is preoccupied, and I have neither the headspace nor time for my focus to drift to other potentially more painful aspects of my life. Indeed, for some clients, "symptom talk" (i.e., an excessive focus on their own symptoms; e.g., the bodily symptoms of anxiety) may itself serve an avoidance function and can, in extreme cases, result in clients' engaging with literally nothing in their life other than their own physical symptoms.

Clients may also interrupt emotion (self-interruption) that is already evoked (particularly primary vulnerable emotions), doing so either intentionally in a manner that they are aware of or in a manner that occurs outside of awareness—for example, dissociation. Emotional self-interruption can be situational, but it can also be a more habitual, traitlike, generalized way of being. Indeed, some clients have developed emotional processing styles such that accessing emotional experience in an aroused way is something they do not do under almost any circumstances. There can be stereotypically gendered and cultural dimensions to this processing style—for example, many men may have learned not to feel and not to express feelings. As we have implied, emotional avoidance strategies are often linked to subsequent behavioral avoidance (not expressing feelings can, e.g., be conceptualized as a form of behavioral avoidance), and various forms of self-interruption often overlap with behaviors that ensure painful feelings are not experienced (e.g., withdrawing from interactions in which there is the potential for me to be disappointed).

Self-harm, compulsion, and rumination can, in various ways, be conceptualized as—at least in part—forms of avoidance. For some individuals, the physical pain of self-harm distracts from a more self-defining psychological pain. It should be emphasized that this is not always the case, and self-harm can, among other things, often also be an expression of harsh self-criticism or self-punishment (Sutton, 2007). Compulsions can be seen as attempts to neutralize and mitigate felt discomfort, typically fear or anxiety but often also shame (e.g., "I am dirty for seeing these images in my head"). Compulsions, in a similar way to worry, may ensure that the client is not living in such a way as to be fully immersed in experiencing the world and their interactions with others, thus protecting the client from potentially painful experiences. Excessive rumination may fulfill a similar function.

Comfort eating, engagement in distracting activities, self-medication through various forms of anxiolytics, and restricted behavior in many ways can be seen as forms of behavioral avoidance. Many forms of behavioral avoidance are not directly enacted in the therapy session and are known to the therapist only through the client's narrative about life outside of the therapy room. However, our research group identified several forms of emotional and behavioral avoidance that actually can be present within the therapy session (O'Brien et al., 2019). For instance, clients may change the topic when the focus of the session is on difficult subject matter; they may have a conversational style that functions to preclude them and the therapist from focusing on painful emotions; they may minimize or laugh off difficult topics; and they may not want to engage in experiential tasks, such as chair dialogues. At times, clients may even be seen as almost wanting to stay in a particular distressing emotional state rather than allow themselves to feel another—for example, they may stay with secondary anger rather than attend to or acknowledge underlying vulnerability.

Emotional and behavioral avoidance strategies may be situational and transient, or they may be more traitlike and defining of the client's way of being. It is mainly those strategies that are persistent, chronic, and almost traitlike ways of avoiding that we target in the symptom-level transdiagnostic work described in Chapter 7. As with some of the other aspects we have already discussed in this chapter, while we do not see various emotional and behavioral avoidance strategies as necessarily defining of a particular diagnostic group as currently conceptualized in the *Diagnostic and Statistical Manual of Mental Disorders* or in the *International Statistical Classification of Diseases and Related Health Problems*, some of those strategies can be more apparent in some presentations compared with others (see Table 3.4).

CORE EMOTIONAL PAIN

Early on in the development of EFT, Les Greenberg (Greenberg & Safran, 1989; see also Chapter 2, this volume) differentiated among primary, secondary, and instrumental emotions. *Primary emotions* are emotional reactions that are discreet, clear responses to triggers. So, for example, the shame felt in response to an experience of rejection (trigger) is a primary emotion. We can also experience primary emotions in response to self-treatment in the context of triggers—for example, "My son is upset [trigger], so it is my fault [self-criticism], and, therefore, I feel shame [primary emotion]." By contrast, *secondary emotions* are often secondary emotional responses to more primary emotions—for example, "My shame will never change, and, therefore, I feel hopeless." Secondary emotions can be diffuse indicators of some underlying discreet emotion—for example, "I feel unhappy in general"; or, they can be

TABLE 3.4. Examples of More Diagnosis-Specific, Emotional and Behavioral Avoidance Strategies as May Pertain to Primary Diagnostic Groups

Diagnostic groups with common symptomatic presentation	Examples of more diagnosis-specific, emotional/behavioral avoidance strategies
Depression	Withdrawal from interactions that might bring disappointment or activate core painful feelings; numbing, distracting oneself from feeling
Generalized anxiety	Worrying about potential situations that would bring unbearable painful feelings; spending time worrying; focusing on own anxiety; using off-label anxiolytic medication
Social anxiety	Worrying about potential social/interpersonal situations that might bring unbearable painful feelings of shame; avoiding those social situations; using off-label medication for social situations
Obsessive-compulsive presentation	Worrying/obsessing about intrusive thoughts/images; engaging in compulsive rituals in an attempt to neutralize the images, thoughts, or related feelings
Posttraumatic stress	Worrying about further traumatization; avoiding situations similar to situations in which traumatic experience occurred
Panic and agoraphobia	Worrying about physiological reactions and the situations in which they may occur; being preoccupied with own bodily reactions/symptoms; avoiding particular places

specific attempts to avoid primary emotion—for example, "I feel and express anger when I am being put down" (primary shame, secondary anger). The relationship between instrumental and primary emotions can be thought off as somewhat similar; an *instrumental emotion*, broadly speaking, hopes to evoke responses to primary emotional experiences—for example, "I showed off my anger [instrumental] so you would respond to my sadness [primary] and the need for closeness."

Les Greenberg also indicated early on (Greenberg, 2017; Greenberg & Safran, 1989) that it is primary emotions, particularly primary maladaptive emotions, that are the focus of therapy precisely because it is the activation of primary maladaptive emotion schemes that underpins the distress and impairment experienced by clients. Primary maladaptive emotions thus became the primary focus of EFT and of the transformational work at the core of EFT. Given that differentiation among secondary, primary, instrumental, and primary adaptive and primary maladaptive emotions is a heuristic judgment—based to a significant extent on clinical experience (and clinically relevant writing as hopefully represented by this book)—the process of making these distinctions is not always clear-cut. Indeed, this chapter, and this book as a whole, constitutes an effort to help with making these differentiations. In broad strokes, however, EFT endeavors to focus on primary maladaptive rather than secondary emotions so that when a client with depression describes their hopelessness and helplessness in a manner that is generic and diffuse, the therapist looks for underlying discreet primary emotions that are clearly linked with particular triggers or self-treatment.

Returning to the example introduced in Chapter 2 of the individual lying in bed feeling hopeless, helpless, and depressed, the therapist might, in this instance, inquire about discreet experiences that may have led the client to resign (e.g., "What are some of those things that make you give up?"), thereby learning about the painful feelings of sadness experienced by that client when not receiving the wished-for closeness and support from their partner. It is this discreet emotion (e.g., unbearable loneliness/sadness), chronic in nature and maladaptive in that it does not inform adaptive action, that the therapist will endeavor to focus on. The therapist thus follows "the core" of the client's emotional experience—the maladaptive emotion—that part of the client's experiencing that is heuristically determined to be most painful. Les Greenberg and Rhonda Goldman (2007) used the term *pain compass* to describe the process by which the therapist follows what is most painful in a client's experience to identify, attend to, and work with what is most therapeutically important. In the famous Les Greenberg demonstration video with Dion (Greenberg & Carlson, 2007), the client first mentions that she feels hopeless (around minute 3), and Les invites her to explore what some of the "disappointments" contributing to that felt hopelessness might be. Eventually, the client focuses on a discreet sense of guilt she feels for having uprooted her son (around minute 11). This then becomes the painful experience (primary maladaptive emotion, core pain) that Les and the client proceed to focus on.

"Core pain" has become a popular term within the EFT community. We use the terms "core pain," "core emotional pain," "chronic painful feelings," and "primary maladaptive emotions" interchangeably. We also use the term *core emotional vulnerability* when pointing to how idiosyncratic maladaptive emotion schemes make us each uniquely vulnerable to particular experiences of emotional pain. We primarily use terms, such as "core (emotional) pain," "chronic painful feelings," and "(core) emotional vulnerability," not because they refer to uniquely distinct processes but, rather, because we feel they convey the nature of client experiences more poignantly than more technical terms, such as "primary maladaptive emotion."

Core painful feelings are thus those painful feelings that are at the center of the problematic emotional processing of upsetting triggers or corresponding problematic self-treatment. They are feelings that are difficult for clients to tolerate; thus, clients can either expend considerable effort seeking to avoid them or collapse into secondary distress when efforts at avoidance are unsuccessful. These painful feelings also indicate that related emotional needs are not being fulfilled (see the later discussion in this chapter on unmet needs).

Given that EFT is a process-oriented and experiential approach in the humanistic tradition of therapies, such as client-centered and gestalt therapy (as opposed to content-oriented approaches, such as psychodynamic therapy, that define the areas of intrapsychic conflict), it has traditionally shared the reluctance of those approaches to theoretically specify the sort of chronic painful feelings that are likely to be at the center of client difficulties. Indeed, although the writing of Les Greenberg and his colleagues offers specific examples of primary maladaptive emotions and specifies that those emotions generally have to do with attachment- (e.g., "How do I feel in relation to others?") and identity- (e.g., "How do I see myself?") related themes (Goldman & Greenberg, 2015; Greenberg & Goldman, 2007), the traditional preference has been to refer in general terms to "primary maladaptive emotions" without elaborating on which emotions specifically might be maladaptive.

Our research group examined clients' in-session presentations through an EFT theoretical lens that specifically inquired as to the core painful emotions underlying more symptomatic client presentations (e.g., Dillon et al., 2018; Hissa et al., 2020; McNally et al., 2014; O'Brien et al., 2019). The result of these investigations was that we could distill three clusters of primary painful emotions: (a) loneliness/sadness-based emotional experiences, (b) shame-based emotional experiences, and (c) fear-based emotional experiences (for conceptual writing, see Timulak, 2015; Timulak & Keogh, 2020; Timulak & McElvaney, 2016, 2018; Timulak & Pascual-Leone, 2015). It has been our observation that a client's emotional pain or vulnerability is typically present in an idiosyncratic way that more or less fits one or other of those clusters. Combinations of experiences fitting two or more clusters are also possible (e.g., "I feel alone [loneliness/sadness] and scared [fear]!" or "I feel unloved [loneliness/sadness] and unlovable [shame]"). We observed that these chronic painful emotions also indicated that specific idiosyncratic embedded needs were being chronically unmet (e.g., for connection, recognition safety).

Primary maladaptive loneliness/sadness-based emotions are characterized by experiences of chronic isolation or loss. In our studies, we observed clients expressing loneliness/sadness-based emotional experiences with language, such as: "I feel lonely," "I feel alone," "I feel not loved," "I feel on my own," "I feel empty," "I have nobody to turn to," "I do not have anybody," "I miss my [close person]," "I never had their love [again, a close person]," and "I feel sad." These experiences also have been observed as pointing to corresponding needs for closeness, connection, love, or caring. Phenomenologically, loneliness/sadness is typically characterized by some or all of the following: tearfulness or crying, a lower voice quality, subdued posture, a sense of emptiness or depletion, and possibly also a primary hopelessness that is distinctly linked to specific loss (as opposed to a more diffuse secondary hopelessness/helplessness about life in general). In therapy sessions, clients vulnerable to feeling intolerable loneliness/sadness may have a tendency to fall into secondary hopelessness, helplessness, or resignation, or they may try to avoid feeling the loneliness/sadness/loss. These emotional experiences are typically linked to historical triggers involving experiences in which loss or exclusion were unbearable. These emotional experiences became chronic through having needs not met in the context of pivotal shaping interactions in the past, and they are now reactivated by more current triggers, such as current loss or exclusion. At times, even current loss or exclusion may give rise to unbearable pain and the formation of a particularly powerful emotion scheme that is difficult to live with in everyday functioning.

Primary maladaptive shame-based emotional experiences are experiences of self-defining, unshakable diminishment, not feeling deserving, or feeling flawed. In our studies we observed clients expressing shame-based core painful emotional experiences with language, such as: "I feel ashamed," "I feel embarrassed," "I feel worthless," "I feel humiliated," "I feel unlovable," "I feel inadequate," "I feel like a failure," "I feel flawed," "I feel guilty," "I am broken," "I can't handle things," "I feel/I am stupid," "I am incompetent," "I am awkward/weird," "I feel small/like a child," "I am immature," and "I am weak." These experiences suggest unmet needs to be seen, recognized, accepted, understood, or respected. Phenomenologically, shame is characterized by a subtle but powerful feeling of discomfort, by self-silencing, and by a strong action tendency to punish oneself or to hide and disappear. The experience is thus often coupled with experiences of loneliness. In therapy sessions, clients may have a tendency to quickly seek to avoid this type of experience, to go silent, to change topic, or to go to secondary anger. Various historical triggers in the form of rejection, judgment, ridicule, or neglect as well as their equivalent current triggers evoke these feelings, which typically are coupled with an ingrained problematic self-treatment characteristic: self-condemnation, self-contempt, self-rejection, or some combination of those. Particularly powerful are triggers and corresponding problematic self-treatment rooted in developmentally sensitive periods of time.

Primary maladaptive fear-based emotional experiences are experiences of overwhelming panic and terror related to feeling that one's safety from physical harm, bodily violation, or life is at stake. Phenomenologically, they include experiences of sheer panic (e.g., as experienced in panic attacks) with all of panic's physiological correlates, such as shaking, trembling, a sense of fainting/lightheadedness, difficulties with breathing, increased heartbeat, palpitations, heightened bodily tension, sweating, involuntary bowel movement, nausea, and various other uncomfortable bodily symptoms. Dissociation may occur, and the action tendency is to freeze or flee. Given that clients typically want to avoid these types of experiences and may do so or may dissociate from them, a therapist may easily miss the significance of particular in-session symptomatic presentations. In our studies, we observed clients expressing fear-based emotional experiences with language, such as "I am afraid," "I am scared," "I feel terrified," "I feel unsafe," "I am overwhelmed/falling apart," "I am unprotected," "I am feeling invaded/have been intruded upon," "I feel terrorized," "I feel dread," and so on. The clients could then identify corresponding unmet needs for safety, protection, and support. Historical and current triggers involve events in which the client's health, physical integrity, or life were in danger—that is, typical experiences of trauma.

In general, we see underlying core emotional pain as not being predictive of particular sets of symptoms corresponding to diagnostic labels as currently conceptualized. However, it is possible that some idiosyncratic forms of underlying core emotional pain may be more characteristic of secondary emotions/global distress and overall symptomatic presentations. Indeed, when looking at examples in Chapter 5, we can see traces of underlying core emotional pain in more surface-level symptomatic presentations. Overall, however, it is the core emotional pain (or core emotional vulnerability) that is more defining of the client's difficulties rather than symptom-level presentation. This idiosyncratic core emotional vulnerability may find expression at a symptom level in a manner that is more typical of one or other diagnostic group, or, more typically, it can cut across many diagnostic groups as currently conceptualized (hence contributing to the high levels of comorbidity mentioned in Chapter 1). In either case, it is this idiosyncratic core emotional pain, or core emotional vulnerability, that is the primary target of treatment in EFT-T.

UNMET NEEDS

Core painful emotions contain in themselves unmet needs that typically are chronic in nature (see Figure 3.1). These needs correspond to the three clusters of core painful emotions already identified. Idiosyncratic variants of needs for connection, love, closeness, and the presence of loved ones (e.g., "I miss you," "I need your presence," "I need your love") are embedded in painful experiences of loneliness/sadness. Idiosyncratic variants of needs for recognition, acceptance, respect, acknowledgment, validation, and understanding (e.g., "I need you to understand," "I need you to see me," "I need to be accepted for who I am") are embedded in painful shame-based experiences. And idiosyncratic variants of needs for safety, protection, control, comfort, support (e.g., "I need to feel safe," "I need you to protect me," "I needed you to hug me and tell me that it would all be alright") are embedded in painful primary fear-based experiences.

The articulation of unmet needs serves as a bridge in the transformational work at the heart of EFT. Unmet needs point toward the sort of emotional response the client needs to mitigate the unbearable pain they are experiencing (A. Pascual-Leone & Greenberg, 2007a; Timulak & Pascual-Leone, 2015). For instance, the statement "I need you to love me for who I am" clearly points to a need for an expression of unconditional love to heal and balance a sense of feeling unloved and unlovable. Articulated needs thus point to the sort of healthy emotional experiences that must be generated through therapeutic facilitation. Articulated unmet needs also bring clarity, helping to differentiate aspects of the core painful feelings. This clarity can help clients to tolerate the emotional experience, thus facilitating emotional regulation. Articulation of needs also has the potential in and of itself to promote a sense of hope because the clear articulation of needs implies and thus validates deservedness of the need (e.g., "I need your love," "I deserve your love").

TRANSFORMATION OF CORE EMOTIONAL PAIN

Acknowledging secondary distress, overcoming emotional avoidance, accessing core pain, articulating unmet needs, and generating emotional responses to those needs are the essential processes involved in transforming underlying emotional vulnerability. As mentioned in the preceding section, the articulation of unmet needs is the bridge from pain to the transformation of that pain. Broadly speaking, adaptive and transformative responses to core pain and embedded unmet needs take two forms: (a) compassion-based emotional responses and (b) healthy (protective and boundary-setting) anger-based emotional responses. Experiences of compassion and of protective anger help to restructure problematic emotion schemes such that where before there was just pain, collapse, and avoidance, there can now also be a growing capacity to self-soothe, stand up for the self, and bounce back. The goal is to build emotional resilience and emotional flexibility (A. Pascual-Leone, 2009). Overall, both compassion and protective anger are equally important, but in particular cases, one may be more central and thus a more important focus of therapy than the other.

Compassion

Compassion-based emotional responses are generated in EFT primarily through the use of imaginary dialogues. In the prototypical form of such a dialogue, the client is facilitated to access core emotional pain and embedded unmet needs (e.g., "I needed you to love me"). Then, from the enacted position of a potentially responsive person or part of the self, the client is invited to see whether compassion toward the vulnerable self emerges naturally (e.g., "How is it to see them in that loneliness, longing so much for love? What do you feel toward them right now?") Typically, witnessing the poignancy of felt and expressed pain and vulnerability invites a caring response in the self—for example, "I see your pain," "I feel caring toward you," and "I love you." Of course, the generation of compassion is a complex process, and clients are often in therapy, in part, because they struggle to access self-compassion. In Chapter 9, we describe in detail the process of generating compassion and working with various obstacles to this process. For the moment, though, we simply note that the freshness of felt and expressed core pain (see Chapter 2 for a discussion about emotional arousal), the poignancy of articulated need, and the capacity to take risks to feel or put aside overprotection or self-criticism are decisive factors in facilitating or inhibiting the generation of self-compassion. Indeed, the manner in which transformational work progresses in imaginary dialogues is very telling from an assessment point of view because client struggles to access underlying pain/unmet needs or to generate compassion inform the therapist's understanding and case conceptualization (we talk more about this topic in Chapters 5 and 9).

An important source of compassion for the client is the compassionate presence of the therapist. EFT therapists are emotionally engaged with their clients. They try to embody and convey a caring presence such that it might feel safer for clients to explore painful feelings. EFT therapists are often genuinely moved by clients' pain as well as by their efforts to cope with that pain. As part of offering a warm, connecting, and engagingly relational presence, EFT therapists do not shy away from expressing when they are moved by their clients' struggles and when they feel for their clients. EFT therapists bear witness to their clients' pain and struggle, and they explicitly validate client unmet needs, acknowledging on a deeply human level the clients' deservingness to have needs for closeness, recognition, and safety met (Timulak, 2014; see also Chapter 4, this volume).

Caring and compassionate presence, whether from the client themselves or from the therapist, also invites the client to access and express more vulnerable feelings (core pain). The dyadic relationship between pain and compassion is not as simple as compassion soothing pain, and often the relationship is one whereby the pain invites compassion, and the compassion invites more pain. Indeed, at times in imaginary dialogues, some clients can only access pain and vulnerability if a caring imagined figure is sitting in the other chair (see Chapter 9). Client-generated compassion also often leads to a natural grieving in relation to past pains. Antonio Pascual-Leone's line of work has demonstrated how compassionate responses invite grieving in relation to past pains (A. Pascual-Leone, 2009; A. Pascual-Leone & Greenberg, 2007a), grieving that can have a healing and letting-go quality (e.g., Dillon et al., 2018; McNally et al., 2014). The compassion–pain dyad thus can, at times, become a pain–compassion–grieving triad. Over time, experiences of compassion allow for and facilitate experiences of connection, closeness, caring, kindness, and love as well as corresponding physiological experiences of relief, calmness, and warmth. They are thus the opposite of, and offer a balance to, core pain and symptomatic distress.

Protective Anger

The second pillar of transformational work is the generation of boundary-setting protective anger in response to hurtful triggers, the pain elicited by those triggers, and the unmet needs contained in that pain. While compassion is elicited by witnessing vulnerability, primary adaptive protective anger is elicited by seeing the mistreatment (e.g., bullying) in the trigger or problematic self-treatment (e.g., harsh self-criticism). Healthy, protective, boundary-setting anger is self-affirming, bringing confidence and inner strength, and needs to be distinguished from secondary anger, which is often reactive and mixed with the pain and upset that it is a reaction to. Protective anger is more measured. It comes in a form that is less aroused but has a subtle firmness (e.g., "I am an adult, so you can't hurt me anymore"). It is validating of the unmet need and brings a sense of deservedness in relation to the need (e.g., "I do deserve to be treated with respect," "I am valuable").

In the EFT literature, this healthy type of primary adaptive anger is sometimes called "assertive anger" (e.g., A. Pascual-Leone, 2009; A. Pascual-Leone & Greenberg, 2007a). We prefer the term "protective" or "boundary-setting" anger because we wish to stress that it is typically not an expansive anger encroaching on the other. Physiologically, it brings less arousal, but it gives a sense of inner strength and firmness. It serves as an antidote to vulnerability, anxiety, fear, and overwhelming upset; thus, it helps with emotional regulation. In EFT, it is typically generated in chair dialogues during which the client stands up for themselves against the imagined/enacted intruder, harmful other (trigger), or problematic part of the self (e.g., self-critic). Felt anger and its enactment in chair dialogues brings an experience of being truly alive. The client is not talking about anger but is truly feeling and expressing anger. The enactment of protective anger brings a sense of agency, empowerment, and inner strength, and research indicates that this is an important outcome of EFT (e.g., Timulak & Elliott, 2003; Timulak et al., 2017). The empowerment is felt experientially and brings an emotional, but also physiological, sense of freedom, resilience, and strength.

Relationally, the therapist validates healthy anger, thus also validating the client's right to have their unmet needs met. An open affirmatory stance is a part of the therapist's empathy and overall relational presence. Again, the therapist is not necessarily hidden with their affirmation but, rather, is an open and transparent supporter of the client. Such open backing and acknowledgment of unmet needs offers relational affirmation. The EFT therapist thus offers both a caring/compassionate and affirming/validating relationship.

THE NECESSITY TO ADDRESS AND TRANSFORM PSYCHOPATHOLOGICAL SYMPTOMS

The conceptualization just presented, which differentiates among the triggers of emotional pain, problematic self-treatment, emotional avoidance strategies, underlying core pain and unmet needs, and compassionate and protective anger-based experiential responses to pain and need, is central to our model of transdiagnostic transformational therapeutic work. We want to access core vulnerability and unmet needs irrespective of client symptomatic presentations—and transform that vulnerability by increasing emotional resilience and flexibility (A. Pascual-Leone, 2009). The particular nature of this underlying vulnerability (e.g., shame- or loneliness-based) is not necessarily predictive of the type of symptoms present in client presentations, although, at times, there is a relationship (e.g., traumatic fear underlying symptom-level anxiety in PTSD). The main focus of any EFT work is thus transdiagnostic in essence; it focuses on the core vulnerability idiosyncratic to each client, the particular nature of which gets unfolded in the therapeutic process.

Despite this primary focus of EFT-T on underlying vulnerability, we currently propose that symptom-level distress needs not only to be acknowledged and then bypassed (although, for the most part, this is how it is) but also needs to be addressed and requires a certain type of therapeutic work. This is based on our learning so far (e.g., Timulak & McElvaney, 2018) given that we have seen how some symptomatic aspects of client presentations are so engrained and habitual that they live a life of their own, directly contributing in their own right to client suffering. Thus, although we see symptoms as developing out of an apprehension to feel core painful feelings in certain contexts (triggers) or from an inability to tolerate those same painful feelings (e.g., collapse to hopelessness), and although we remain primarily focused on healing that core pain and vulnerability, we propose that there frequently may also be a need to address symptom-level distress. Indeed, this may be necessary not only because such symptomatic processes have become habitual and cause suffering in their own right but also because symptoms may have become obstacles to transformational work (e.g., avoidance preventing the accessing of core pain).

In Chapter 8, we address the most common ways of working with the varied symptoms of depression, anxiety, and related disorders. For now, we will say briefly that symptom-level work follows a certain pattern. We try to bring to client awareness their agency with respect to symptom-level difficulties (e.g., "How do you worry yourself?"), the function of the self-treatment process playing a role in symptom-level difficulties (e.g., "What drives your worrying?"), and the impact of this self-treatment process on the self (e.g., "How does it make you feel when you are being worried like this?"). We then try to facilitate the client's capacity to generate compassion toward the affected part of themselves (e.g., "How is it to see yourself so impacted by the worrying?") or set a boundary to the problematic self-treatment (e.g., "What will you do if that part keeps worrying you?"). As can be seen, this process is not that dissimilar from the core pain-related transformational work. The only difference is that it focuses on the secondary symptom-level distress generated by those processes engaged in by the client to unsuccessfully protect the self from underlying pain and vulnerability.

CONCLUSION

In this chapter, we presented a detailed description of how we think about cases from a EFT-T perspective. Our approach is based on the work of A. Pascual-Leone and Greenberg (2007a) and has been further informed by our own clinical and research experiences. We propose that past painful experiences leave clients emotionally vulnerable to current triggers. Fear of the pain that these triggers could activate combined with problematic self-treatment in the face of these triggers drives emotional and behavioral avoidance processes.

Although clients typically present to therapy in a state of global distress characterized by secondary emotions, the task of therapy is to facilitate the client's accessing of the core pain underlying this distress to identify attendant unmet needs related to that pain and to facilitate the generation of adaptive emotional responses within the session to that pain and the unmet needs. In addition to targeting this core emotional vulnerability, which we propose underlies the various specific disorders clients present with, a subordinate but parallel process targets those self-treatment processes that give rise to persistently problematic aspects of symptomatic presentations.

PART **II** BUILDING BLOCKS
OF DELIVERING
TRANSDIAGNOSTIC
EMOTION-FOCUSED
THERAPY

4 OFFERING A COMPASSIONATE AND VALIDATING RELATIONSHIP

In this section of the book, we focus our attention on clinical practice, that is, on how we actually work with clients in transdiagnostic emotion-focused therapy (EFT-T). We begin by looking at the nature of the therapeutic relationship as conceptualized in EFT. As a humanistic *relational* psychotherapy in the tradition of Rogers (1951, 1961), the development and provision of a therapeutic relationship characterized by authenticity, warmth, and empathy is a cornerstone of EFT. These relational qualities are also seen as the building blocks of the trusting relationship that is both precursor to, and necessary for, the work of therapy. A trusting therapeutic relationship provides the safety necessary to allow clients explore and express emotional vulnerability, and it is in the context of such a relationship that it becomes possible for core chronic painful emotions to be accessed and ultimately transformed in therapy. The therapist's authentic presence also can have a soothing effect for the client, serving as an antidote to painful interpersonal encounters experienced elsewhere by the client. In addition, it can offer a more direct corrective emotional experience when, in the context of activated core painful emotions and unmet needs, the therapist both responds compassionately to, and validates the deservingness of, the unmet needs being responded to.

https://doi.org/10.1037/0000253-005
Transdiagnostic Emotion-Focused Therapy: A Clinical Guide for Transforming Emotional Pain, by L. Timulak and D. Keogh

RELATIONAL QUALITIES

A prerequisite for a trusting therapeutic relationship is therapist *authenticity,* the therapist's capacity to be genuinely present with the client in a relational encounter rather than to remain hidden behind a facade of professionalism (Rogers, 1957, 1961). Such authenticity has both intrapersonal and inter-personal dimensions (Lietaer, 1993). To be authentically present to the client, the therapist must be aware of their own emotional processes both before and during the session. The therapist must also be fully open to hearing and understanding the client's experience without abdicating their own values or beliefs but being sufficiently aware of such processes that they do not obstruct empathic attunement to the client. This awareness may involve a reflection of the therapist's identity and background that may interact with the client's identity and background as well as the therapist's privileges that may interact with "invisible" barriers experienced by marginalized clients (Levitt et al., 2019).

On an experiential level, Geller and Greenberg (2012) outlined a variety of practices that can be useful for therapists to increase awareness of their own processes before and during sessions. In addition to self-awareness regarding such internal processes, it is important that the therapist also assess when it is important to put aside their own processes so as not to adversely affect the therapeutic process. And, conversely, the therapist needs to be willing to be open regarding their own experience in the session to aid the therapeutic process. For example, it might be therapeutic in a particular context for the therapist to disclose that they are moved by the client's experience such that the disclosure validates the client experience in a manner that facilitates acknowledgment and a sense of connection.

In addition to being authentically present and open to the client's experience, the therapist actively and openly communicates that they care for the client. Such interpersonal warmth is valued by many clients (Timulak et al., 2017). It contributes to the client's trust that the therapist has their best interests at heart, thus facilitating trust in the therapeutic process as a whole even as that process involves touching on and working with previously avoided or dreaded painful emotions. In attending openly to the client's experience, the therapist is especially attentive and compassionate toward any vulnerability that the client might experience.

Although empathy is central to most psychotherapeutic approaches, it is especially important in EFT. In particular, the EFT therapist works to be empathically attuned to client affect (Greenberg, 2019). To do so, the EFT therapist draws on a wide repertoire of empathic interventions (Elliott et al., 2004; see also Chapter 2, this volume). The therapist uses a range of empathic interventions, from simple empathic reflections that communicate understanding of what the client is saying, to evocative reflections that communicate understanding but use evocative language or imagery that heightens emotional experiencing, to empathic conjectures in which the therapist draws on their knowledge of human emotional experience to tentatively conjecture what the client might be experiencing. Throughout the process of therapy, the therapist balances empathic exploration of the client's experience with communicating their understanding of that experience to the client. The communication of understanding may also involve affirmation that has an experiential focus ("It must have been very difficult. I can imagine it must have been so draining").

The therapist's empathic presence helps to modulate the client's experience. The therapist is cognizant of pacing within the session. They ensure that space is left for vulnerability to take form, modulate vocal quality so as to empathically connect with vulnerability or affirm adaptive anger, and focus not just on words and expressed feelings but also on experiential and bodily felt aspects of experience. The therapist's presence thus offers a regulating holding (see Chapter 6) but also helps to bring optimal levels of emotional arousal and an optimal focus on core painful feelings while simultaneously facilitating emotional experiences with the potential to transform this core pain.

The therapist's relational skills also show in how the therapist scaffolds the therapeutic process and, in particular, experiential tasks (see the next section), and the actual form of their engagement and interventions varies at different points within the session and across therapy. For example, it is different when the therapist is trying to help the client get in touch with core emotional vulnerability compared to when the therapist is helping the client to engage in different stages of therapeutic tasks or different stages of symptom-level or emotional vulnerability–level transformation. In the instance of emotional vulnerability–level transformation, for example, the therapist's approach frequently is more directive. The relationship is also pivotal in facilitating emotional transformation because problematic emotion schemes often involve processing of interpersonal encounters; in such work, the therapeutic relationship can provide a corrective emotional as well as interpersonal experience.

TASKS AND GOALS AGREEMENT

The therapeutic relationship is forged not only through the therapist's skill at responding to the client's emotional experience but also through the therapist's expertise at easing the client into therapy, at providing a rationale for therapy and therapeutic tasks, at scaffolding those therapeutic tasks, and at facilitating client reflection not only regarding emotional experiences but also regarding therapy itself. The therapist's expertise, interpersonal skills, and comfort dealing with emotionally charged issues help the client trust and go along with the therapeutic process. Those factors help to form a solid alliance that can especially support the client's engagement during particularly emotional or interpersonally difficult moments in therapy. The EFT therapist is therefore a multilayered expert capable of dealing with the wide variety of issues that therapy can bring. This expertise ranges from the ability to provide a rationale for therapy or tasks to the capability for handling therapeutic relationship ruptures, and from proficiency in variants of specific therapeutic tasks to skill in dealing with crises that may arise (whether related to therapy or not). To be able to provide this level of expertise, the therapist remains a learner throughout their career and seeks support through further training, consultation, and supervision.

Providing Rationale

Early on as well as in an ongoing manner throughout the therapeutic process, the therapist seeks to build a trusting alliance with the client so that the latter is willing to focus on their painful emotional experiences and engage in such therapeutic tasks as might allow the restructuring of chronic painful feelings. The provision of a rationale early on in therapy and at critical junctures in the therapeutic process may be important to facilitate the client's continuing engagement in therapy. Many clients may have reservations and anxieties about the idea of exploring painful subject matter and feelings precisely because it is so painful. They may arrive at therapy expecting or wishing to work only at the level of symptomatic distress, wanting simply to learn to live with their depression or to reduce symptoms of anxiety. For such clients, the idea of touching on core painful issues in their lives and relationships might be especially daunting, and they need appropriate guidance and explanation from the therapist to overcome apprehensions or reluctance. For others, avoidance of their own emotional experience may even be a central process underpinning psychological difficulties; thus, the emotion-focused work that might counteract this avoidance needs to be offered in a way that is understandable to the client.

Provision of a rationale that resonates with the client also requires the therapist to have some understanding of how the client relates to their own emotional experience, how they are or are not able to stay with emotions, and how the client understands the role emotions play in their difficulties and in life more generally. The therapist may thus tweak the rationale provided so that it fits with the client's outlook, thus facilitating a joint understanding of the goals and tasks of therapy (Bordin, 1979). At times, clients may directly ask about the rationale for an emotion-focused approach. In such instances, the therapist can offer a generic rationale that can then serve as a basis for a personalized one (see the example in the next chapter on individualized case conceptualizations). In general, though, the therapist offers an explanation of the therapeutic process in language that the client understands and in a manner that takes into account the client's presenting issues and goals for therapy. In addition, when clients arrive at therapy with prior diagnoses, think about their difficulties in terms of symptomatically defined diagnoses, or have queries in some way related to these issues, it is important that the therapist can offer a coherent explanation of how working with painful emotions in therapy is relevant to that particular diagnosis or can lead to a reduction in symptomatic distress. As mentioned earlier, the rationale is not provided once but may also be offered at other junctures that require the client's reengagement.

The therapist also seeks information about the client's expectations of therapy as well as information about previous experiences of therapy, especially past experiences that the client describes as unhelpful. This information may be an early indicator of potential challenges to the therapeutic process, including relational challenges. If the client says that their previous therapist did not understand them, it is important to begin by checking what it was that the previous therapist did not get. Although these initial inquires may not offer much, they can start to orient and sensitize the therapist to how core painful emotions may be triggered in interactions between the therapist and client (we assume here that client sensitivities in this respect are linked to their emotional vulnerability).

Facilitating Experiential Tasks

The therapist's relational skills also show in how the therapist scaffolds experiential tasks. The therapist needs to offer the client a rationale for experiential tasks, such as imaginary chair dialogues (see Chapter 2 and Chapters 6–9), and part of the therapist's expertise is shown in the ease with which they introduce such tasks. Novice EFT therapists are often anxious and may be especially apprehensive when introducing potentially evocative tasks. This anxiety, however, can undermine client confidence and trust in both tasks and the therapist, and it therefore is important that the therapist has enough experience with tasks to be comfortable both introducing them and guiding client through them. It is our experience that the ease with which tasks are introduced and the ease with which clients are facilitated to engage in them are predictive of client engagement in those same tasks.

Each task has its own unique structure (see Chapters 6–9), and the EFT therapist needs to be sufficiently familiar with tasks so that, at different stages in the task, they can offer the appropriate instructions to the client. The therapist seeks to ensure that the client stays in the dialogue with the other chair and does not venture elsewhere, for example, by starting to talk to the therapist. The therapist also endeavors to facilitate an optimal pace or rhythm in the work often characterized by a "dance" (or sequence of steps) involving focusing inside, naming the experience, and expressing that felt experience to the other. This dance is essentially the same whether the other is a part of the self or an enacted other person. Depending on the stage of the task, the therapist may guide the client in unfolding emotional experience or enact a perceived part of the self or an imagined other. In later chapters, we describe in detail the processes involved in working with particular chair tasks, but it is important to say here that the therapist in their knowledge and expertise holds the overall structure that facilitates transformation whether at a symptom level or at the level of underlying emotional vulnerability.

Especially in tasks, it is through relational presence and skill that the therapist facilitates access to core painful feelings and to the emotional toll of symptoms, and it is through this same relational presence and skill that the therapist then orchestrates possibilities for adaptive responses to those painful emotions and to the toll of those symptoms. One aspect of this presence is manifest in the manner in which the therapist does not give up on the client. That the client has sought treatment in the first place suggests that problematic emotion schemes or symptoms are entrenched. The therapist thus needs to acknowledge stuck points as they arise while also pointing to and facilitating potentialities. When adaptive experiences are generated, the therapist wants to support and consolidate any changes, which can be then further supported by reflection and potential homework (see Chapter 10).

Making Sense of Therapy

The use of case conceptualization (see the next chapter) is also pivotal in forging a good therapeutic alliance. The therapist co-constructs their case conceptualization with the client and is transparent about this case conceptualization. Throughout therapy, the therapist openly, albeit very briefly in terms of actual time, discusses their evolving understanding of the client's difficulties and shares their thinking about how best to work with these difficulties in therapy. This process of transparency, dialogue, and checking continues over the course of therapy, contributing to the therapist's evolving understanding of the client and the client's process as well as facilitating client engagement with the therapeutic process. It also helps the client to make sense of their therapeutic experience and thus generate a coherent narrative that can help further consolidation of potential changes (Grafanaki & McLeod, 1999). Again, it should be emphasized that while this dialogue is important and constitutes one of the continuous threads running through therapy, these discussions are brief and do not take center stage. The emphasis in therapy is on experiential work, and care is taken to avoid fruitless intellectualization that not only is not the work of therapy but can also constitute, or contribute to, avoidance of engagement with emotion (Timulak & McElvaney, 2018).

THE USE OF RELATIONSHIP THERAPEUTICALLY IN EFT-T

As should be evident from what we have said so far, EFT is profoundly a relational therapy. However, as we have also elaborated on, it is relational in a particular kind of way, and there can often be a misunderstanding when EFT is taught to therapists whose primary therapeutic training or orientation is not humanistic. For example, the relational focus in EFT is very different from a psychodynamic perspective that sees the in-session therapeutic relationship as an opportunity to explore the client's general interpersonal relational style. Simply put, this is not a focus in EFT. While in EFT, the use of therapeutic relationship and the focus on the client's relationships come in several forms (discussed shortly), in-session interpretation of what is happening between the therapist and client is not one of them. Rather, the default position is that the therapist uses the therapeutic relationship to facilitate the client's capacity to stay with emotional experiences and to transform chronically painful emotions through the generation of adaptive emotional experience, primarily, as a result of the client's intrapsychological processes (e.g., self-compassion or protective anger accessed, experienced, and expressed in the context of imaginary dialogues).

Although the process of reworking and restructuring problematic emotion schemes is a profoundly intrapsychological process, it does, of course, have interpersonal connotations on several levels. First of all, the historical triggers and experiences that give rise to core pain are typically interpersonal in nature, and so, working with and transforming problematic emotion schemes typically involves the processing of primarily interpersonal interactions. Thus, whether implicitly or explicitly, there are always others present in experiential exploration and imaginary dialogues. Secondly, this intrapsychological work happens in the context of the therapeutic relationship, and the quality of the therapist's presence contributes to the restructuring of emotion schemes in a number of ways: (a) through helping modulate emotion, (b) through corrective emotional-interpersonal experiences the client experiences with the therapist (e.g., the therapist offers compassion and validation), (c) through the processing of relational difficulties that arise in the therapeutic relationship, and (d) through the therapist's empathic exploration and understanding of relevant aspects of the client's interpersonal functioning. We turn our attention now to each of these four dimensions.

Emotional Modulation

The therapist's relational presence, warmth, and caring for the client, as demonstrated verbally but also through facial expression and voice quality, contribute to the coregulation of emotional experience. The therapist's empathic presence indirectly helps regulate dysregulated experience but also supports specific interventions in which the therapist explicitly facilitates the client to regulate overwhelming emotional experience (see Chapter 6 on modulating the dysregulation). The therapist thus offers a soothing presence when dysregulation is too much for the client, while this warmth and caring presence also facilitates a client sense of safety that allows for vulnerable emotions to be accessed in the session and used by the client or transformed as needed.

As we have mentioned a number of times already, the work of transforming chronic painful feelings requires optimal levels of emotional arousal and expression (see also Warwar & Greenberg, 1999). The therapist endeavors to facilitate such optimal levels of arousal and expression. Although, at times, this can mean downregulating overwhelming emotion, at other times, it may involve helping the client to let down their guardedness to allow themselves to feel and express more emotion. Again, the therapist can do so explicitly via the particular use of specific tasks and interventions, but they do so implicitly through their attentive presence as well as through empathic interventions that invite the client to feel emotions followed by supportive invitations to express them (see Chapter 7 on overcoming emotional avoidance).

Corrective Emotional-Interpersonal Experience

While the most important corrective emotional experiences are generated by the clients themselves (see Chapter 9 on transformational experiences in imaginary chair dialogues) and one of the main goals of therapy is that clients are able to self-generate adaptive emotional experiences in the context of activated chronic pain, these new experiences are further consolidated by the client's experience of the therapist's response to such experiences. There are essentially two types of corrective experiences that the therapist can offer in the context of activated chronic pain and unmet need: (a) a compassionate caring that is authentically expressed toward the felt pain (e.g., "I see your pain, and I care") and (b) validation of unmet needs and the healthy anger stemming from them (e.g., "I can see what you went through. You deserved your mom being there for you"). The therapist thus witnesses and acknowledges the client's pain and is both authentically compassionate toward the pain and validating of a sense of deservingness (Timulak, 2014). The therapist's relational stance here echoes the intrapsychological processes of client-generated self-compassion and client-generated protective anger. Their expression of compassionate presence in the context of core pain and articulated unmet needs has a potentially healing effect while also fostering and affirming client self-compassion. The therapist's relational validation of the client's articulated needs or experienced protective anger further supports this self-affirming stance in the client.

It should be clear, therefore, that the EFT therapist does not stay behind a facade of professionalism, dispassionately remaining on the sidelines while the client struggles through painful emotional turmoil. The therapist both empathically connects with the client in their pain and is willing to disclose their own frame of reference by, for example, speaking openly from a heartfelt compassion for the client. What we are talking about here is the direct expression of the therapist's own feelings for the client as well as disclosure of the therapist's perspective on the context within which the client's painful experiences have come to be. So, for example, the therapist may share how touched they are by the client's pain while also offering the perspective that it was not okay for a child to experience what the client experienced as a child. In our previous writing (Timulak, 2015), we gave an example of such an exchange in the context of a client presenting with generalized anxiety and comorbid depression. During experiential work, the therapist was moved by the poignancy of the raw pain expressed by the client who, as a child, had been neglected by an inattentive and emotionally unavailable mother. The therapist expressed to the client:

> It shouldn't have happened. Yeah? . . . I'm telling you. . . . And I'm powerless to go back in time. . . . But you shouldn't have gone through it. Yeah? Nobody should. It's not only that, it's you. Yes? No girl [should have to go through that].

To be met in an authentic, compassionate, and validating way while feeling deep pain is a powerful experience, and such experiences in therapy can constitute a corrective and transformational emotional-interpersonal experience for the client (Greenberg & Elliott, 2012). Rather than experiencing intense loneliness in their pain, the client can touch on their pain while feeling deeply connected to a caring, protective other. The pain can thus be experienced in the context of a deep human connection. Instead of experiencing rejection, abuse, invalidation, disinterest, or neglect, the client in their vulnerability experiences another human's attentive, compassionate, and validating care. In the here and now of deeply felt pain, such experiences are poignant for the client, and in contexts of high emotional arousal, such experiences can be transformative, leading to the transformation of emotion schemes and the reshaping of emotional memory (Lane et al., 2015). These in-session experiences can also serve a future protective function: The client internalizes the therapist's compassionate, protective presence in such a way that it serves as a buffer at times of vulnerability and distress.

The therapist's judgment regarding when to actively use the self in a direct response to the client is often intuitive and guided by the poignancy and the relational context of the client's internal work. Although facilitating the intrapsychological work of the client (even while such work has interpersonal connotations) is the therapist's default position, whenever the therapist has a strong sense that sharing their authentic care and validation may further solidify that internal work, they may offer it. All human suffering and striving are only human in the extent to which they are mirrored in the perspectives of other humans. To be human is to exist in relation to other humans, and to feel emotional pain is to feel that pain in the context of how we experience others witnessing us in that pain. The difference between feeling the pain of abandonment in the context of others whose disinterest or invalidation implicitly communicates that we deserve such pain, and that same pain felt in the presence of someone who communicates their valuing of us, is immeasurable. This is the level of shared humanity that the therapist engages in. Such work inevitably brings the therapist out of their comfort zone because there is a vulnerability involved in sharing one's own internal reactions toward the pain and unmet needs of another person. However, it is in this way that the therapist bears witness to the client's striving.

At times, the therapist may use themselves as an instrument to facilitate the client's emotional-interpersonal work—for instance, to facilitate client experimentation with, or consolidation of, new emotional experiences. For example, having witnessed the emergence of adaptive anger expressed toward an abusive other and the subsequent articulation by the client of a sense of self-worth and self-esteem ("I'm not going to let anyone treat me that way. I deserve respect, and I feel proud of myself as I say this"), the therapist might invite the client to repeat this expression, stating it directly to the therapist and noticing what it feels like to state it. An example of this intervention can be found in Les Greenberg's American Psychological Association video *Emotion-Focused Therapy for Depression* (Greenberg & Carlson, 2007). In the context of an imaginary dialogue with her mother, when the client expresses pride in her accomplishments, Les Greenberg invites her to repeat this directly to him. He then responds by authentically sharing his appreciation of the client's struggles.

Ruptures as Opportunities for Emotional and Interactional Transformation

No matter how hard therapists work to be authentic, attuned, and to provide a caring and validating presence, they are not infallible, and it is thus likely that most therapists will have moments when they are misattuned, incongruent, or invalidating of their clients. In many instances, clients may not notice these moments or may tolerate them without much problem. In other instances, such moments have the potential to be especially painful for clients. It may be particularly so if such moments interplay with the client's emotional vulnerability (e.g., a yawning therapist seen by a socially anxious client who vigilantly observes others for any signs of disinterest). In many instances, the client's idiosyncratic emotional sensitivity may not only be triggered by the therapist but can also itself play a role in shaping how clients experience and process interactions with their therapist. For example, a therapist who empathically stays with a client's core painful emotion both out of a respectful appreciation of the client's pain and a firm belief that helping the client to stay with that pain will eventually lead to the articulation of needs and the possibility of adaptive responses to that pain, may be experienced by the client as cruel and not caring precisely because the therapist does not endeavor to immediately reassure the client and sooth the pain; this perception is rooted in past painful experiences of being unsupported at times of great distress. Similarly, a client with a painful guilt or fear that they have trespassed against others, such as parents, may experience therapist encouragements to express boundary-setting anger to an enacted parent as disrespect on behalf of the therapist toward the parent.

Therapy is such a complex emotional and interpersonal process that it is impossible not to experience ruptures in the therapeutic relationship (e.g., studies by Rennie, 1990, on the client's experience of the therapy hour). Those ruptures that are tightly linked to client underlying vulnerability are particularly important therapeutically. In such instances, the therapist needs to focus on this underlying vulnerability. The therapist needs to be aware that the client feels hurt by the therapist's actions or inactions, needs to help the client give voice to that hurt, and needs to nondefensively acknowledge and own the role the therapist's own actions or inactions played in causing the hurt (Elliott & Macdonald, 2020; Elliott et al., 2004; Safran & Muran, 2000). There is then an opportunity to explore the client's experience and hurt in the context of the client's core pain, idiosyncratic vulnerabilities/sensitivities, and life story. The therapist's genuine, nondefensive exploration and validation of the hurt, and the unmet needs the hurt points to, can thus become an opportunity for a corrective emotional-interpersonal experience.

Equally important are those ruptures that are experienced as upsetting for the therapist. It may well be that some clients' relational positions and actions may be upsetting for the therapist (e.g., a client who persistently tries to make contact with the therapist on social media). It is likely in such an instance that the therapist will have to manage their own upset and will therefore be less optimally therapeutic in their skills. A problematic cycle of interaction can even begin. It is important here that the therapist becomes aware of what is happening and tries to restructure the interactional cycle into a more constructive form within which the therapist constructively shares with the client their own vulnerable experience while also focuses on the client's underlying emotional experience that is being played out in the cycle.

Learning from the EFT for couples literature (Greenberg & Goldman, 2008) is useful. For instance, the client who does not respect the therapist's boundaries (e.g., by contacting them outside the therapy office), thus upsetting the therapist, can be engaged in a frank discussion during which the therapist may share the effect this behavior has on them. The therapist may genuinely set a boundary to that behavior and still inquire as to what it was that drove the client's behavior (e.g., longing for connection), which can then be focused on in the session. Although the effect of the therapist's boundary-setting behavior also needs to be processed, the underlying vulnerability that gave the rise to the client's behavior is primary and thus is the primary focus of attention.

It may well be that, for some clients, these types of interactions are more likely to occur. In any case, these instances are opportunities for emotional transformation as well as rupture or alliance repair by which the client is facilitated by the therapist to get involved in an authentic engagement that may help to process the core chronic painful feelings as well as offer opportunity to restructure the relational interaction. Again, the process may be akin to EFT for couples work. The therapist and the client may need to understand their cycle of interaction—for example, "You contact me outside the hours, and I do not respond. You feel hurt that I am cruel, and I feel intruded upon, so I am unable to respond" is reformulated into "I need to set a boundary because I am anxious and feel intruded upon, but that does not mean I want to be cruel. I also see that there is something you need in the attempt to contact me. Can we have a look at what it is?" This understanding may facilitate efforts to engage differently in terms of interaction but also frees up opportunity to focus on the underlying vulnerability that is the natural focus of the therapy. Again, this approach offers the potential for both a transformational and corrective emotional-interpersonal experience (i.e., alliance repair) and a reset of the focus on further emotion transformational work centered on processing the client's idiosyncratic vulnerabilities and sensitivities in the context of the client's interactions with others.

Interpersonal Learning in EFT-T

EFT therapists do not offer interpretations of the client's interpersonal functioning. Increasing client insight into the nature of their own interpersonal functioning or ways of relating to others or increasing insight and awareness per se are not the primary goals of EFT. While insight and awareness are, of course, important (e.g., A. Pascual-Leone & Greenberg, 2007b), and meaning making and reflecting on experience, including interpersonal experiences, are important aspects of EFT, in general, they are seen as supplementary to the primary experiential work of accessing and transforming core pain. This focus is quite different from that taken in some other approaches, and some therapists trained in other approaches (e.g., an insight-oriented psychodynamic approach) can understandably struggle to remove their focus from a curiosity about the client's relational functioning both in relation to the therapist and also out there in the world.

Of course, the EFT therapist is observant and inevitably notices interpersonal aspects of the client's stories that are central to the client's emotional processing. Internal client emotional experience is linked to perceptions of others and others' behavior, and client narratives about their emotional experience include stories about their emotional expression and behavior toward others in salient interactions outside the therapy room. The therapist's understanding of interpersonal functioning, which is shaped by conceptualizations from couples and family therapy variants of EFT, informs their empathic interventions. The therapist, together with the client, tracks the client's perceptions of the other's interactional positions; instrumental, secondary, and primary emotions; behaviors; and messages the client sees the other as giving the client while also tracking the client's own internal emotional reactions to those messages, emotions, interactional positions, and behaviors. This process of exploration, and the resulting understanding of the others' actions, experiences, and intentions, typically occurs in the context of imaginary chair dialogues with salient others in which the client is facilitated by the therapist to describe and enact the perceived behavior and intention of the other (often those who trigger the client's painful feelings). The process of enactment helps differentiate the client's perception of the other and evokes the core painful feelings that are to be worked on and transformed in therapy. This process also, however, indirectly facilitates a complex construal of the client's interpersonal life, giving rise to many interpersonal observations that contribute to a better understanding of the others' actions, emotional experiences, and motivations, thus facilitating emotional and conceptual processing of complex interpersonal interactions.

At times, when the client and therapist's exploration of a client's experiencing leads to an exploration of interactions with others in which the client's actions may be contributing to the dynamic in a particular way that the client does not appear to be aware of (e.g., a client's romantic partner feeling blamed by the client), the therapist may share their observations. However, it is imperative that the therapist offer these observations in an empathic way that does not leave the client feeling judged or criticized. Observations of this nature are most likely to be constructive when the client is inquisitive about the nature of the interaction rather than when they are simply expressing their own pain. Such empathic observations need to be timed properly, and their utility and success depends on the context of where therapy is at that point and on what the client is focusing (e.g., whether the client is interested in understanding the interaction versus processing the pain they feel). In any case, any observations shared by the therapist are offered in the spirit of openness and as suggestions rather than authoritative statements. They constitute the therapist's contributions to, rather than expert interpretation of, the client's exploration.

CONCLUSION

In this chapter, we looked at the nature of the therapeutic relationship as it is conceptualized within EFT. A relationship characterized by authenticity, warmth, and empathy is a cornerstone of EFT because these qualities allow for the development of trust between the client and therapist, thus creating the safety necessary to explore and express painful emotions.

In EFT, the relationship is seen as both healing in and of itself and as facilitative of therapeutic tasks. Although the relationship facilitates emotional modulation and can constitute a corrective emotional experience, a strong therapeutic relationship also underpins optimal client engagement with the challenging experiential tasks central to the emotional transformation process. The relationship can become even more central when processing relational difficulties that may arise in the therapeutic relationship. The client's interpersonal functioning can also become a natural part of the therapeutic exploration.

5

USING TRANSDIAGNOSTIC CASE CONCEPTUALIZATION

In Chapter 3, we presented our case conceptualization framework that helps us understand client presenting issues but also outlines theoretically possible pathways for emotion transformation. Here, we focus on the practical use of case conceptualization over the course of therapy. In doing so, we look at examples of client presentations across the diagnostic spectrum. While the examples we offer are based on real clinical work, to facilitate anonymity and thus protect confidentiality, we use composite cases—that is, each case is not be based solely on one particular client. These real-life but composite case examples illustrate our thinking about how case conceptualization can be used when reflecting on client presenting issues.

Historically, case conceptualization has been conspicuous by its relative absence in humanistic approaches to therapy. Seen as the domain of psychodynamic/psychoanalytic therapies in which the therapist knew the real "cause of the problem" and the client did not, case conceptualization has been viewed with deep suspicion by humanistic therapists. Rogers (1951) vocally opposed any diagnostic/assessment efforts on the part of the therapist and saw such activities as potentially hindering the establishment of a warm,

https://doi.org/10.1037/0000253-006
Transdiagnostic Emotion-Focused Therapy: A Clinical Guide for Transforming Emotional Pain, by L. Timulak and D. Keogh

caring relationship. Client-centered therapy was therefore not known for elaborate case conceptualization frameworks. Furthermore, from the perspective of experiential therapy, a case conceptualization seemed to be too much of a static thing, something fundamentally at odds with the ever-changing nature of an evolving experiential exploration. The whole business of case conceptualization was also suspected of falling victim to therapist fallibility, both regarding therapist error as well as therapist defensiveness. It was felt that a defensive therapist could easily attribute difficulties with therapeutic progress or difficulties in the therapeutic relationship to the client, and use an elaborate case conceptualization for that purpose. It was not until the work of Les Greenberg and Rhonda Goldman (Goldman & Greenberg, 1997; Greenberg & Goldman, 2007) that emotion-focused therapy (EFT) writers (and indeed any writers within the humanistic-experiential paradigm) offered a thorough, elaborate, and systematic case conceptualization framework (Goldman & Greenberg, 1997, and Greenberg & Goldman, 2007, used the term "case formulation" rather than "case conceptualization").

Goldman and Greenberg's (2015) formulation offers a comprehensive guide to therapist considerations in EFT. It puts an emphasis on an interplay between narrative and emotion, as well as on optimal arousal (e.g., optimal client exploration requires a certain level of emotional arousal), and it differentiates between attachment (relational) and identity (self-perception) themes. All provide context for pursuing poignancy and emotional pain in the client's narrative. Then, in a manner similar to that outlined in our Chapter 3, they focus on underlying emotions, unmet needs, more symptom-level emotions, and emotional interruption. These considerations are positioned in the context of the client's in-session presentation and in-session markers (e.g., self-criticism) that offer opportunities for the use of specific therapeutic tasks (see the following chapters). They also provide a guide for working within the outlined tasks. We recommend Goldman and Greenberg's work because it provides a comprehensive summary of the various processes and heuristics that an EFT therapist considers in the course of doing therapy, and our own case conceptualization framework needs to be seen in the context of the broader considerations outlined by Goldman and Greenberg. The outline we offer in Chapter 3 roughly matches a subset of considerations outlined by Goldman and Greenberg in Stage 2 of their framework (e.g., underlying emotions, needs, secondary emotions, interruption).

In the rest of this chapter, we present considerations pertaining to the case conceptualization framework outlined in Chapter 3. We focus primarily on moment-to-moment considerations but also give some attention to session-to-session considerations. Other considerations, such as particular in-session markers, level of client arousal, stage of therapy, and use of homework, are further outlined over the course of the remaining chapters of this book.

EMPATHIC EXPLORATION AND CREATION OF FOCUS

Many moment-to-moment tasks are constantly at play within an EFT session. For instance, the therapist is working to ensure that the client is in a self-exploratory mode, that a constant focus is on the client's emotional experiencing, and that this experiencing is present in an activated or aroused manner. The attunement of the therapist's empathy to affect helps ensure that both therapist and client are focused on the client's inner emotional experiencing. While the therapist acknowledges the client's perceptual field (e.g., "This is what happened," "This is what is happening"), the therapist focuses primarily on how the client felt during particular interactions with their environment (e.g., "And this is what you felt," "And this is what you feel"). The therapist facilitates a process of emotional exploration, unfolding what happened as perceived by the client but also how it affected the client emotionally (e.g., "So, this is what happened . . ., and that made you feel . . .?"). In support of this process, the therapist's empathic repertoire can be thought of as consisting of two key types of responses: (a) an exploration propelling empathy and (b) an understanding communicating empathy (see Chapter 2).

An example can be seen in the following transcript in which client Paula,[1] who presents with mixed anxiety and depression, describes her worries about losing her aging father:

CLIENT: It is so painful to see him in any pain or to see him in any discomfort. It'd be . . .

THERAPIST: It's like world is kind of falling apart or something? This is how it feels when you see him in pain.

CLIENT: The head gets squashed, kind of. It's like . . .

THERAPIST: That it's just unbearable. Yeah?

CLIENT: I feel anguish.

---

[1]Chapters 5 through 9 include several case studies. Some are based on real clients, and others are composite sketches. Permission to use client data is on file with the authors.

THERAPIST: Anguish. What's in the anguish?

CLIENT: Is he going to. . . . Is he going to . . .? It's like every time he's in pain or that he's sick or he's in the hospital, it's another step closer to being dead.

THERAPIST: Okay. Okay. And then he wouldn't be here? Yes? "And I will miss you so much." Yeah? Just let those tears come. These are important tears. Yeah?

Although exploration of the client's experiencing happens in a moment-to-moment manner, the therapist, by following what is most poignant in the client's narrative and by attending to in-session markers, attempts to create a focus for the session or for part of the session. The constant interplay between narrative (theme, description of triggers, or description of problematic self-treatment in the context of triggers) and the client's internal experiences means that any given session—but, subsequently, also therapy as a whole—consists of multiple islands of potential foci, any of which could become the focus of therapeutic work (whether in the form of particular therapeutic tasks or other EFT skill, such as empathic affirmation or emotion coaching). These islands of focused therapeutic work can, in turn, be seen as existing within an ocean of care, validation, and understanding support as provided by the therapeutic relationship (here, we are paraphrasing Les Greenberg's spoken words heard during trainings). While it is hypothetically possible that islands of work may pertain to discrete and unrelated client experiences, these various foci (e.g., difficult aspects of the client's relationship with a significant other) tend to oscillate around overlapping triggers (e.g., narratives of similar difficult aspects in other relationships) that point to particular underlying emotional vulnerabilities (e.g., not feeling seen, supported, or validated in important relationships).

This underlying vulnerability (or core pain), in its idiosyncratic client-specific variant, defines both the client's presentation and our conceptualization. We can thus discern and distinguish the underlying emotional vulnerability and its triggers, problematic self-treatment in the context of those triggers, apprehension, emotional and behavioral avoidance, and so forth. We can explore and identify chronically unmet needs and assess which transformative processes postulated by our framework (i.e., compassion and protective anger) are difficult to facilitate. Here, we make the point again that the part of Figure 3.1 (see Chapter 3) from the top down through the "Unmet Needs" box is considered as constituting our case conceptualization framework, whereas the lower part of the figure (including "Compassion" and "Protective Anger") consists of those emotional processes that we try to facilitate in therapy to transform emotion schemes centered around core painful feelings.

THE ROLE OF CASE CONCEPTUALIZATION

The case conceptualization framework that we present in Chapter 3 (see Figure 3.1) organizes therapists' thinking about their clients. For example, it can serve as a basis for note taking after the session, when it can be helpful to note what triggers were touched on by the client during the session, whether any forms of problematic self-treatment or interruption/avoidance were present, what secondary emotions were present, what underlying emotions/core pain was accessed, whether unmet needs were identified, and whether the client was able to access and express self-compassion or protective anger. The framework may also be used by supervisees as a basis for presenting cases in supervision. Indeed, we recommend it to supervisees as a framework that can help organize and guide their presentation of cases to supervisors and, in the context of group supervision, also to fellow supervisees. In addition, the framework can serve as a basis for presenting cases in other formats, such as academic papers, and we and our colleagues have used this case conceptualization framework as the basis for all the case study writings coming from our lab (e.g., Connolly-Zubot et al., 2020; Dillon et al., 2018; Hissa et al., 2020; McNally et al., 2014; O'Brien et al., 2019; Timulak, 2014, 2015; Timulak & McElvaney, 2018; Timulak & Pascual-Leone, 2015).

The framework presented here can also be used for the therapist's own assessment of in-session processes. It can serve that function within the session but also across sessions and, thus, also across therapy as a whole. For instance, as sessions progress, the case conceptualization framework orients the therapist to attend to what secondary emotions (global distress) the client typically experiences, what forms of problematic self-treatment are present, what typically triggers emotional pain, what is the core pain that gets triggered, what chronically unmet needs are articulated, and what forms of self-interruption or avoidance manifest in the face of difficult emotions or triggers. The therapist can also observe whether the client has difficulty standing up for themselves in the face of mistreatment or whether the client can soften toward the self when witnessing their own pain. The framework thus can inform the therapist's moment-to-moment process— for example, checking for what anxiety/protection drives the interruption/

avoidance of emotions. It can also inform the therapist's session-to-session thinking—for example, that the client tends to collapse into hopelessness when they try to stay with assertive, healthy anger out of fear that the anger will hurt their close ones and result in even further painful experiences of rejection. The case conceptualization can serve as a basis for in-session reflections shared with the client, particularly toward the end of the session when there is a space for reflecting on the experiential work that happened during the session. It can also serve as a basis for discussing homework with clients, something we refer to in the forthcoming chapters, particularly in Chapter 10.

Of course, case conceptualization is not everything the EFT therapist focuses on; the EFT therapist takes into account many other considerations. For instance, in later chapters, we provide maps for facilitating various EFT tasks (see also the original formulations in Elliott et al., 2004; Greenberg et al., 1993). While Goldman and Greenberg's (2015) case formulation framework considers tasks to be a part of case formulation, we see case conceptualization more narrowly; therefore, we conceptually do not consider other EFT considerations, such as task structures to be part of case conceptualization per se. That said, we suggest that the therapist's approach to specific tasks with a particular client can be meaningfully informed by the therapist's overall thinking about the case.

In terms of transdiagnostic thinking and diagnosis, we see the generic case conceptualization framework presented in Chapter 3 (see Figure 3.1) as cutting across diagnostic presentations. Symptomatic distress, as characteristic of a particular disorder, is present mainly in the form of prevailing secondary emotions, and so there may be diagnosis-specific patterns regarding secondary emotions (e.g., hopelessness and irritability in depression, anxiety in anxiety disorders) but also forms of avoidance (e.g., avoidance of places associated with traumatic events in posttraumatic stress disorder [PTSD]), triggers (e.g., the social/interpersonal situations in social anxiety), problematic self-treatment (e.g., specific type of worrying in respective anxiety disorders, compulsive behavior in obsessive-compulsive disorder [OCD]), and so forth. However, we contend that although some disorder-specific patterns may be discernable, underlying core emotional pain and core emotional vulnerability are not always clearly linked to a specific symptomatic, and thus specific diagnostic, presentation. Underlying core pain is always idiosyncratic (albeit cutting across clusters of loneliness/sadness-based, shame-based, and fear-based emotions) and is not necessarily predictive of symptom-level presentation.

A similar core pain may be shared by various clusters of symptoms, and similar clusters of symptoms may cut across several diagnostic labels (giving rise to the problem of high comorbidity). Thus, an individual with underlying shame (e.g., "I am unworthy") may symptomatically (i.e., diagnostically) present with depression (hopeless/helpless—e.g., "I am unworthy, and nothing can be done about it"), social anxiety (anxiety about, and avoidance of, social situations—e.g., "I am unworthy and therefore avoid social situations where others might see that"), or a mixture of both depression and social anxiety (hopeless/helpless and anxious about social situations—e.g., "I am unworthy, and nothing can be done about it; I avoid situations rather than risk anybody finding out"). We also know that diagnoses "travel" such that although, one time, depression might be dominant for a person, at another time, social anxiety might become dominant (e.g., Lahey et al., 2017).

We believe that the interplay between underlying pain and symptom-level presentation is multifactored and may include biological factors (see Chapter 1). While it may be possible to speculate as to why a particular underlying vulnerability, such as shame (e.g., "I am unworthy"), presents in one person as depression, in another as social anxiety, and in yet another as a mixture of the two, such speculation is not our primary focus. Here, we prefer to focus on giving examples of variations of symptomatic (diagnosis-specific) presentations and the underlying core pain/vulnerability those symptomatic presentations spring from. Again, while we suggest that both of these layers need to be addressed in therapy, we argue that the underlying vulnerability is at the core of client distress, and thus is the most critical layer to address. We argue that it is this vulnerability that plays a major role in the development (although not necessarily maintenance) of symptomatic presentations. We look now at several case examples to illustrate constellations of symptomatic presentation and their relation to underlying emotions. To protect the identity and confidentiality of individual clients, the examples offered are composites of real cases.

AN EXAMPLE OF A CLIENT WITH DEPRESSION

Josh (see Exhibit 5.1), a client in his late 30s, meets criteria for a primary diagnosis of depression. He comes to therapy because of low mood and a sense of profound unhappiness and sadness. He feels very alone. Within the session, he is subdued and becomes emotionally expressive only at particular moments when he touches on specific core painful feelings. Josh describes

EXHIBIT 5.1. A Summary of Josh's Difficulties Using the Conceptualization Framework: Example of a Client With Depression

Triggers

Historical Triggers

- Father's high standards and critical, punitive nature
- Mother protective but also vulnerable

Current Triggers

- Highly demanding work environment
- Performance appraisals at work
- Feeling distant to partner
- Recent loss of father
- Conflict with teenage son

Self-Treatment

Self-criticism (e.g., "I am not achieving as I should," "The problems in our marriage are my fault," "I am a bad father"), perfectionism (e.g., "I should work more to achieve"), self-worry (e.g., about financial security, performance appraisals, son)

Global Distress

Hopelessness, helplessness, profound sadness, occasional irritability, tiredness, exhaustion

Apprehension/Anxiety

Of assessment at work, of being judged by people who have high standards, of disappointing others in close relationships (losses)

Behavioral Avoidance

Working hard to make up for shortfalls, not seeking closeness (out of anxiety about being disappointed), engaging in intellectual debates during sessions, controlling behavior with son

Emotional Avoidance

Resorting to speculation and purely meaning-oriented explorations, using humor to avoid pain

Core Pain

- Shame based—for example, "I am not as good as others," "I have failed to achieve," "I am not a good parent," "I am not a good partner"
- Loneliness/sadness based—for example, "There is nobody on my side," "I feel alone," "I miss connection," "I miss the relationship with my father that I never had [this can be present in an aroused manner]"
- Fear based—for example, "Our financial situation is precarious and unsafe," "I won't be able to look after myself and family," sensitive to his children's fear

Unmet Needs

To be valued, accepted, approved of; to be loved, connected to; to feel confident, capable, and resilient having always had a difficult relationship with his father. His father held high standards and could be critical and contemptuous of his son, whom he frequently appraised as underperforming. At times, Josh's father also resorted to physically disciplining him. This difficult relationship was further complicated when Josh's father died a few months previously with Josh feeling like he never had a chance to earn his father's esteem. Josh reports feeling closer to his mother. However, he describes her as a timid, vulnerable person who is not always available to him during times of difficulty. Josh's siblings are of different ages, so he is not particularly close to any of them, and he did not have any particularly close friends growing up.

Current triggers of emotional pain include his situation at work and difficulties within his marriage and family. Josh works in a highly competitive company at which he is constantly compared with his peers. At home, Josh feels he has grown apart from his partner, who he experiences as quite distant from him, leaving him feeling alone in the relationship. He has a teenage son, who is quite critical of him, and arguments often escalate between them. Many of these arguments arise in situations in which Josh tries to protect his son and becomes somewhat controlling. Josh then feels responsible for the conflicts that arise.

Josh is very self-critical. He has a sense that he is inferior compared with his colleagues. He criticizes himself for being the kind of father he is. He sees his father's standards as reasonable and feels that he essentially failed his father. In his romantic relationship, he feels as if he is failing his partner. At work, he is anxious around any upcoming performance appraisals. He works incredibly hard and thus often feels exhausted and tired. In terms of symptomatic distress, in addition to exhaustion, Josh feels depressed, hopeless, helpless, and occasionally irritated.

During sessions, it is difficult for Josh to stay with underlying feelings of failure and loneliness; instead, he prefers to spend time engaged in meaning-oriented, intellectual debates. At times, he deflects exploration of his own experience by minimizing or joking about it. At work, he reports working to the point of exhaustion to avoid a sense of failure. He does not seek close friendships or relationship because he does not trust they could develop.

Josh's underlying vulnerability is a painful sense of being a failure, of being inferior to others, and of being a disappointment to his parents and to himself. He feels profoundly alone. When he touches on this loneliness, he can become more emotionally aroused and expressive. He is fearful of financial instability and particularly anxious about financially providing for his son. He longs for recognition, appreciation, relational connection, and love as well as for a sense of internal resilience.

AN EXAMPLE OF A CLIENT WITH SOCIAL ANXIETY AND COMORBID DEPRESSION

Joanna (see Exhibit 5.2), a client in her late 40s, meets criteria for a primary diagnosis of social anxiety and also criteria for comorbid depression. She comes to therapy because of feeling very isolated and socially anxious. She has strong physiological reactions in social and interpersonal interactions. For years, she has avoided such interactions wherever possible, instead choosing to stay at home to spend time on the internet.

When Joanna was growing up, she experienced her mom as judgmental and dismissive of her (criticizing both her academic capabilities and overall "life resilience"). Occasionally, her mother could also be physically abusive. As a child and teenager, Joanna experienced her dad as warm but often unavailable. However, with old age, he has changed and become quite irritable—even with her, at times. As a child, she was diagnosed with dyslexia. She felt that she was different from her classmates and that she was letting her parents down. She developed anxiety, initially around her academic performance but, later on in her teenage years, around being seen as anxious. This began in the context of school before eventually generalizing to other social situations. She had a sense that friends left her, and she attributed this to her anxiety. She experimented with drugs in her late teens, which compounded her anxiety because she had strong physiological reactions that scared her.

Joanna is self-critical and self-contemptuous. She judges herself for her dyslexia but also for the high levels of anxiety she experiences in social and interpersonal situations. She is extremely avoidant of social and interpersonal interactions. She has a job that involves minimal interpersonal contact, over-prepares for any social outing she cannot avoid, and self-medicates through the use of beta blockers or alcohol. She avoids romantic pursuits out of an anxiety that she will not be found attractive enough. In session, she tends to give a detailed overview of her anxiety symptoms in particular interactions to such an extent that it is difficult for the therapist to focus on underlying feelings. She is also highly emotionally constricted, and with the exception of talking about her anxiety, she is not emotionally expressive.

Her core pain is revealed in chair dialogues and centers on feelings of inadequacy (e.g., "I am a weirdo," "I am awkward," "I am disabled"). She feels very lonely and has a huge longing for approval, acceptance, and connection. She wants to feel loved and lovable. She also wants to feel safe because she can still recall how scared she was as a child when her mother's dislike of her was expressed in physical assaults.

EXHIBIT 5.2. A Summary of Joanna's Difficulties Using the Conceptualization Framework: Example of a Client With Social Anxiety and Comorbid Depression

Triggers

Historical Triggers

- Mother very judgmental, dismissive, and (at times) physically abusive
- Father warm but often unavailable and, increasingly lately, fragile and quite irritable
- Dyslexia and resulting underperformance in school
- In early 20s, friends turning against her for being too avoidant (e.g., not going out)
- Traumatic experiences when experimenting with drugs in late teens

Current Triggers

- Conflict with critical mother (e.g., where she is in life: single, no steady job)
- Father irritable and less warm
- Job instability
- Challenges in work (e.g., to be smart, social)

Self-Treatment

Self-criticism (e.g., "I am a weirdo," "I am not normal," "There is something strange about me and about how I am with others"), worry about social/interpersonal situations (e.g., "They will see what a weirdo I am")

Global Distress

General sense of anxiety, specific anxieties in advance of or during any social/interpersonal situations, hopelessness/helplessness that life will never change

Apprehension/Anxiety

Of any social and interpersonal situation, of being judged by others as a "weirdo," of the disappointment she would bring to any relationship

Behavioral Avoidance

Overpreparing for social situations, taking beta blockers to calm herself before interpersonal/social situations, not going to social situations, focusing in session on the details of anxiety in social situations

Emotional Avoidance

Focusing in session on the details of anxiety in social situations, offering frequent explanations to the therapist that are purely symptom focused

Core Pain

- Shame based—for example, "I am a weirdo," "There is something fundamentally flawed about me socially," "There is something wrong with me cognitively," "I have a disability"
- Loneliness/sadness based—for example, "I feel alone," "I will never have close friendships," "I will never have a romantic relationship"
- Fear based—for example, "I am so dislikable that I can be physically assaulted [by my mother]"

Unmet Needs

To be accepted as I am, to be loved as I am, to feel closeness in a relationship, to feel safe

AN EXAMPLE OF A CLIENT WITH OBSESSIVE-COMPULSIVE DISORDER AND COMORBID DEPRESSION

John (see Exhibit 5.3), a client in his early 20s, presents with OCD symptoms and low mood. Since finishing school, he has had a number of jobs. He receives little support from home because his parents are unable to offer him any financial support. He is the son of immigrants, and the family has experienced much financial hardship. When he was young, they moved often from place to place as his parents sought various forms of employment. He frequently had to adjust to new schools and new classmates, something he found difficult. He also wondered about how much he differed from the majority of his classmates, particularly those not from an immigrant background.

From a young age, John had to look after his younger brother while his parents worked long hours. He often felt overwhelmed by the responsibility, and from a young age, he began having images and thoughts of horrible things that might happen—for example, that he would harm his brother by mistakenly poisoning him with food, that the family would get murdered, that the house would blow up, that his parents would never come back from work and would abandon them, and that his parents would die in a car accident. These images and thoughts were often so vivid that he believed the thing in question had actually happened. He figured out that he could "neutralize" the resulting fear or distress by engaging in various rituals—for example, by counting objects in the room to a certain number within a prescribed time or tidying items in the kitchen in a prescribed pattern. He never told his parents about what he was going through because he did not feel they would understand, and he did not want to further burden them. His father was strict, believed in a hard work ethic, and expected his boys to be tough. His mother was stressed and overwhelmed, and often was in a low mood. He had few friends, and those friendships he did have were quite superficial because he always had things to attend to at home or with his brother. He was very fond of and caring for his brother.

Recently, John moved to a new city to find work. In doing so, he moved from the town he grew up and left behind his few friends. He feels very isolated in the new city. It is the first time he has lived alone. He misses his brother and is in constant contact with him over the phone. He has had a few server, bar, and supermarket jobs, but they frequently have not lasted long. Accordingly, with any change in his job situation, he has had to change accommodation because of affordability or access to the necessary public transportation. Limited employment opportunities and expensive rent have made the city a challenging place for John to live.

EXHIBIT 5.3. A Summary of John's Difficulties Using the Conceptualization Framework: Example of a Client With Obsessive-Compulsive Disorder and Comorbid Depression

Triggers

Historical Triggers

- Being left at an early age to look after himself and his younger brother because parents were out of the home for long hours at work
- Father's firm beliefs about strict discipline
- Mother often overwhelmed and depressed
- Left to own devices and unable to approach parents if feeling overwhelmed with responsibilities
- Frequent family relocation giving rise to worries about adjusting to new school, new peers, and new environments
- Sense of being different to others as a result of being a son of immigrants
- Early distressing childhood experiences of intrusive thoughts and images

Current Triggers

- In a transitionary period in life
- Move to new city
- Stress of job-hunting, short-lived employment, and concerns about financial stability and ability to support himself
- Lack of personal support in the city (e.g., friends)

Self-Treatment

Self-criticism (judges self for experiencing intrusive thoughts and engaging in rituals, judges self for not having a stable job or friends), obsession/self-worrying (obsesses/worries self about distressing intrusive thoughts and images), self-compulsions (engages in various rituals to mitigate the feared danger)

Global Distress

General sense of tiredness and disorientation/dysregulation resulting from self being defined by intrusive thoughts, images, obsessions, worries and the rituals engaged in to mitigate/neutralize them; secondary shame about self for being this way—that is, having these symptoms; hopelessness about the present and future

Apprehension/Anxiety

That the images and thoughts he has will cause damage; that his engagement with others in work or elsewhere will cause harm; that others will perceive him negatively or react negatively to him; that he will fail in work, in his living situation, or in interpersonal contexts

Behavioral Avoidance

Engaging in rituals to mitigate the effect of "bad" images or thoughts, overworking in job to mitigate anything that could go wrong, overly placating others (e.g., bosses, friends, potential friends, landlord)

(continues)

EXHIBIT 5.3. A Summary of John's Difficulties Using the Conceptualization Framework: Example of a Client With Obsessive-Compulsive Disorder and Comorbid Depression (Continued)

Emotional Avoidance

Spending hours obsessing/worrying about intrusive thoughts and images, engaging in rituals aimed at "neutralizing" these dangers, worrying about mistakes he might make in work, worrying about things he might do wrong within friendships, ruminating about past mistakes or things that did not go as well as he would have wished

Core Pain

- Shame based—for example, "Something is wrong with me," "I have these weird thoughts and images"
- Loneliness/sadness based—for example, "I feel alone," "I will never have a close relationship [friendship or romantic]"
- Fear based—for example, "There are imminent dangers to me, to those close to me [particularly my brother], to others"

Unmet Needs

To be looked after, to be protected, to be relieved of responsibility, to be accepted as I am, to feel closeness in a relationship

At work, John often experiences intrusive images, vividly seeing how he has caused major damage—for example, poisoning customers or making major losses at the counter. These images and thoughts are often so vivid that he believes the thing has already happened. He then engages in a variety of rituals unrelated to the "damage" he believes has happened (e.g., counting steps and ensuring that their number is identical every day). He also often finds himself worrying that he has caught some illness or disease from customers at work, and he responds by washing his hands excessively. He is embarrassed about his behavior and is afraid to meet new people in town because he feels he would come across as weird.

During sessions, John frequently talks about his symptoms. He is not emotionally accessible, but when he touches on underlying feelings of loneliness and insecurity, he can get emotionally activated and expressive. Deep down, he wants to be protected, looked after, reassured, and accepted, and he wants to feel close to others.

AN EXAMPLE OF A CLIENT WITH PTSD AND COMORBID GENERALIZED ANXIETY

Kate (see Exhibit 5.4) is a client in her early 50s. She sought therapy for post-traumatic stress symptoms after an assault 6 months before that involved her being hit twice in the face by a robber and needing medical treatment.

EXHIBIT 5.4. A Summary of Kate's Difficulties Using the Conceptualization Framework: Example of a Client With Posttraumatic Stress Disorder and Comorbid Generalized Anxiety

Triggers

Historical Triggers

- Father not emotionally accessible
- Father's terrifying temper "outbursts," targeting mother but, at times, also Kate and her siblings
- Mother timid and, although worried about children, incapable of standing up to husband
- Continuing open conflicts with father through late teenage years
- Older brother dying in car accident
- Mother diagnosed with cancer and dying a short time later
- Traumatizing experience of caring for mother through illness and treatment

Current Triggers

- Increasingly independent teenage children (whose safety and welfare she worries about)
- Husband's work as a taxi driver (whose safety and welfare she worries about)
- Violent assault 6 months previously

Self-Treatment

Self-worrying about potential further assaults on herself or on her close ones (children, husband), self-criticism (e.g., "Something about me invites these distressing events")

Global Distress

General sense of distress, hypervigilance, sleeplessness, irritability, difficulty concentrating, flashbacks from the assault

Apprehension/Anxiety

"Leaving the house is dangerous," "My children are in danger," "My husband is in danger," fear of potential illnesses or adverse events

Behavioral Avoidance

Not leaving the house, not going anywhere alone, constantly checking on children and husband

Emotional Avoidance

Watching television to distract self, spending time in therapy recounting symptoms, seeking to persuade the therapist about the severity of dangers in her life

Core Pain

- Fear based—for example, "Dangers to me and to those close to me [particularly children and husband] are imminent," "The danger is seeking me"
- Shame based—for example, "Something is wrong with me that these things happen to me"
- Loneliness/sadness based—for example, "I miss my brother and my mom"

Unmet Needs

To be safe, to be protected, to have predictability in life, to have a sense that she is alright, a longing for connection with brother and mother

In session, she presents as anxious but is otherwise not emotionally expressive; instead, she talks predominantly about her symptoms.

Kate grew up in a busy family in which her dad often lost his temper and could become angry and scary. He particularly targeted Kate's mother, but at times, he also targeted Kate and her siblings. Kate had a number of frightening exchanges with him, particularly in her late teenage years when she tried to stand up to him. Her mother was timid and afraid of her husband, and she was generally anxious and worried a lot. Kate was close to her brother who died in a car accident when she was just 16. She was traumatized by this experience, and her brother's death was a big loss for her. When Kate was in her early 20s, her mother was diagnosed with cancer and died after a few years. During her mother's illness, Kate supported her and was vicariously traumatized by the endless medical procedures and by the frequent ups and downs in her mother's health and prognosis. The loss of her mother compounded the loss she still felt for her brother. Apart from the aforementioned difficulties, Kate enjoyed good relationships with her remaining siblings and friends. In her early 20s, she met and married her current husband; together, they have two children, one boy and one girl.

In recent years, Kate has become preoccupied with the safety of her two teenage children when they started to live more independent lives and as her capacity to shield them from potential dangers became correspondingly limited. Her husband is a taxi driver, and she worries about his safety and welfare. She worries about herself or a family member getting a life-threatening illness. All these anxieties and worries have been compounded by the assault during which she was physically attacked by a stranger who stole her handbag. Since the assault, she no longer leaves the house for walks. She insists on being dropped to and collected from work by her husband. She is hypervigilant, anxious, and distressed, and she cannot sleep, she experiences flashbacks, and she reports that her worries for the safety of her family are greater than they used to be. She tries to distract herself by watching a lot of television but has difficulty concentrating even on the programs she likes. Within sessions, she mainly talks about her anxiety and is not expressive of other underlying emotions (e.g., underlying fear, loss).

Kate reports feeling a sense that it must be something in her that is responsible for the bad things that happen to her and to those close to her. She longs for a sense that she is alright and that it is not her who brings these traumatic experiences on herself or others. She is preoccupied with dangers and with her symptoms. Deep down, she is frightened, feels unsafe, and feels that she cannot be protected. She misses her brother and her mother, and she longs to feel a connection with them. Her relationship with her dad, who lives nearby, is much better than it was when she was younger. However, although she worries about his health, she cannot walk to visit him because of her anxiety.

CONCLUSION

The case conceptualization framework presented in this chapter and in Chapter 3 can organize the therapist's thinking about cases and can serve as a basis for note taking, discussing the case in supervision, and reflecting on clients during and in between sessions. It also can inform in-session collaborative reflections with the client and possible in-between session client work.

The framework is not a static document. Rather, it needs to be further coupled with observation regarding the client's progression in therapy. For instance, the therapist may assess whether the client is capable of generating self-compassion or protective anger, whether the client benefits from the therapist's compassion and validation, whether natural grieving occurs, whether emotional interruption and avoidance become less dominant as sessions progress, and so forth. The therapist also can focus on progress regarding the degree of symptomatic distress experienced and on the clients' capability to benefit from therapeutic tasks. In the upcoming chapters, we focus on those micromarkers (see Chapter 2 for the definition) that the therapist considers.

6 MODULATING EMOTIONAL DYSREGULATION

Clients often present in therapy in an emotionally dysregulated manner—that is, they experience global distress–level emotions in a highly aroused and upset way. Although the diagnostic criteria for depression, anxiety, and related disorders imply that clients who meet criteria for these diagnoses have difficulties with emotions (the term *emotional disorders* is also used to refer to these difficulties; see Bullis et al., 2019), counterintuitively perhaps, this does not mean that all such clients necessarily experience emotions in an overwhelming, highly aroused, or dysregulated form. For instance, in a small but intensive qualitative study by O'Brien et al. (2019), only about 30% of clients presented as regularly dysregulated in the session (with highly aroused emotions typically in the form of global distress and anxiety). An additional nearly 15% presented, at times, as dysregulated but more generally quite constricted and avoidant. In contrast, more than 50% of clients presented as generally emotionally constricted. Despite use of the term *emotional disorders*, therefore, it is important to remember that all clients are not necessarily excessively expressive or easily emotionally dysregulated. In the next chapter, we look at how to work with clients who present as overly emotionally constricted or avoidant.

https://doi.org/10.1037/0000253-007
Transdiagnostic Emotion-Focused Therapy: A Clinical Guide for Transforming Emotional Pain, by L. Timulak and D. Keogh

While not all clients struggle with emotional dysregulation, many clients presenting with depression, anxiety, and related difficulties either regularly or occasionally do experience overwhelming distress. They can experience heightened emotion that is not only painful but can variably feel uncontrollable, undifferentiated, or unclear. We are talking here primarily about types of emotional experience that we have already defined as global distress or symptomatic-level distress. The emotional experience in such instances is too painful for the client to be able to differentiate, reflect on, or articulate in narrative. The level of emotional arousal is high, and voice and speech patterns can often be broken (see Stages 6 and 7 on the Client Arousal Scale in Warwar & Greenberg, 1999).

Although overall, in emotion-focused therapy (EFT), we do want clients to access emotional experience in an aroused manner, and this is particularly the case with primary emotions, in the case of overwhelming (and typically) secondary emotions, the task of the therapist is to help the client regulate or modulate such experiences so that they can be productively used by the client. The regulation and modulation of otherwise dysregulated emotional experiences allows the client to tolerate, explore, and reflect on their experience, thereby increasing clarity for the client and increasing their ability to articulate in narrative and to communicate what they are experiencing. The experience of being soothed within the session reveals to clients that they can be in contact with emotional experience in a bearable manner and points to the possibility that emotional experiences can be regulated and modulated in their life more generally.

When clients are facilitated in session to down-regulate otherwise overwhelming experiences, perhaps even access a sense of calm, they may subsequently be capable of focusing on the originally upsetting emotional experience in a more productive manner. In this way, working to help clients regulate overwhelming emotional experience allows the work of therapy to progress. Often, however, it takes the full session to help the client regulate and modulate an overwhelming experience. Even this, however, is therapeutically productive because the client can internalize the therapist's calming presence or learn to draw on the relevant experiential task (e.g., clearing a space) outside of therapy whenever they feel emotionally overwhelmed.

WAYS TO REGULATE AN OVERWHELMING EMOTIONAL EXPERIENCE

We look now at four ways in which the EFT therapist can help clients to regulate an upsetting and overwhelming emotional experience: (a) empathic holding, (b) explicit regulating and grounding, (c) the clearing a space experiential task, and (d) the soothing of global distress through use of an imaginary dialogue.

Empathic Holding

To begin with, the therapist's warm, caring presence and empathic attunement to client affect has in and of itself a soothing effect. That soothing effect is especially present when the client is overwhelmed and uncontrollably upset. In such moments, the therapist offers a particularly active approach to soothing empathic communication. When such moments in therapy are looked at (e.g., in the context of supervision or research), it is noticeable how the therapist naturally leans forward as if offering even closer contact to the client. The therapist's already soft voice often softens further, and the therapist may repeat words the client says, staying in contact even when the client themselves have stopped articulating the experience in words.

The therapist essentially feeds the client the words they themselves might be struggling to access at those moments—for example, "It brings all this upset. It is just so, so painful"—thus naming the experience, something that has a regulating function on its own. If there is a clear context to what has caused the client's upsetting experience, the therapist offers a narrative that captures it—for example, "So, he left you, and it brings all this upset. It is such a loss." The therapist persists in staying with, leaning into, and putting words on the client's pain. Even if the client's presentation signals hopelessness, the therapist stays equally attuned, soothing, and calming. If the client's experience is one of anxiety or panic, the therapist offers a firm presence rather than anxious reassurance.

Grounding and Regulating

Building on this empathic presence and holding, the therapist can also offer gentle instructions that facilitate grounding and regulation. The most common guidance is the instruction to breathe: "Yeah, maybe take a breath. Yes, like that . . . just take a breath." Regular breathing facilitates the regulation of experience. Other examples of such instructions orient the client to what it is that brings the distress (e.g., "So, you are telling me all this, and it brings all this upset") or focus the client's attention on objects that may offer to facilitate a grounding experience (e.g., "Yeah, have a sense of your feet on the ground; as you are sitting in the chair, have a sense how it holds you"). Regulating and grounding instructions are usually offered within the context of soothing, empathic holding. As such, they are embedded within the therapist's caring, soothing empathic presence and are part of their empathic communication.

The Clearing a Space Task

Clearing a space is an experiential task that the therapist can introduce when there is a marker of uncontrollable, overwhelming distress. It is a task that comes from the practice of focusing (Gendlin, 1981, 1996; Leijssen, 1998), which has itself been adopted as a task within EFT to facilitate the unfolding of an unclear felt sense (see Chapter 2). Within the focusing therapeutic tradition, clearing a space is an initial step whereby the client is guided to concentrate and focus attention inward toward the middle of the body, where we generally feel feelings. Robert Elliott (Elliott et al., 2004) adapted these steps into a format that is possible to use as an end in and of itself to facilitate emotional regulation. What follows is our variant of the task based on his formulation.[1]

Step 1. Feeling Overwhelming, Uncontrollable Upset

The marker for the intervention is the client's overwhelming and uncontrollable upset. Optimally, the client also clearly recognizes the feeling as causing a physiological discomfort in the middle of their body. We suggest introducing this task only if the upset is preventing the client from engaging in any other way within the session. If, for example, the client is capable of tolerating and working with the distress, then this is what the therapist should facilitate.

Step 2. Paying Attention Inward Where the Distress Is Felt

Once the marker is established, the therapist asks the client to focus inside and pay attention to the middle of their body—roughly from the throat to the bottom of the stomach (e.g., "How does it feel inside? Pay attention to the middle part of your body"). It is typically in this part of the body, an area that includes the solar plexus, a huge network of radiating nerve fibers involved in autonomous nervous system functions, that we sense the physiological aspects of distress. At this point, some clients may begin by referring to other parts of their body like their head ("I have a headache"), back ("My back is tense"), or limbs ("My hands feel shaky"). Some symptomatic presentations, particularly those involving anxiety and related difficulties, include aches in the back, neck, or other muscles, perhaps stemming from a long-lasting history of vigilance.

---

[1]Our variation is an adaptation of Box 8.2 from *Transforming Generalized Anxiety: An Emotion-Focused Approach* (p. 122), by L. Timulak and J. McElvaney, 2018, Routledge. Copyright 2018 by Routledge. Adapted with permission.

However, although uncomfortable, these physical and often muscle-related feelings are not the focus of the clearing a space intervention. When the client reports such feelings, the therapist acknowledges the discomfort but focuses the client back on attending to the middle part of their body. The therapist asks the client to identify where in the body they are feeling the upset (e.g., "Can you show me where you feel the feeling?"). The task can be optimally engaged in when clients close their eyes because this can facilitate the process of concentrating on internal experience. However, for some clients, the direction to close their eyes may in and of itself give rise to additional anxiety, so it is generally helpful to suggest but not require this, saying something like, "You can close your eyes if it is okay with you. It may help to keep your focus inside."

Step 3. Describing the Bodily Aspects of the Feeling

After the client focuses inward and identifies where they feel the physiological discomfort, the therapist asks the client to show them the boundaries of the feeling (e.g., "Can you show me from where to where you have this feeling?") and then to describe the feeling and its qualities (e.g., "If you were to describe that feeling inside, what is it like?"). Establishing the boundaries of the feeling is important because the therapist will later suggest to the client to imagine the feeling being put aside, and, to do so, it is helpful if the client has a sense of the feeling that is clearly distinguished and tangible. This establishment of boundaries is further facilitated by inviting the client to describe the qualities of the feeling as if the feeling was a distinct, external object in their body. The therapist will want to later point out to the client that the client is more than just the feeling, and the less nebulous and more tangible the visualization of the feeling, the easier it is for both the feeling to be put aside and for the client to feel that they are more than it.

Step 4. Naming the Feeling and Linking It to the Client's Life Situation or Issue

As the client describes the bodily aspects of the feeling, the therapist asks them to give it a name (e.g., "What would we name this feeling, for now?"). The client may call it, for instance, "a heavy boulder in my stomach." The therapist then checks whether "the heavy boulder" (i.e., the difficult feeling) is linked to something happening in the client's life. If the client is able to identify such a link (e.g., "It's linked to my worries about my sick dad"), the therapist, in subsequent instructions, uses both the label assigned to the feeling and the link to what that feeling relates to in the client's life (e.g., "This heavy boulder you are feeling in your stomach that is somehow linked to how your dad is doing"). We suggest probing for this link because narrative or meaning regarding what is triggering the feeling may be of use in later exploration or may point to other possible foci or markers for subsequent work. That said, clients are not always able to link bodily feelings with what is happening in their life. They may feel upset inside without having a clear sense as to what it relates to. In such cases, the therapist respects that this is how it is for the client and stays with describing and naming only the physical quality of the bodily feeling.

Step 5. Putting Aside the Feeling
After the client names the feeling (and potentially what it relates to in their life), the therapist invites the client to imagine the physical feeling (e.g., "the heavy boulder") being put aside somewhere. When giving this instruction, the therapist uses neutral wording so that the client is not under pressure to imagine that it is themselves who must somehow put the feeling aside (e.g., "Can you imagine that this heavy boulder is being put aside?"). This neutral phrasing implicitly acknowledges that it can be difficult to put such feelings aside. The very fact that the therapist and client are engaged in this task is itself indicative of how all-encompassing such feelings can be for the client, and it is thus assumed by the therapist that the client may have difficulty imagining that it could be in their agency to put such feelings aside. Furthermore, the therapist may stress the temporariness of the feeling being put aside so that the client feels further validated that the feeling is linked to serious issues needing attention and cannot be that easily disregarded.

The therapist then invites the client to imagine where the feeling may be put, saying something like: "Imagine that this feeling—this heavy boulder somehow linked to your dad—is going somewhere or is being put somewhere for a moment. Where would it be good for it to be or for it to be put?" The actual place nominated by the client can be anywhere, either real (at the bottom of their yard) or imagined (at the bottom of an ocean), close by (beside their chair), or distant (outside the door). As the client nominates the place, the therapist asks them to imagine that the feeling is going there. Then the therapist asks check-in questions: "Can you see it there?" If the client says yes, the therapist says, "So, it is there, and you are here" to stress the distance and to help the client variously move their attention between the externalized feeling/object, in this case the "boulder," and the self.

Step 6. Inviting the Client to Again Focus Inside
Once the client reports that they can see or visualize the feeling as put aside, the therapist redirects the client's attention internally, asking them to check

inside again: "So, the boulder is out there in the corner of the room, and you are here. Is that so?" [The client says, "Yes."] "So, what is the feeling inside now?" Typically, clients at this stage report a sense of change and some relief, saying something like, "The feeling is not that heavy anymore." "Not that heavy" implies that there is still some discomfort. The therapist thus checks and probes further: "So, is the sense fully relaxed, or is something not fully okay? You are saying 'not that heavy.'" If the client indicates some discomfort, Steps 2 to 6 are repeated. Typically, it takes several iterations of this process for clients to get a sense of calm and relief, and, in some cases, it may take the whole session.

Troubleshooting

At times, particularly with anxious clients, the task may initially appear not to be working. After the initial round, clients may report feeling more upset, more distressed. For some, this can occur because, in trying to put an issue or feeling aside, they feel as if they are neglecting something to which they feel a compulsion to attend to (i.e., they are driven by an apprehensive anxiety that is organizing them to be prepared to deal with the issue in question). They may then feel unprepared to deal with the issue that the feeling relates to, and because of that unpreparedness, they become more upset.

For instance, a client's initial feeling may be overwhelming anxiety that her father will become unwell on vacations because his health depends on taking medications that she usually manages for him, and she will not be on the vacation to look after him. The client may describe a radiating fist-sized ball around her solar plexus, linking this to her father's not being under her day-to-day care. Asked to imagine this put to one side, she may become even more anxious, panicking that if she were to put that worry aside, she might forget to call him, thus leaving him even more unprotected and at risk. In such instances, we encourage clients to visualize feelings as being put aside but close by—at a certain distance (e.g., not in their lap because we still want to stress the distance) but within reach. We reflect that they are put aside but highlight that the feelings (and thus the issue that may need attention) are available and within reach. We also stress that the feelings are put aside only temporarily, that the client is not seeking to forget or disregard these concerns; rather, in this moment, they simply need some space from the overwhelm. We also point out that such feelings do have a strong tendency to come back easily (as evidenced by the fact that the client was so overwhelmed in the first place). With strategies of this kind, the process tends to proceed relatively smoothly, even with those clients who initially reported feeling worse.

In our experience, the clearing a space task is most useful when a client is overwhelmed to such an extent that the session cannot have any focus other than achieving some level of regulation. It is one of the strategies that the therapist has available to them should a client be overwhelmed, and it is often not the strategy first resorted to. For some clients, however, for whom getting overwhelmed is a routine experience, it may be quite a central task. Such clients can learn the task and use it as homework. Indeed, we have experience of clients benefiting from the task within session and spontaneously drawing on it as a self-help strategy when overwhelmed outside of the therapy room, even without it being suggested by the therapist. Other clients have reported using this task at specific times, for example, to put worrisome, intrusive, or distressing thoughts and memories aside at nighttime so they can sleep.

At times, clearing a space may need to be used more creatively. For instance, some clients may have difficulty focusing inwardly, and, for them, the task needs to be introduced gradually with emphasis placed on focusing on particularly distinct physical feelings. For other clients, it may be difficult to focus on the middle of their body if they feel acute distress in other parts of their body, such as their back, neck, head, or limbs. Here, we suggest acknowledging this distress, and in cases in which it is chronic, we recommend a checkup with a general practitioner or physiotherapist but with an explanation to the client that within the session, we will endeavor to retain a focus on the front part of the middle section of the body because that is where we most typically feel the acute physiological aspects of emotional distress. Other clients may have difficulty putting the feeling aside. Here, we can offer images that might help with the task. For instance, feelings can be put into a box (which has a lid, thus helping to contain the feeling), or there may be some force that helps the feeling go to the assigned place (e.g., wind). Some clients, no matter how productively they engage with the task, are likely to feel some residuum of the uncomfortable feeling. For them, we can work to activate some soothing force that might engage with and sooth the remnants of the uncomfortable feeling—for example, "What would feel good to have in response to the feeling you feel inside? Can you imagine it [what the client named] doing that?"

The following transcript illustrates an example of a short clearing a space task in the middle of a session. The client, Peter, presents with social anxiety and, at times, has found it difficult to focus on internal exploration because he has felt uncomfortable in the session.[2]

---

[2]Chapters 5 through 9 include several case studies. Some are based on real clients, and others are composite sketches. Permission to use client data is on file with the authors.

THERAPIST: Yes, yeah, this is for anxiety. It's to regulate it a little bit. So, if you, try to sit as freely as you can and if you describe to me where do you feel that anxiety, where in your body you feel.

CLIENT: In the gut area . . . and it spreads out to the arms up here as well.

THERAPIST: Okay, okay, okay. Mainly stay with the stomach area, gut area, and, um, if you describe that physical feeling to me a little bit [focusing on the middle of the body].

CLIENT: It's a—it's a kind of, um . . . it's a heavy feeling, ya know. It kind of stifles me rather, it makes me stiff. . . . It's tightening, stiffening feeling as well.

THERAPIST: Okay.

CLIENT: It's hard to know where the thoughts end and the physical symptoms begin . . .

THERAPIST: I see, I see. Just stay with that physical sense in your body. Now, if we were to label it somehow, yes, it's maybe either a physical thing, you know, stiffness, or it may be stiffness connected to what happened in the shop [somebody gave Peter a compliment in his job, which subsequently made him anxious].

CLIENT: It's related to the whole up and down of what went on, for me having this horrible feeling that, you know, she picked up on the anxiety to, what happened afterward to where she was delighted with me like . . .

THERAPIST: So, all of it—it's like a lot of it, yeah.

CLIENT: All of it, yeah.

THERAPIST: It's like a lot of—all of it can link to the interaction in the shop, and that brings that stiffness inside. And, could you even describe to me the borders where you sense that stiffness, how big is that feeling?

CLIENT: Maybe about that size (*points to his stomach and signals with his hand the size of the stiffening feeling*).

THERAPIST: So, let's stay with this. We call it "the compliment-related stiffness" or something like that.

CLIENT: "The compliment-related stiffness."

THERAPIST: And if you—now let's try to almost, you can close your eyes if you feel comfortable, and if we were to put it aside, that stiffness in your stomach, for a moment, it's somehow related to the compliment you got, maybe in the room. Where would it be good to put it for a moment, aside—it won't go away—but where would it be good to put it?

CLIENT: In the bag beside me.

THERAPIST: Okay. So, imagine it almost going to the bag beside you, okay?

CLIENT: Yeah, zip the bag up then.

THERAPIST: Yeah, okay. Can you imagine it going to the bag?

CLIENT: Yeah.

THERAPIST: So, it's there in the bag, yes, and you're sitting here, and it's there in the bag, that "compliment-related stiffness." So, you are here, and it's there in the bag, yeah. If you check inside now, what's the sense like inside now, in your body?

CLIENT: Feels like there's been a bit of a shift.

THERAPIST: Okay, okay. So, enjoy the shift. Let's see what else is there. You can even breathe into the shift, yeah, yes, it's nice, yeah. So, what else is there? How is it in the body now?

CLIENT: (*Pauses*) It's less than what it was, um . . .

THERAPIST: Okay, but roughly in the same area? Or . . .

CLIENT: Mmm, but not so much.

THERAPIST: Okay, so that's important, yes, that's great. So, if you stay with it, so now if you describe physically how that feeling feels. I mean, you say it's somewhat shifted, so how does it sense now?

CLIENT: It's still slightly uncomfortable, some stiffness, but it's not overwhelming or anything. It's, um—it's kinda like a very mild physical feeling, but . . .

THERAPIST: Okay, okay. Could you physically almost give me the borders of it? With your hands, show me where it is almost like.

CLIENT: Just in around here (*points to the middle of his stomach*).

THERAPIST: Somewhere here. So, it's somewhat smaller as well physically, okay. So, yeah, maybe close your eyes and stay with it, with that feeling. If you were to label it, somehow, I mean, it may be something specific about the compliment situation, or it may be something else?

CLIENT: Um, it's almost linked now to the fact that there's another 5 weeks with the same person.

THERAPIST: Okay. "Another 5 weeks with the same person," yes . . .

CLIENT: Like, there's more of a chance that I'll get found out, but . . .

THERAPIST: Okay, just . . .

THERAPIST: Okay, so it's "another 5 weeks," yeah, and a "mild stiffness" that it brings, yes. "Maybe I will be found out." So, now where would it be good for it to go for a moment, if we were to put it aside, where would it be good to put?

CLIENT: Um, under the chair maybe.

THERAPIST: Okay. So, yeah, imagine it going under the chair or being there. Can you imagine it going under the chair?

CLIENT: Yeah.

THERAPIST: Okay, so imagine it's under the chair, yeah. It's not that far, but it's not where you are. It's a little bit further from you under the chair. Can you get a sense that it's there?

CLIENT: Yeah.

THERAPIST: Okay, so you are here, and it's there, yeah. And what's the sense like inside your body now?

CLIENT: It's calm.

THERAPIST: Okay, so enjoy that, yeah. Breathe into it and enjoy it, yeah . . . (*takes a moment of silence*).

CLIENT: It's almost like I'm not—I don't have to think about it now.

Use of an Imaginary Dialogue to Soothe Global Distress

One EFT task used primarily in the context of transformational work aiming at the core painful emotions (see Chapter 8) is self-soothing. It is most typically used in the context of an "unfinished business" dialogue, but it can also be used in any context (e.g., self-critic dialogues) in which underlying client vulnerability is activated and unmet needs are expressed. The enactment of a caring figure who responds to the wounded, vulnerable self in an imaginary dialogue is the prototypical form of self-soothing in EFT. Although the term "self-soothing" implies that the client enacts the caring position from self to self, it also covers instances in which the client enacts another caring person who responds to the client's vulnerable self (see Chapter 9). As such, the task can variously involve client expressions of care and compassion from their own adult self to their vulnerable self; from their own adult self to an imagined, developmentally younger self; or from a caring, enacted, imagined other (e.g., grandparent) to their vulnerable self.

In the context of dysregulated, overwhelming, or uncontrollable upset, we may also use a variant of this task as an alternative to clearing a space. Indeed, for some clients, it can be easier to enact and use an internalized caring other than to engage in and use an intrapsychological task, such as clearing a space. It can also be a better fit to the context of a session in which the client's distress has some clearly relational component (e.g., "I am alone with my distress"). In this variant, when the client is particularly distressed, they can be asked to nominate a person who has—or has had in the past—a soothing presence that they could draw on when in need of calming and soothing. (Clients often nominate people who are no longer alive, e.g., a cherished parent or grandparent, so it is important to be aware that, in cases in which the nominated person is relatively recently deceased, the client may experience the pain of loss as well as the enacted other's caring presence.)

Global distress–level soothing differs from more transformational soothing in that, although transformational self-soothing is enacted to elicit a compassionate response to core painful feelings and core unmet needs, global distress–level soothing is aimed only at providing a regulating and modulating presence to distress present on the level of secondary emotions and symptoms. We sometime use the term "symptom-level" self-soothing or "global distress level" self-soothing to distinguish that what is happening is not on the level of core emotional pain (see Timulak, 2015; Timulak & McElvaney, 2018). This task can be used not only in the context of overwhelming, dysregulating, or uncontrollable symptomatic distress but also potentially as a task to close sessions when clients might otherwise feel too raw emotionally.

In this task, at a marker of overwhelming undifferentiated distress/upset, the therapist asks the client to identify someone whom they can imagine being soothed by: "When you feel all this upset here, now, who comes to mind who would have a calming presence, or who would be good to have around when you are so upset?" After the client nominates a person, the therapist invites the client to move to the other chair and enact that person— to look at themselves in the other chair and express what that other person would do or say if they saw the client so upset: "Come here . . . be your grandmother. What would she say if she saw you so upset, what would she say now? What does she feel toward you? Convey her presence." As the client enacts that caring person, the therapist asks them to pay attention inwardly to how it is to convey that caring presence. The therapist wants the client to savor how it is to enact and express that calming presence. The therapist then asks the client to move back to their chair (the self's chair) and notice how it is to receive that calming presence. The therapist may say, "She is saying that everything will be alright, she is here with you, she feels loving and caring toward you. How is it to get it? To hear it? How is it to be a recipient of it?" As the client expresses the effect, which is often to feel cared for, soothed, or calmed, the therapist encourages the client to express what it feels like to the caring other (e.g., the client says, "I feel soothed"; the therapist says, "You feel so soothed, so tell her 'it is so soothing to receive this from you'"). Attending to, acknowledging, and expressing the sense of being soothed and calmed allows the client to bathe in the feeling and brings it further into the client's attention, thus consolidating the experience.

An example of this task is offered by Les Greenberg in his work with the client "Marcy" in the American Psychological Association demonstration video *Emotion-Focused Therapy Over Time* (Greenberg, 2007a). In that video, he invites the client to enact the presence of her father, who had a calming effect on her when he was still alive. The client enacts her father's expression of loving care toward her imagined self. After she moves back to her own chair, she is able to let in the caring presence she expressed when enacting her father. While this brings a sense of loss at missing her father, the client also reports feeling both calmed and supported.

Here, we offer another example of the use of this task in the context of a client's meeting diagnostic criteria for generalized anxiety disorder. The client, Anne, has difficulty regulating the distress that she touches on in the session (e.g., worrying about the welfare of her children and worrying about her own health). When asked by the therapist, she nominates her husband as the caring person whose presence she finds calming.

CLIENT: *(Appears distressed, cries, and is overwhelmed)* And I couldn't get them feelings out of my head and out of my body. And every time I turned around, there is another drama. And I said I fixed that, and then I turned around, and another drama. I need to get all that back down. I need to get it to a level where I can go just (*takes a breath*): "Right. Okay. Keep going. Get through it and keep going. You will get out the other side."

THERAPIST: Yeah.

CLIENT: But at the moment, I cannot see the other side. It was down there (*points at her forehead*) because I think every parent has fear about their children. But it just went above there (*points hand above her head*). And I need to get it back down. And I need to get it down and fast before it takes over my life and that is all I have.

THERAPIST: So, what does it feel like inside: Is it shaky or overwhelmed?

CLIENT: Overwhelmed.

THERAPIST: Okay. What would that feeling need right now in this moment?

CLIENT: For somebody to tell me that I am not going to die any time immediately in the future. And that somebody who belongs to me would not be hurt [the client implies the presence of somebody else who would calm her].

THERAPIST: Who can convey this presence?

CLIENT: Like God maybe. No, James [husband].

THERAPIST: (*Points to the client to swap the chairs and sits in the other chair opposite the one the client is sitting in*) Could we bring him here? Picture yourself here (*points to the chair in which the client was sitting in just a second ago*). You are James. And Anne is saying, "I am scared, overwhelmed. I am scared that it's spiraling out of control, that it's escalating. I just want to hear, 'I'll be fine, the children will be fine . . . we'll live, we'll be happy, nothing bad will happen. . . .'" What do you say to her, as James? What's the message you convey.

CLIENT: (*Speaks as James*) He just says, "Take it as it comes. There's no point in worrying about tomorrow because you don't know what it's going to bring."

THERAPIST: What do you feel toward her? As James, what do you feel toward Anne when you see her so upset?

CLIENT: I want to hug her.

THERAPIST: Can you imagine you are hugging her? What is that feeling? It's like, "I look after you"?

CLIENT: (*Enacts husband*) "You'll be safe."

THERAPIST: Tell her again, "You'll be safe. I'll keep you safe." And the sense is like, "I am conveying the safety. I keep you safe." [By saying "and the sense is," the therapist tries to bring an experiential quality to the client's awareness.]

CLIENT: "We'll be okay."

THERAPIST: And it's like, "I can be firm. I'll be here for you. I am strong enough to keep us safe." [Again, the therapist focuses on the felt quality of the client's expression.]

CLIENT: "We can deal with it as it comes. And we can get through it."

THERAPIST: "I will comfort you."

CLIENT: "I'll comfort you."

THERAPIST: As you say it, try to see if you can sense some of that strength he gives you: "I'll be there to hold you." [Again, the therapist brings an experiential focus.]

CLIENT: "I'll comfort you. I'm here for you. I'll always be."

THERAPIST: Could you come back here (*points to the self chair*)? So just see him: "I'll hold you. I'll keep you safe." Just imagine all this coming from him. How does it feel?

CLIENT: I do feel safe.

THERAPIST: Now imagine it here. What does it feel?

CLIENT: Love.

THERAPIST: Could you tell him?

CLIENT: (*Appears visibly calmer*) I feel loved, and I feel secure with you. And I know we will get through anything. We have been through so much.

THERAPIST: So, you appreciate it? [The therapist wants the client to further stay with the felt quality.]

CLIENT: I do appreciate it.

CONCLUSION

In this chapter, we looked at ways of working with emotional dysregulation within the session. While we do wish to activate and work with aroused emotion, it is important that clients are not dysregulated or overwhelmed by their emotional experiences. When clients are overwhelmed or emotionally dysregulated, it is important that the therapist is able to help them regulate or modulate their experience such that painful emotions can be tolerated and productively worked with. We presented four ways of modulating and soothing global distress–level emotional dysregulation within the session: empathic holding, explicit regulating and grounding, clearing a space task, and use of an imaginary dialogue to soothe global distress.

7

OVERCOMING AVOIDANCE

Because chronically painful emotions are so difficult, it is understandable that clients want to avoid both those feelings and the triggers that could evoke them. Equally, when such painful emotions are experienced, it is understandable that clients will want to stop them, interrupt them, dampen them, or find other ways to lessen the pain. These are natural, self-protective processes that, in many instances, may fulfill adaptive functions. However, such self-protective processes become issues when they do not allow the client to process painful emotions, articulate the unmet needs in them, or organize the self to respond with adaptive emotions and actions to those needs. Thus, work with self-protection and emotional avoidance becomes the focus of emotion-focused therapy (EFT) when these processes hinder the healthy processing of painful chronic emotions.

In this chapter, we discuss the evocative nature of EFT and how this runs counter to the emotional avoidance that can present, either occasionally or pervasively, within the therapeutic process for various clients. We also discuss working directly with avoidant, self-interruption processes using an experiential task specifically designed to address these processes. This task,

https://doi.org/10.1037/0000253-008
Transdiagnostic Emotion-Focused Therapy: A Clinical Guide for Transforming Emotional Pain, by L. Timulak and D. Keogh

the *two-chair dialogue for self-interruption*, can be used at a specific moment in the therapeutic process when emotional experience or expression is interrupted, but it can also be used in cases in which a client is chronically emotionally constricted. It also can be used when the client stops themself from getting into situations that would potentially elicit painful emotions. Before looking at this task, though, we explore other means by which EFT facilitates the optimal accessing of emotions in therapy.

FACILITATING ACCESS TO EMOTIONS IN EFT

Although therapists do validate the self-protective function of emotional avoidance and related processes, ultimately in EFT, they seek to access the core painful emotions at the center of the client's distress to facilitate transformation of these emotional states. Obviously, this can only happen if the client is not too overwhelmed, in which case they need to help the client become capable of regulating and tolerating the distress so that it can be worked with (see the previous chapter). In a similar way, therapists cannot work with painful emotion if the client is so overregulated or avoidant that such emotional experiences cannot be accessed and, in such instances, need to find ways to work with overregulation and to overcome avoidance.

In general, therapists bypass client emotional avoidance by the simple process of remaining empathically attuned to client affect and, in particular, to primary emotions. Thus, when a client engages in narrative or intellectualization in a manner that appears avoidant of what is poignant or painful, they focus on that poignancy or pain—for example, by empathically conjecturing, "I imagine that was painful to hear." In this manner, they simply bypass avoidance to focus first on the core painful emotions at the center of the client's vulnerability and focus later on the primary adaptive emotions that can potentially transform this vulnerability. Client emotional avoidance only becomes the central focus in therapy when it persistently poses an obstacle to accessing core painful feelings or those adaptive emotions, the accessing and expression of which might constitute an emotional transformation process.

In terms of our case conceptualization in this book, we capture avoidance processes explicitly under the headings of "apprehensive anxiety" and "emotional and behavioral avoidance," but they can also be captured under the heading of "problematic self-treatment processes" (see Chapters 3 and 5 for details). We postulate that clients are apprehensive of both triggers that could potentially bring emotional pain (e.g., being judged and rejected by a significant other) and of the pain itself (e.g., the shame of feeling defective). Clients thus engage in behaviors to mitigate the potential impact of triggers (e.g., placating the other to avoid rejection and judgment) as well as engage in strategies so they do not feel any pain that might be activated (e.g., trying not to pay attention to the shame, expressing secondary anger rather than underlying shame). All occur as a result of symptomatic-level, problematic self-processes (e.g., self-worrying or overpreparing the self for potential rejection, compelling the self to engage in rituals to mitigate the pain of rejection). The case conceptualization framework offered thus allows avoidance processes to be captured from a number of perspectives and can serve as a basis for therapist reflections on these processes.

In the actual moment-to-moment interactions of therapy, the EFT therapist generally seeks to facilitate optimal levels of emotional arousal. The focus on underlying vulnerability—on those chronic painful emotions that need to be accessed to be transformed—is, in general, accomplished through the therapist's empathic exploration with the client of that client's experience. The therapist attends to narrative but offers an empathic attunement that is specifically attentive to affect (see Chapter 2). They acknowledge secondary emotions but focus primarily on underlying more primary emotions. The therapist combines empathic exploration with the communication of understanding, all while endeavoring to keep emotions evoked by using an attuned, sensitive voice quality (e.g., that speaks to client vulnerability); focusing on the client's felt experience (e.g., "I can imagine it must bring an ache in your body. How does it feel?"); and by using evocative empathy (e.g., "It must have been so painful"). The therapist may also use more direct interventions, such as explicitly guiding the client to what they feel inside of their body. When approaching adaptive experiences, such as compassion and healthy boundary-setting anger, the therapist empathy may take a more validating form (e.g., "It brings all that anger in you," which they say using a firm voice quality). Again, they may use direct instructions to evoke a more vivid experience—for example, "Say it again: 'I am angry.'" The overarching picture here is that the therapist seeks to ensure that both chronic painful emotions and new adaptive emotional experiences are felt as fully as possible within the session both to optimally facilitate emotional transformation and to ensure the most vivid experience for the client of these transformational processes within the session itself.

Apart from the therapist's general empathic and emotion-focused style, which implicitly overcomes or bypasses emotional avoidance, the therapist also engages the client in, and guides the client through, a variety of EFT tasks (Elliott et al., 2004; Greenberg et al., 1993), many of which by their nature (and design), invite and amplify emotional experience. For instance, systematic evocative unfolding (see Chapter 2) is a task specifically used to facilitate client tracking of their own emotional reactions to external situations. It involves a vivid reimagining of the situation in question such that the client's emotional reactions are activated and thus made amenable to reflection (e.g., "How does it feel inside as you look at the disappointment in her eyes?").

Similarly, in focusing (see Chapter 2), the client is asked to focus their attention inward, but instead of putting feelings aside as in the clearing a space task, the client is asked to name various noticed aspects of the felt experience and, if possible, to link this felt experience to what is taking place in their life. Again, focusing seeks to bypass avoidance by focusing attention on the felt quality. With focusing, it is important to encourage the client to put felt experience into words and to express it, thus allowing it to be what it is. This emotional expression is important because, in our clinical experience, some practitioners of focusing trained in this method can, at times, use the method to dampen experience and thus interrupt feeling or expression by overly engaging in a reflective and introspective process (e.g., instead of expressing "I am angry," the client may say something like, "Let me see what I actually feel," thus essentially interrupting the anger).

Transformational tasks, such as the two-chair dialogue for problematic (self-evaluative) self-treatment (self-criticism) and empty-chair task for interpersonal emotional injury (unfinished business), are naturally focused on accessing underlying chronic painful feelings in an emotionally aroused manner. Moreover, the introduction of such tasks typically is sufficient to facilitate the accessing, expression, and exploration of emotional client experience. These two central EFT tasks also serve as a means for generating adaptive emotions, such as (self-) compassion and protective anger, which, again, the therapist seeks to facilitate access to, and expression of, in an emotionally aroused manner.

Apart from the just mentioned EFT tasks, several others in EFT have been specifically developed to target avoidance, the interruption of emotional experience, or the interruption of behavior that could bring painful emotions. Given that many of these tasks target specific clusters of symptomatic presentations (e.g., worry), we focus on them in Chapter 8 when we look at common symptoms (and related self-protective processes) of mood, anxiety, and related presentations. Specifically, we look at worry, rumination, avoidance of feared objects/situations, obsessions and compulsions, and trauma-related symptoms that may have elements of emotional avoidance. For now, in the remainder of this chapter, we turn our attention to focus on the generic process of emotional constriction and related behavior, which, in the EFT literature, is termed "self-interruption" (Greenberg et al., 1993).

WORKING WITH SELF-INTERRUPTION IN EFT

Self-interruption, and the process of working with self-interruption, has been written about in EFT from early on (Greenberg et al.,1993). Building on strategies for working with self-interruption adapted from gestalt therapy, early EFT writing described and defined the two-chair dialogue for self-interruption (Elliott et al., 2004; Greenberg et al., 1993). In contrast to other major EFT chair tasks, such as the two-chair dialogue for problematic (self-evaluative) self-treatment (self-criticism) and the empty-chair task for interpersonal emotional injury (unfinished business)—which, although adapted from gestalt therapy, were reformulated on the basis of empirical work that studied processes in successful versus unsuccessful use of the tasks (e.g., Greenberg, 1979; Greenberg & Dompierre, 1981; Greenberg & Foerster, 1996; Greenberg & Higgins, 1980; Greenberg & Malcolm, 2002)—the self-interruption task is based purely on clinical experience. However, although it is not directly informed by empirical task analysis, the self-interruption task has constituted part of "the whole package" of EFT as studied in various empirical studies that have tested EFT efficacy (e.g., Goldman et al., 2006; Greenberg & Watson, 1998; Shahar et al., 2017; Timulak et al., 2017, 2018; Watson et al., 2003).

Our formulation of this task, as presented here, is based on the writing of Greenberg et al. (1993; see also Elliott et al., 2004) and also on our own experience with the task in practice and in clinical research trials. We have also outlined this formulation in previous writing (see Timulak & McElvaney, 2018; see also Table 7.1).

Markers of Self-Interruption

For two reasons, we suggest focusing on self-interruption only when it is a major obstacle to therapeutic process or when it is an almost traitlike feature of the client. First, and as we have already elaborated on, avoidance and self-interruption can often be worked with and bypassed more economically. Second, two-chair dialogue for self-interruption is a difficult task for clients to engage in. For instance, the therapist offers instructions such as, "How do you stop yourself from feeling?" While the therapist assists the client in this process, engaging in it can, at times, be quite abstract and difficult

TABLE 7.1. Stages in the Two-Chair Dialogue for Self-Interruption

Stage	Experiencer Chair	Interrupter Chair
1	Experiencing the marker: Stopping oneself, experiencing the tension	
2		Enacting the interruption (highlighting its function and what drives it—e.g., fear of the emotional experience or expression)
3	Accessing and differentiating the effect of the interruption (i.e., tension)	
4	Articulating and expressing the need for freer emotional experience and expression	
5		Probing for compassion, seeing the effect or cost of the interruption (highlighting the protective function of the interruption)
		Stage 5A—if no compassion is coming: Going with the increased interruption/tensing/suppression
		Stage 5B—if compassion is coming: Facilitating resolve to let go of protection
6	Building the resolve to set a boundary to the interruption and experience emotions more freely, allowing the emotional experience and expressing it	

Note. From *Transforming Generalized Anxiety: An Emotion-Focused Approach* (p. 108), by L. Timulak and J. McElvaney, 2018, Routledge. Copyright 2018 by Routledge. Adapted with permission. The original source also cited Elliott et al. (2004).

for the client. For this same reason, we do not recommend using this task as the first chair task in therapy. In addition, for some clients, some forms of self-interruption or emotional avoidance can be present on an almost continuous basis, so it can be tricky determining whether interruption at a particular moment constitutes enough of a marker for it to become the focus of the session. We therefore reiterate the point that occurrences of self-interruption within the session should not in and of themselves be taken to indicate that a focus on self-interruption is warranted, nor should they be automatically taken as markers to introduce a two-chair dialogue for self-interruption. Rather, self-interruption in the session should only be focused on if the interruption is a major obstacle to accessing emotional experience (whether chronically painful or adaptive) that is important for therapeutic progress within the session and across therapy.

Markers of self-interruption (i.e., in-session client presentations indicating that self-interruption is occurring) may be present in various forms. We now look at subtypes of self-interruption markers that indicate use of the task may be productive. The simplest example is a *situational interruption of expression*. This marker occurs if, in the context of another chair dialogue, the client begins to feel emotion but, at some point, becomes unable to express or feel the emotion that is arising. This form of marker most frequently occurs in the context of the empty-chair task for interpersonal emotional injury in which the client is speaking with the imagined other, such as an enacted parent. Our clinical and theoretical understanding here is that this often happens out of self-protection because allowing the feeling or expression of that feeling could lead to a worse experience (e.g., pain caused by the other's reaction). However, while there is a self-protecting aspect, there is also a cost: typically a sense of interruption, obstruction, resignation, and a giving up on one's needs or perspective. An example can be found in Les Greenberg's American Psychological Association demonstration video on EFT for depression (Greenberg & Carlson, 2007) in which the client begins to access anger toward her mother but that anger dissipates. Les then asks the client to move to the other chair and enact the Interrupter, that part of herself that somehow stops the anger in the Experiencing Self.

A second type of self-interrupter marker pertains to the client's baseline ability to access and express emotion. It occurs when a client is *chronically constricted*, that is, unable in general to access or express emotion in an aroused way. This is a traitlike quality that usually develops over years. Such clients may, in essence, have given up on trusting emotional experiences, even those experiences that might be positive or inform them about important needs. Instead, they settle—for reasons of self-protection—for limited and obstructed experiencing. This constricted emotional experiencing, albeit safe and predictable, gives rise to a sense of not being fully alive. Within therapy, this sense can constitute a major obstacle to change in that chronic constriction limits access to freshly experienced painful emotions. Subsequently, it is difficult for clients to access core emotional vulnerability in an aroused way, which, in turn, inhibits the likelihood of new transformational emotional experiences with the potential to restructure problematic emotion schemes. Although, in such instances, the therapist follows the same EFT process/strategy as they would with a less constricted client, the therapeutic work may be more limited as to what can be achieved. A more explicit focus on emotional avoidance, such as the use of self-interruption dialogues, is therefore warranted. This work can also be supplemented by homework encouraging emotional experiencing and expression. For example, the client may be asked to watch a poignant movie and observe both how they become emotional (for instance teary) and how they begin to engage in various methods of dampening that emotion (e.g., through distraction). They are encouraged to practice letting go to allow themselves both to feel and express emotion (e.g., let the tears drop).

A third type of interruption is *behavioral (action tendency) interruption,* markers for which are most typically present in client narrative accounts of keeping themselves out of situations in which core painful feelings could get triggered. An example of this type of self-interrupter marker can be found in Les Greenberg's (2007a) video *Emotion-Focused Therapy Over Time* (see Session 2) in which the female client describes how she protects herself from getting hurt by withdrawing behind a (metaphorical) wall of protection. Essentially, she remains emotionally withdrawn in close relationships so that she does not get hurt. The self-interrupter part of the self ensures that the client does not engage in certain types of behavior/actions (e.g., seeking closeness) that might bring painful emotional experiences (e.g., feeling rejected). Although on one level, the client appreciates the safety this affords her, she also identifies the cost of this self-protecting self-interruption as a sense of isolation that, in part, results from giving up on those behaviors that could lead to her needs for closeness being met.

Two-Chair Dialogue for Self-Interruption

We now describe the two-chair dialogue for self-interruption task (see also Table 7.1). While the actual work may differ somewhat depending on the subtype of self-interrupter marker present and, thus, the type of self-interruption that is the focus of therapeutic work, here, we describe the generic model. We also use illustrations to depict how the task may look within the therapy session.

Stage 1. Seeing That the Marker of Self-Interruption Is Present

Any of the subtypes of self-interruption (e.g., situational interruption of emotional expression, chronic interruption/constriction, behavioral interruption/constriction) may be present when initiating the self-interruption chair dialogue. In general, we suggest initiating this task only with more chronic emotional or behavioral interruption/constriction. Situational interruption can often be dealt with in alternative ways (e.g., empathic attunement to affect, emotion guiding, facilitation of the felt experience and its expression; see discussion at the beginning of this chapter). We only focus on situational interruption within the session when it may be helpful to bring to the client's awareness the function and manner of this interruption. More chronic emotional or behavioral interruption/constriction can also be productively worked with in a variety of ways other than with the two-chair dialogue for self-interruption task (again, see the beginning of this chapter). Indeed, EFT as a therapy is developed around facilitating emotional experience and expression. Specific homework (like the aforementioned example of watching a movie) can also be used to facilitate the client's development in this area.

However, given that, in cases of chronic interruption, self-interruption is omnipresent in the client's functioning and a powerful self-protective process is involved, it is good to make that interruption the focus of some self-interruption dialogues over the course of therapy. It is important that the marker for such work be present in a fresh manner. The client should refer to the interruption in the here and now (e.g., mentioning the major role it plays in their difficulties in life), or the client's emotional experiencing should be constricted in a significant way within the session. The therapist may reflect the significance of what is happening for the client and suggest the task as a way to explore what is happening (the therapist may say, e.g., "Maybe we could look at this process. It sounds like there's a part of you wanting to keep you safe, and this part somehow ensures that it's difficult to know what you feel or to express how you feel"; the wording for situational interruption or more behaviorally oriented interruption would be tweaked accordingly).

Stage 2. Enacting the Interruption

As the marker is established, the therapist asks the client to move from their own chair (from here, we refer to this as the "Experiencer Chair") to sit in the other chair (from here, we refer to this as the "Interrupter Chair") and enact the interruption (e.g., "How do you stop yourself from feeling? How do you stop yourself from seeking connection" [in case of behavioral interruption/constriction]?). The goal is to bring to the client's awareness how they actually stop themselves and what the function of this stoppage is (e.g., to protect oneself from feeling pain). The client can thus get a sense of what drives the interruption. Once the client enacts the interruption and articulates the function of it (e.g., self-protection), the therapist brings to the client's awareness the manner and the function of self-interruption (e.g., "So this is how you stop yourself from feeling. This is how you try to protect yourself").

The following example of the enactment of an Interrupter is from a session with Fiona, who presented with social anxiety and a comorbid depression, and who described literally freezing herself in social situations.[1] Here, the therapist asks her to enact that freezing/interruption:

THERAPIST: So how do you freeze yourself? How do you bring it on? Let's do it.

CLIENT: [In the Interrupter Chair] I will make you so uncomfortable that you won't be able to look at me in a relaxed way.

THERAPIST: Show her how she'll look! Make her look . . .

CLIENT: I am able to change the way you think . . . so it locks you into a position where you can't . . . it's almost like I . . . you're mind controlled. I'm able to mind control you for as long as I want. And I am able to do it. As soon as I trigger you into thinking that the other person is picking up on it. And I can do it whenever I want!

THERAPIST: So, it is like I will intrude on you.

CLIENT: I will be able to change every aspect of your body language, you know. Even the way you speak with people will change. And you will talk in a very guarded way, and you will look uncomfortable and rigid.

THERAPIST: And my function is like . . . I tighten the control or something like that?

CLIENT: I do it to protect you in so many ways. I limit the exposure and the potential for interactions that might go wrong [referring to socially embarrassing situations].

THERAPIST: So, eventually, people won't engage with you.

CLIENT: I'll take you off the situation. If you get into a situation where you would get hurt in some way, I will automatically take over how you think, and I will automatically induce that particular way of eye contact and that closed body posture, and all of that kind of stuff.

THERAPIST: So, this is what you do to yourself [brings to the client's awareness what she does to herself].

---

[1]Chapters 5 through 9 include several case studies. Some are based on real clients, and others are composite sketches. Permission to use client data is on file with the authors.

Stage 3. Accessing and Differentiating the Impact of the Interruption

Once the client has enacted the interruption and articulated its function, and once the therapist has brought this to the client's awareness, the therapist invites the client to move back to the Experiencer Chair and check inside to see what impact the enacted interruption has on them experientially (e.g., "What happens inside when you get that?"). In the case of situational interruption, the client may feel blocked or tense or may have some other physiological symptoms, such as headache. In the case of chronic interruption, the client may report a familiar or "known" sense of constriction or blockage that possibly coexists with a posture typically associated with efforts to control feelings (e.g., a rigid sitting). In the case of more behavioral (action tendency) interruption, the client may feel resigned, blocked, or stopped.

Alongside these various types of unpleasant effects, which can be seen and experienced as costs of the interruption, clients may also report positive aspects of being interrupted, usually in the form of feeling protected, or a sense of a safer engagement with the environment because it has a known or predictable quality (i.e., known evil vs. unknown evil). At times, especially in cases of chronic interruption, clients may have a sense that this has been their reality for as long as they can remember. They may also have a sense that this is who they are and that they cannot be different to this. As the experienced impact is articulated and differentiated, the therapist encourages the client to do so not only internally but also in the dialogue with the Interrupter in the other chair (e.g., "So it brings that sense of being tensed and stopped inside. . . . Can you tell him this part of you?").

Returning to our previous example, in Fiona's case, the impact of the Interrupter was explored and revealed in the following exchange:

THERAPIST: Just see here what happens. Just here at this moment. It's like I'll take over, and you will be like frozen, staring . . . and you can't shake me off or something. . . . What does it do to you to get it here?

CLIENT: [In the Experiencer Chair] It's so demoralizing.

THERAPIST: It's almost like I can't resist you, right?

CLIENT: You're all-powerful and you . . . you have so much control over me.

THERAPIST: It's almost like I physically feel how you intrude upon me and take me over.

CLIENT: Like, you're in charge. I am just there. It's suffocating and it's . . . um . . . demoralizing and . . .

THERAPIST: So, tell her, tell her! I feel suffocated by you.

CLIENT: I feel stifled. It's stifling, it's very stifling. There's not even a point in me even fighting back here because it's hopeless. I'm not going to win with you.

THERAPIST: You have such a power over me. Tell her, right. You have so much power over me!

CLIENT: I'm disempowered. I am literally frozen. Even if I tried to move, I may as well hold my hands behind my back . . . my hands in handcuffs and my legs in leg cuffs . . . and then trying to move, because I can't move.

Stage 4. Articulating and Expressing the Need for Freer Emotional Experience, Expression, and Engagement

As the impact of the Interrupter is felt, differentiated, and expressed, the therapist asks the client to articulate what it is they need from the Interrupter (e.g., "What do you need from this part of yourself?"). In the case of a *Situational Interrupter*—that is, the interruption occurs in the context of an empty-chair dialogue with an imagined significant other—clients at this point are often not only capable of expressing what they need but are able to allow themselves feel and express what was previously interrupted (thereby actually moving to Stage 6 in Table 7.1). In such cases, work with the Interrupter may finish at this point with the therapist and client reengaging with the task within which the interruption had initially occurred. When the therapist chooses to continue with the self-interruption task, the client at this stage is encouraged to express what they need to the Interrupter. After the expression of the need to the Interrupter, the client is then asked to move to the Interrupter Chair and invited to respond to the self in the Experiencer Chair (see Stage 5, which follows shortly).

The expression of the need in Fiona's case looked as follows:

THERAPIST: What is it that I need in this moment from her (*points to the Interrupter*)?

CLIENT: [In the Experiencer Chair] Um, I need, um . . . at this stage, I need you to just completely back off.

THERAPIST: And if she doesn't understand? [indirectly facilitates a firmer expression of the need and an expression of healthy boundary-setting anger; see Stage 6 shortly].

CLIENT: If you do not want to hear that, I can't tell you to just ease off. I need you to back off.

Stage 5. Probing for Compassion: Seeing the Impact or Cost of the Interruption

As the client is asked to sit back in the Interrupter Chair, they are invited to respond from within to the expressed impact and need of the client/self in the Experiencer Chair. The actual instruction may include a probing for how the client in the Interrupter Chair feels toward the affected part of the self and the need expressed in the Experiencer Chair (e.g., "What is your response from inside? What do you feel toward the impacted part of yourself?"). Clients who are chronically constricted typically get more panicked at this stage and enforce their interrupting process (Stage 5A; e.g., "You would be unsafe if I let go. I cannot relent"). The therapist validates this escalated self-protection and validates the function of it (e.g., "I want to keep you safe") but also asks the client to enact the escalation (e.g., "So tell him/her I will keep stopping you because it is so scary to feel").

At times, clients may soften at this point and express both a wish to stop interrupting the self (Stage 5B) and a cautiousness or sense of not knowing how to stop because the interrupting is so engrained (e.g., "I see you need to feel and breathe and to express yourself, but I do not know how to let go of stopping you"). Often there is a mixture of the two responses (Stages 5A and 5B combined)—that is, some understanding and some enhanced control (e.g., "I see what you need, and I understand that, but I have to keep you safe. I am too scared to let go, and, therefore, I will keep stopping you"). It is important here to highlight the motivation behind the self-interruption process, situating it within the Interrupter's process regarding their own vulnerability/fear.

In Fiona's case, the Interrupter showed some softening but mainly a reluctance to let go of interrupting:

CLIENT: [In the Interrupter Chair] I can't back off. If I allow you to see that aspect of yourself, you might enjoy it, you might take more risks. I see how it would feel nice to you [in the direction of Stage 5B]. But when I see you potentially getting to that point, I have to really stop you [Stage 5A].

THERAPIST: But this is important, yes, to be more aware of how you do it.

CLIENT: I am making you smaller.

THERAPIST: To ensure that you don't try anything.

CLIENT: I am doing it to protect you. I am taking you out of the situation and it's—it's a form of protection.

Stage 6. Building Resolve to Set a Boundary to the Interruption and Experience Emotions More Freely; Allowing the Emotional Experience and Expressing It

As the therapist highlights the Interrupter's insistence on interrupting emotional experience in the client (Experiencer), albeit to protect the self, the therapist points to the controlling and dominating position of the Interrupter and checks what the client (in the Experiencer Chair) wants to do with it (e.g., "What is your response to that—'I will keep stopping you'—right now? What do you want to do with it, here and now?"). Often, clients at this stage express increased determination to assert their needs for fuller emotional experiencing and freedom to be emotional expressive. Even clients who report feeling unable to do so in the moment often express determination to find a way to stand up for this need in the future, a not insignificant moment of self-assertion that in and of itself can bring hope.

In Fiona's example, a boundary to the interruption was expressed from the Experiencer to the Interrupter (see the aforementioned Stage 4):

THERAPIST: So, see what's the response right here, right now. It's like this part of you (*points to the Interrupter*) is saying, "I'll do it even more. You start to talk about what you need and how you want to be free, but I can't let you, I can't let you. I'll squeeze you even more, I'll get a grip." What's your response to that?

CLIENT: [In the Experiencer Chair] Just to stop doing that.

THERAPIST: Say it: "Stop doing it" [supports the client's boundary setting].

CLIENT: Back off.

THERAPIST: See what's the feeling as you are saying this "back off" [wants the client to savor her standing up the Interrupter].

CLIENT: There's mixed feelings. On one level, I am scared. And on another level, it's like I know it's the best thing for me [oscillates between her determination to stand up for herself and fear of being out and about].

THERAPIST: So, tell him: "I'm scared, but I know it's the best thing for me."

CLIENT: I am scared. It's almost like I feel like I'd have to go into the unknown. . . . But I know that, in the long run, it's definitely going to be much better for me.

Overall, the process in a two-chair dialogue for self-interruption task is fluid and not as linear as outlined in the stages here (see Table 7.1).

We present these stages primarily for didactic reasons (see also the steps outlined in the original formulations in Greenberg et al., 1993, and in Elliott et al., 2004) and have found them useful as reference points in supervision, in teaching, and in our conceptual thinking. The process is also always exploratory and so, for many reasons, may divert from the stages we outline. An important point here is that interruption has a protective function and either served adaptive purposes in the past or continues to serve them currently. Therefore, both positions—that enacted in the Interrupter Chair and that enacted in the Experiencer Chair—may have value and need to be respected. In addition, we emphasize that EFT is a client-centered therapy, and so it is central to an EFT way of working that the client's own pacing and own assessment of what they want are respected by the therapist.

As with the other tasks that we present in the following chapters, we offer a handout (see Table 7.2) the therapist can use when reflecting on the client's experience in the task. It can also be used as the basis for devising homework that the client may engage in (see Warwar & Ellison, 2019). We are not prescriptive in any way regarding the use of this handout and leave it to individual therapists and their clients to ascertain whether and in what format the framework might inspire reflection on the in-session experience or inform any possible homework.

CONCLUSION

While it is natural that clients seek to avoid painful feelings and the triggers that might evoke such feelings, self-interrupting processes can become problematic when they adversely affect client emotional processing. When these processes impede therapeutic work within the session, they thus become the focus of EFT. In this chapter, we looked at ways of working with and overcoming client emotional overregulation and avoidance. We identified several types of self-interruption, including situational interruption of expression, chronic constriction, and behavioral (action tendency) interruption. We discussed how a wide range of generic EFT strategies for working with emotion are often sufficient to overcome such processes but also how, in particular instances, specific work targeting these processes may be clinically indicated. Finally, we described a task specifically developed for addressing such processes: the two-chair dialogue for self-interruption.

TABLE 7.2. A Framework for Reflecting on the Self-Interruption Task or for Homework

Parts enacted in the Experiencer Chair	Parts enacted in the Interrupter Chair
	How do I stop myself from feeling? (Increasing awareness of the ways one stops themself from feeling)
	What drives my efforts to stop my feelings? (Focusing on the underlying fears of the painful emotions)
What effect does the interruption have? (Highlighting the emotional toll of the interruption)	
What do I need in the face of the interruption? (Articulating the need with regard to the interruption)	
	What do I feel toward the impacted part of me? (Bringing a reminder of compassionate experiences that may help one let go of the interrupting process)
How can I face the interruption? (Reminding one of the resolve in the session to allow and express emotion)	

Note. From *Transforming Generalized Anxiety: An Emotion-Focused Approach* (p. 110), by L. Timulak and J. McElvaney, 2018, Routledge. Copyright 2018 by Routledge. Adapted with permission.

8 DEALING WITH ANXIETY AND OTHER COMMON SYMPTOMS

In the previous chapter, we looked at avoidance of emotion as well as at the self-interrupting of emotional experience. We mentioned that various emotional and behavioral processes play into emotional avoidance, particularly the avoidance of core painful emotions. In this chapter, we focus on those self-processes that play a role in generating and maintaining anxiety (e.g., worry) or other symptomatic processes (e.g., compulsions). Many of these processes either directly or indirectly also serve an avoidance function. Specifically, we focus on worry processes as present in generalized anxiety disorder (GAD), social anxiety, specific phobias, and panic disorder; on rumination as present in depression; on obsessions, worries, and compulsions as present in obsessive-compulsive disorder (OCD); and on flashbacks, traumatic memories, and avoidance as manifesting in posttraumatic stress disorder (PTSD; see Table 8.1). Some of the descriptions we present in this chapter have previously been offered in the emotion-focused therapy (EFT) literature, whereas some are a unique contribution of this book. What they have in common is that they focus primarily on symptom-level difficulties (see Chapters 1 and 3) rather than on the underlying and non-disorder-specific core vulnerability that gives rise to those difficulties.

https://doi.org/10.1037/0000253-009
Transdiagnostic Emotion-Focused Therapy: A Clinical Guide for Transforming Emotional Pain, by L. Timulak and D. Keogh

TABLE 8.1. Symptom-Level Tasks and Their (Typically) Corresponding Diagnostic Groups in EFT-T

Task	Common in diagnostic group
Two-chair dialogue for self-worrying	GAD, social anxiety, specific phobias, panic disorder, PTSD
Two-chair dialogue for self-rumination	Depression
Two-chair dialogue for obsessions (self-worrying) and compulsions	OCD
Retelling of traumatic emotional experiences (images, memories)	PTSD, OCD
Two-chair dialogue for behavioral self-interruption (avoidance)[a]	PTSD, panic disorder, social anxiety, GAD, specific phobias
Two-chair dialogue for emotion self-interruption[a]	Common in many presentations

Note. EFT-T = transdiagnostic emotion-focused therapy; GAD = generalized anxiety disorder; PTSD = posttraumatic stress disorder; OCD = obsessive-compulsive disorder.
[a]In Chapter 7, we covered these two tasks under the name "two-chair dialogue for self-interruption."

The interventions described in this chapter thus target symptoms. Although the targeting and treatment of symptoms have historically not been a direct focus of EFT and, within the current model, are still not our primary focus, we believe for two reasons that this level of presentation cannot be fully bypassed. First of all, symptoms such as excessive worrying typically develop over a long period and thus become embedded in the client's functioning. Second, problematic and unpleasant symptoms are often what clients bring to therapy as their presenting issue. Thus, we believe that symptom-level presentations need to be addressed in therapy to provide some respite from these symptoms. Given that clusters of symptoms are idiosyncratic to a client while also shared across diagnostic groups, we propose a "modular" approach to treating symptom presentation. In other words, we propose that while the underlying client vulnerability centered on core loneliness/sadness, shame, and fear as well as corresponding unmet needs remains the main focus of therapy, symptom-specific tasks can be introduced in response to common symptomatic presentations when appropriate in-session markers for those tasks emerge.

Many symptom-level presentations either directly or indirectly fulfill an avoidance function. If I worry excessively about how I will be perceived in social situations, I do not have time to focus on anything else that matters to me. Thus, preoccupation with symptoms is, in a way, a secondary process that has a similar function to secondary emotions. It either tries to mitigate felt underlying pain or prevent it. The tasks presented in this chapter thus have to be used with caution; they should only be introduced if symptoms present a major obstacle to the therapeutic process or are a major focus of the client's in-session or overall functioning. The therapist has to be aware that spending too much time focused on symptom-level presentation risks contributing to avoidance of the underlying vulnerability that needs to be healed and transformed. Thus, we recommend that therapists focus primarily on attending to underlying vulnerability, core chronic painful emotions, and unmet needs, and only address symptom-level presentation to the extent that it is inevitable or necessary (e.g., symptoms present an obstacle to the therapeutic process or persist despite progress in emotion transformation of the underlying vulnerability). We focus here on several tasks targeting clusters of symptoms typically shared by some common diagnostic groups (see also Table 8.1). Again, any given task should only be introduced if a marker for its use is vividly present in the session.

TWO-CHAIR DIALOGUE FOR SELF-WORRYING

Worry is a common process in anxiety and related disorders. Clients may worry about a wide variety of subjects: about social situations (social anxiety), about many idiosyncratically relevant subjects (GAD), about their own symptoms of anxiety (GAD, panic disorder), or about specific situations or objects (specific phobias, PTSD). They may also engage in processes, such as obsessing, that may, in turn, involve or give rise to an element of worry (e.g., the obsessive thought "My hands are contaminated" can be followed by the worry "I will pass it on to my children"). Although the task of working with worry has been described in the EFT literature (Elliott, 2013; Greenberg, 2015), it was not initially studied empirically. Our research group then studied work with worry in the context of clients presenting with a primary diagnosis of GAD (e.g., Murphy et al., 2017; Toolan et al., 2019), and we have previously described the use of a worry task in our clinical writing on working with GAD (Timulak & McElvaney, 2018). Further description can also be found in Watson and Greenberg (2017) and Watson et al. (2019). Elliott and Shahar (2017) also described the use of a two-chair dialogue for working with worry in the context of social anxiety. Here, we present a formulation based on work in our own lab (as summarized in Timulak & McElvaney, 2018) and further informed by our transdiagnostic project examining the efficacy of the model presented (Timulak et al., 2020). We outline stages involved in addressing worry using a two-chair dialogue (see Table 8.2). The reader is reminded that the actual process of EFT is nonlinear. The stages are presented in the following order to orient the therapist; however, they may not follow this exact order within therapy.

TABLE 8.2. Stages in the Two-Chair Dialogue for Self-Worrying

Stage	Experiencer Chair	Worrier Chair
1	Experiencing the marker: Worrying, feeling exhausted	
2		Enacting the worrying: The experiential quality
3	Accessing and differentiating anxiety and tiredness (potentially also core pain)	
4	Articulating and expressing the need for freedom, for less limited life	
5		Probing for compassion, seeing the impact and need (highlighting the protective function of worry)
		Stage 5A–If no compassion is coming: Going with the increased worry (unable to control)
		Stage 5B–If compassion is coming: Savoring it experientially and expressing it
6A	Building protective anger, setting a boundary to the worry	
6B	Letting compassion in, savoring it experientially but still insisting on a boundary	

Note. From *Transforming Generalized Anxiety: An Emotion-Focused Approach* (p. 90), by L. Timulak and J. McElvaney, 2018, Routledge. Copyright 2018 by Routledge. Adapted with permission.

Stage 1. Seeing That the Marker of Worry Is Present

Typical in-session worry markers include the client worrying in-session or describing recent worry in the session (e.g., "I was up all night worrying about . . ."). The client may also report the exhaustion and anxiety that worrying bring. In the case of GAD, clients may worry about various idiosyncratic issues that are somehow, although not necessarily clearly, linked to their underlying core pain (O'Brien et al., 2019); by comparison, in the case of social anxiety, worries are more clearly linked to the underlying pain of feeling flawed and being seen as such. Clients may worry about specific concerns, such as illness (e.g., recurrence of cancer; Connolly-Zubot et al., 2020; Hissa et al., 2020), panic attacks, or something traumatic happening.

At times, the object of worry may be somewhat displaced, and rather than pointing directly to underlying vulnerability, the worry may be an expression of more symptom-level distress. Worrying and anxiety in a manner similar to other emotion-inducing processes are associative, and, thus, worry that is more directly linked to underlying vulnerability may generalize and get displaced onto other areas. For instance, a client who chronically worries about how they are perceived by close friends (social anxiety) may start to feel worried and anxious in nonsocial situations (e.g., health anxiety). Some clients may start to worry about potential harms the worry might give rise to.

Worry should be distinguished from similar but different processes, such as rumination (in which the client goes over and over past upsetting situations) and obsession (in which the client feels invaded by unwanted thoughts or images). We focus on these processes later in this chapter. The worry process is often accompanied by a self-critical process. Indeed, in a study from our lab (Toolan et al., 2019), we saw some form of criticism in all 55 inspected worry dialogues. This self-criticism was seen in either a relatively superficial form related to symptomatic presentation ("I should not worry, it is not normal to be a worrier") or on a deeper level clearly linked to core underlying vulnerability (e.g., "I worry about other people's judgment because I am flawed"; "I worry that I cause harm because I am incompetent"; "I worry about potential challenges as I am too weak to face them"; "I worry that I will neglect something, and if something bad happens, it will all be my fault because I am bad/inattentive").

Given that the process of working with self-criticism is much better elaborated on in the EFT literature (e.g., Greenberg et al., 1993) and has been written about for many more years, it is understandable that EFT therapists often digress from the "unknown" territory of worry dialogues to the more familiar "known" territory of self-critic dialogues (we describe two-chair dialogue for problematic self-treatment [self-criticism] in the next chapter). In general, this is not a major problem. Because work on self-criticism (with the exception of secondary or superficial self-criticism, e.g., blaming oneself for one's own symptoms—e.g., for being a worrier) generally cuts to the core of client vulnerability, it constitutes the central work of therapy—that is, transforming core vulnerability and core painful emotions. Therefore, we consider a focus on criticism relevant and important, and, in general, we advocate following the experiential path from worry to this deeper and more transformative work in therapy. We recommend working specifically with the worry process only when it is an obstacle to such transformational work or when the worry process has become such an ingrained aspect of the person's day-to-day functioning and symptomatic presentation (as in anxiety disorders) that, albeit linked in its development to the client's attempts to prevent underlying emotional pain, it now lives life on its own, independent of that core vulnerability.

Another consideration for the therapist when thinking about introducing a worry dialogue task is where in the therapy process the worry marker occurs. We do not recommend a worry dialogue be the first imaginary chair dialogue a client engages in—and for the same reasons that we do not recommend a self-interruption dialogue be the first dialogue engaged in. Both types of dialogues can be particularly challenging for clients to experientially engage with because the concept of worry or self-interruption as forms of self-treatment can be difficult to comprehend. In contrast, empty-chair dialogues for emotional injury (unfinished business), which involve dialogues with imagined significant others, or even two-chair dialogues for problematic self-treatment (self-criticism), which involve dialogues with the critical self, are typically easier for clients to engage in. In both instances, it is simply easier for most clients to enact and engage with the imagined other or the critical voice. Both of these processes tend to feel more tangible to clients, whereas with worry, clients may struggle to differentiate between eternal stressors and events and the message to the self (i.e., the manner in which they worry themselves about these events). For this reason, although with some clients worry dialogues is indicated, we advise that they are not the first dialogues engaged in. Where markers for a persistently problematic worry process arise in early sessions, the therapist can simply make a note that this is work that may be returned to in later sessions.

Stage 2. Enacting Worrying: The Experiential Quality

As the worry marker is clearly established and the client and the therapist agree to look at the worry process in a chair dialogue, the therapist invites the client to move from their own chair (hereafter called the Experiencer Chair) and sit in a second chair facing their own (hereafter called the Worrier Chair; see Stage 2 in Table 8.2). The therapist introduces the dialogue and instructs the client to enact the worrying—that is, how they worry themselves (e.g., "We will have a look at how you worry yourself. . . . Please sit in this chair, and let's see how you worry yourself." The therapist continues: "How do you actually do it? Let's have a look, worry yourself, it is like . . . [here, the therapist offers examples of worries already expressed by the client earlier in the session, the expression of which constituted the marker to initiate the worry dialogue in the first place] others will judge you; they will see through you?"). The therapist wants to ensure that the client actually engages in the dialogue. The client is thus instructed to visualize their Self in the Experiencer Chair and actively worry themselves by directly expressing the worries to the Self in front of them (e.g., "Worry him/her," "Tell him/her,"

"Make him/her worried about what can go wrong"). The therapist also wants to ensure that the client engages in the worrying process as fully as possible, actually activating viscerally felt worry, anxiety, and agitated energy in the Self in the Experiencer Chair (e.g., "How do you make him/her anxious" (*points to the Experiencer Chair*)? "How do you scare him/her? Let's do it").

Although not necessary at this stage (it more typically takes place at Stage 5), the therapist may then probe for the function of worrying. The therapist may ask, "What drives this self-worrying? Tell him/her. . . ." Or, is it like, "If I do not worry you . . . what would happen then?" Generally speaking, worry serves a similar function to self-interruption (i.e., somehow protecting the self from emotional pain), and clients in the Worrier Chair typically express that they want to ensure that the Self in the Experiencer Chair is ready for any danger or threat that could bring emotional pain. The therapist brings to the client's awareness this (typically self-protective) function but also emphasizes the manner (e.g., agitating, insisting, controlling, frightening, conveying, urgent) in which the Worrier goes about this (e.g., "So, this is how you want to protect yourself, and you do it in this agitated manner").

The following dialogue from a session with Fiona, a client presenting with social anxiety and depression, illustrates how the enactment of worry in a two-chair dialogue for self-worry (for short, we refer to it hereafter as the "worry dialogue") might look[1]:

CLIENT: I have this anxiety that people are going to look at me and think, "There's something wrong with her. She's not right," you know?

THERAPIST: So, if you come to this chair (*points to the Worrier Chair*). How do you worry yourself? Is it like they are going to look at you and will see that something is wrong with you? Let's do it [asking Fiona to enact the worrying].

CLIENT: [In the Worrier Chair] You are going to look awkward. They will be asking themselves what is wrong with you? They may be asking you whether you are okay.

THERAPIST: So, do it a bit more.

CLIENT: They will be wondering what is wrong with you? They will start to look at you and wonder about you.

---

[1]Chapters 5 through 9 include several case studies. Some are based on real clients, and others are composite sketches. Permission to use client data is on file with the authors.

THERAPIST: And you bring all this worrying and energy [pointing out the experiential quality of the Worrier]. So, this is what you almost do to yourself. You come up with all those scenarios like: They will be wondering what is wrong with you. You almost prepare yourself for the people's judgment [the function of the worrying]. Okay, could you swap now? [The therapist here brings to Fiona's attention what it is that she does to herself.]

Stage 3. Accessing and Differentiating Anxiety and Tiredness (Potentially Also Core Pain)

Once the client enacts the worry process in its full experiential manner and, in doing so, possibly identifies its function, the therapist asks the client to move back to the Experiencer Chair (see Stage 3 in Table 8.2). The therapist invites the client to focus inside and notice the impact, or toll, of this worrying self-treatment: "What happens inside when you get this . . . this can happen, or this, or this." Here, the therapist uses as examples the most agitating worries voiced from the Worrier in the Worrier Chair and also seeks to emulate any relevant aspect of the Worrier's voice quality (e.g., agitated, harassing). The therapist wants the client to slow down and attend to the effect of the worrying self-treatment on them in the here and now. Usually, in cases of chronic worrying, clients in the Experiencer Chair report that the worrying evokes in them a sense of anxiety and tiredness (e.g., "I feel anxious, exhausted"). Chronic worrying and the attendant sense of agitation delivered by worry eventually wears clients down, so the fresh enactment of self-worrying in this task typically brings both the anxiety and the tiredness (exhaustion or a sense of tension).

The therapist then directs the client to speak from the anxious feeling: "Tell him/her (*points at the Worrier*), 'I feel anxious, exhausted.'" The therapist wants to ensure that the client feels these feelings in the here and now, names the feelings, and expresses them directly to the Worrier Chair. Doing so facilitates an optimal level of emotional arousal but also facilitates the client staying in the dialogue. In particular, the expression of feelings is pivotal because it helps maintain arousal.

While the worry dialogue is a symptom-level task, emotions are associative; thus, it is often the case that, at this stage of the dialogue, clients may touch on those underlying painful emotions that are at the core of anxious apprehension. For instance, in the case of GAD, the worrying and overprotective mother who worries about the welfare of her children (e.g., "Something bad might happen to my children") may get in touch with underlying vulnerability (e.g., the too familiar pain of being unprotected). Often, this happens as part of the exploration of the anxiety triggered within the task by self-worrying (e.g., the therapist may check: "What is the worst of it all? What would happen if the worries were fulfilled?"). The therapist and the client may digress here to focus on the underlying vulnerability—for example, exploring the client's experience of being unprotected by initiating an unfinished business dialogue (see the next chapter). The work can thus be divided into two interrelated processes: (a) the more superficial, symptom-level work as targeted in the worry dialogue task itself (i.e., "Something can happen to my children") and (b) deeper work focused on the core vulnerability targeted in an unfinished business dialogue for emotional injury (i.e., "I felt so unprotected"). In some instances, both can be tracked and worked on within the same session by, for example, working first within an unfinished business dialogue before returning to a worry dialogue. Alternatively, one of these can be focused on within the current session (unfinished business), and the other (worry), bookmarked as something to return to during a subsequent session.

Generally, in EFT, we prioritize deeper work focused on core painful emotions and core vulnerability, but with clients presenting with anxiety difficulties and chronic worry, it has been our clinical experience that it is important to focus at some point in therapy on the level of symptomatic self-worrying. We believe this is important because these experiences are central to the client's day-to-day experience, are debilitating in their own right, and almost live life on their own (Timulak & McElvaney, 2018). In our research projects targeting GAD in which intervention typically consisted of 16 to 20 sessions of EFT (Timulak et al., 2017), the course of therapy usually included three to five worry dialogues, not all of which ran their full course. Instead, they often digressed into work with deeper intrapersonal (e.g., self-criticism targeted with two-chair dialogue for problematic self-treatment [shortly, self-critic task]) or interpersonal emotional processes (e.g., empty-chair dialogue for an interpersonal emotional injury [shortly, unfinished business task]). For the remainder of this chapter, however, we do not comment on this deeper, core vulnerability–level work (which we explore in the next chapter); rather, we focus on the worry task is its pure form.

Returning to the previous case example involving Fiona: After she enacted the self-worrying process, Stage 3 proceeded as follows:

THERAPIST: As you swap the chair (*Client moves to the Experiencer Chair*), see what it does to you when you worry yourself . . . almost to your body. What's the sense? [Here, the therapist is checking for the impact of the worry on Fiona.]

CLIENT: [In the Experiencer Chair] I feel jittery.

THERAPIST: Speak from the feeling to that part of you (*points to the Worrier Chair*). Speak to her.

CLIENT: I feel shaky, I feel insecure. I feel . . . you kind of talking to me in a way where the outcome is decided before I even . . . there is no other way.

THERAPIST: I am anxious? What's the sense?

CLIENT: I'm terrified. It's almost like you don't trust me to kind of take the challenge on. You don't trust me.

THERAPIST: What's the feeling like?

CLIENT: It is tiring. You are constantly at me. It's overwhelming. I am going to embarrass myself [linking to underlying vulnerable feelings of shame and corresponding self-critical judgment of Self as inept that are worked on in self-critic and unfinished business tasks].

THERAPIST: So, tell her.

Stage 4. Articulating and Expressing Need

Once the client in the Experiencer Chair feels the effect of the worrying and expresses this to the Worrier, the therapist invites the client to articulate what they need when feeling this distress—for example, anxiety and tiredness (see Stage 4 in Table 8.2). The articulation of need should be expressed directly to the Worrier, and the therapist explicitly guides the client to do so: "Tell him/her (*points at the Worrier*) what is it you need from him/her when you feel so anxious and exhausted?" The typical response here from clients is that they need a break from the worrying, or they need the Worrier to stop worrying them (Murphy et al., 2017). Some clients may elaborate further— for example, by stating that they need to feel freer or that they need to not feel under constant threat. Often, in the first worry dialogue in therapy, clients struggle to express need in an assertive manner, instead pleading with the Worrier. In contrast, in later dialogues, clients at this stage may tap into assertive/protective anger (see Stage 6A in Table 8.2).

Fiona, in one of her later dialogues, also expressed the following at this stage:

THERAPIST: What is it that you need from that part? From her, from that part that scares you and worries you? That wants you to be prepared for the judgment of others?

CLIENT: I need you to give me a break. I need you to kind of maybe not be so quick to jump in and put that protection there because it's not helping. I want to be free from you preparing me for everything that may go wrong because it is tiring, and I cannot take it anymore.

Stage 5. Probing for Compassion

Once need (e.g., for a break from the worrying, for more freedom, for some variant of these) is expressed by the client in the Experiencer Chair to the Worrier, the client is asked to move to the Worrier Chair, from which they are asked to respond to the expressed need: "What is your response from inside to what [he/she] is saying: 'I am too anxious; I need you to give me a break'?" The therapist may also check what the client feels toward the distress experienced by and articulated by the Self in the Experiencer Chair: "What do you feel toward [him/her] when you see [him/her] so distressed and anxious?" This intervention probes for softening and compassion from the client in the Worrier Chair toward the vulnerable Self, essentially inquiring as to whether the Worrier is willing to let go of scaring and worrying the Self.

Typically, in the first worry dialogues in therapy, clients in the Worrier Chair become even more worried and scared by this plea. Some clients have the sense that it is a request to lessen self-protection, thus leaving the self exposed and endangered. Typically, therefore, clients respond at this stage (see Stage 5A in Table 8.2) by worrying more: "No, I cannot stop worrying you. I have to do this to protect you." When this happens, the therapist goes along with this fear and highlights the relentlessness of the Worrier's position: "Tell him/her, 'I will keep doing it. I will keep scaring you and controlling you by doing this to you.'" This position will then be pointed to by the therapist in Stage 6A, and it can then be used as a basis for building health boundary-setting anger (e.g., "I won't let you control me").

Our study of worry dialogues (Murphy et al., 2017), however, showed that in later dialogues, clients with GAD were more likely to soften their self-worrying at this stage (see Stage 5B; e.g., "I see how you suffer; I want to stop doing this to you"). At times, clients offered a mixture of softening (Stage 5B) and continuation of the worry (Stage 5A; e.g., "I see how you suffer, but it is so difficult to stop. I want to keep you safe"). When a mixture of softening and insisting on worrying is felt and expressed by the Worrier, the therapist aims to skillfully capture both: the compassion (e.g., "I see your suffering, and I care . . .") and also the inability or unwillingness to let go of worry (e.g., ". . . but I am unable or unwilling, for your safety, to let go").

When there is an inability to let go (e.g., "I see your point, but this is automatic; I am unable to let go") in the context of an otherwise compassionate stance (e.g., "I don't want to be limiting you. I feel for you"), the therapist can stress the client's desire to stop (e.g., "So, I don't know if I can, but I see that you need me to . . . there is this inability but also a lot of understanding . . . tell [her/him]").

In Fiona's case, she struggled to let go of the worry in the context of its expressed impact (anxiety) and the need for her to let go of it:

THERAPIST: Here at this moment . . . what do you feel toward her now (*points at the Experiencer*)?

CLIENT: [In the Worrier Chair] You are fooling yourself. You are not thinking clearly. [The client is not softening, not letting go of worry.]

THERAPIST: Tell her. Somehow, it's like, "I can't give you that freedom." [The therapist rolls with the client's not letting go.]

CLIENT: Once you start getting yourself into situations where there's a potential danger, I can't accept that. I cannot give you a break.

THERAPIST: What are you scared of most [aiming at the function of the worry]?

CLIENT: I'm scared that you will get yourself into a situation where your mental health will take such a bashing from it that you won't be able to recover.

THERAPIST: Such as?

CLIENT: There have been situations where you have tried to express yourself, and it has backfired. . . .

The client elaborates on a situation at work in which she was ridiculed:

THERAPIST: . . . It's like, "I'm still traumatized" . . .

CLIENT: And therefore, I need to prepare you that it may happen . . . you need to be prepared to respond quickly.

THERAPIST: It's like . . . "I know how quickly I can make you think like this (*snaps fingers*) . . . I can supply those scenarios that . . . But I do it out of the fear that you get hurt. . . ." There's a part of it that produces all those thoughts, right . . .? That scare you more, yeah . . . or something, and they scare you, but they make you to focus just on that rather than try to take a risk and take small steps to live more freely or something.

CLIENT: Yeah.

THERAPIST: Therefore, "I need to protect you, and I'll keep doing it, and I can't relent or stop . . . I can't let you go and let you take a risk or something. I will keep worrying you about what may happen." [The therapist highlights the function of the worry and the client's continuation of the worrying despite seeing the painful impact it has.]

CLIENT: Yeah. I will keep doing it. It is too dangerous.

Stage 6A. Promoting Protective Anger

After the Worrier responds, the therapist asks the client to move back to the Experiencer Chair. If the client in the Worrier Chair has softened (Stage 5B in Table 8.2; this stage is not present in the preceding Fiona example), the therapist focuses the client in the Experiencing Chair on letting that compassion in (see the next section on Stage 6B; see also Table 8.2). If, as in Fiona's example, the Worrier has not softened (see Stage 5A in Table 8.2), the client in the Experiencer Chair is asked to address the Worrier's inability and, in particular, unwillingness to stop worrying. The therapist wants to see whether the client is able to set their own boundary (protective anger) to the worrying process. The therapist may instruct the client: "What is your response to this 'I won't let go. I will keep scaring you'? What is your response to that right here, right now?"

Here, the client may spontaneously set a boundary to the worry and the Worrier: "I won't let you." Or the client may struggle and collapse: "I cannot do anything." In the case of a collapse, the therapist validates the client's response: "So, it is like 'I am unable to face you; I'm unable to stop you'"; but, then, the therapist points to the need: "But what is it that you really need?" When the client expresses, "I need a break," the therapist brings to the client's awareness the feeling the statement of need brings: "How does it feel to say it: 'I need a break'?" The client usually feels some resolve: "I feel stronger." The therapist wants to capitalize on and further consolidate this emerging strength: "Tell him/her (*points at the Worrier*): 'I feel stronger.'"

Another way to facilitate boundary-setting when the client collapses is to focus on what the client would do if they had the power to stand up for the Self: "What would you do if you had the power to stand up to [him/her]?" As the client expresses it (e.g., "I would tell him/her to shut up"), the therapist asks the client to say it to the Worrier (e.g., "If I had the power, I would tell you to shut up") and see how it feels to say this (e.g., "How does it feel when you say that?"). Clients usually feel somewhat more empowered (e.g., "It feels good to say it"). The therapist can seek to consolidate this sense of empowerment by asking the client to express again the new feeling that was felt (e.g., "Tell him/her it feels good to say it to you") thus gradually building more resolve. Even in such cases, however, the therapist validates where the client is actually at—for example, it feels good to try to stand up to the worrier, or to do so by proxy, but, in reality, it is difficult.

Another strategy that can help facilitate healthy boundary-setting anger is to amplify the collapse—for example, "So you are saying I am unable to set a boundary to you. Tell him/her you can worry me as much as you want. I am unable to set a boundary to you." As the client says it, the therapist asks how it feel to say this. Clients often report that it is unpleasant—for example, "It feels horrible"—and the therapist then encourages the client to express this to the Worrier—for example, "So tell him/her: 'It feels horrible.'" In the context of this horrible feeling, the therapist again asks after the need, directing the client to express this to the Worrier: "So, what is it that you really want? Tell him/her." The client can thus gradually build some resolve to face the unrelenting Worrier.

Whichever way it proceeds, this process is complex. As with other experiential tasks, it is important not to forget that this is a nonlinear process. The stages outlined here are a map of potential trajectory; not a journey the client must be forced on. The therapist follows the client's process and, although offering suggestions, ultimately respects the client's pace. The client's inability to stand up for themselves can thus simply be acknowledged as an impasse, noted as something important that may be returned to in the future. Indeed, it usually takes a number of dialogues to get a good grasp of the process and for the client to become capable of standing up to the worry. Whatever the process, though, the ability to set a boundary is important because it gives clients a sense of empowerment that in and of itself is a direct antidote to worrying and anxiety. The ability to stand up for the Self in the face of worry (i.e., stand up to the Worrier) is also important in terms of assessment: Clients who stand up for the Self with relative ease likely have a better prognosis.

An example of Fiona standing up to her Worrier in one dialogue included the following sequence:

THERAPIST: So, what is your response to that? Right here, right now. She [the Worrier] is saying, "I won't stop. I will keep scaring you" [checking to see whether Fiona can stand up to the Worrier].

CLIENT: I just want to be free of this. I want to be free of you. It's not helpful anymore.

THERAPIST: And what's the sense inside [trying to get Fiona to see whether she feels any resolve on an experiential level]?

CLIENT: Defiance . . . I have to challenge you now. I don't trust you anymore. I don't believe that you have my best interest at heart. It is too much. I could make a breakthrough.

THERAPIST: It's like, "I need to set a boundary or something."

CLIENT: There has to be a distance between us. You can't just keep jumping over the wall, trying to drag me back in. It has to be on my terms! You spend all your time trying to dictate to me how to keep safe, almost like a means of keeping you occupied and safe.

THERAPIST: What's the sense inside as you are saying it [wanting to validate Fiona's apparent resolve and bring it to her attention]?

CLIENT: Strength.

Stage 6B. Letting Compassion In

If some softening is expressed by the Worrier, the client in the Experiencer Chair is asked by the therapist to try and let that softening in and to attend to how it is to receive it (see Stage 6B in Table 8.2): "How is it to hear this, 'I do not want to worry you. I see how you suffer'?" In the context of the worry dialogue, it is usually not a problem for clients to let such softening and compassion in. In contrast, in the context of self-critic dialogues, the self-critical process can itself inhibit clients' letting in any compassion expressed by the Critic (e.g., "I do not deserve for you [the Critic] to care about me"; see Chapter 9). However, should the client have difficulty letting in compassion from the Worrier (e.g., "It is too scary to imagine you not worrying me. I know my anxiety"), the therapist validates that experience (e.g., "It would be too scary. [*Points to the Worrier*] Tell him/her") but still invites the client to check-in inside (e.g., "But how is it to hear the Worrier saying that [he/she] sees your suffering and wants to stop making you feel so anxious?"). Often, in the context of further probing that acknowledges the struggle, clients are able to let in the softening from the Worrier, thereby experiencing some form of relief (e.g., "It feels good. I feel relieved"; see Murphy et al., 2017).

Again, we wish to emphasize that the process highlighted (Stages 1–6) is in no way linear and that the stages we delineate (see Table 8.2) are used primarily for didactic purposes in teaching and supervision. Clients may go through the outlined stages nonlinearly, in an iterative manner, or partially—for example, by digressing to other tasks (e.g., working with the Critic in Stage 2 or 5A or working with the Critic or unfinished business in Stage 3). It is also the case that some stages may not occur at all—for example, compassion expressed from the Worrier as outlined in Stage 5B. Indeed, in our clinical experience, the experiencing and expression of protective, boundary-setting anger (Stage 6A), are more important in this task than softening of the Worrier. The mobilization of assertive anger brings an experience of the Self as having the potential to be strong, expansive, or empowered, an experience that constitutes a significant antidote to worry and anxiety. Indeed, therapists may further facilitate Stage 6B (protective anger) by reenacting the Worrier's position in Stage 5A or Stage 2 (relentless worrying; e.g., "Try to worry [him/her; the Experiencer] now when [he/she] is standing up to you. Get under [his/her] skin") repeatedly while simultaneously seeking to support the client in holding on to their boundary-setting position (e.g., "Can [he/she; the Worrier] scare you now?").

The two-chair dialogue for self-worrying is a major symptom-level task common to a variety of anxiety and related disorders. The version of the worry task that we describe here is particularly useful in the context of social and generalized anxiety. However, we also use variants of this task with specific phobias, panic disorder, and PTSD (discussion follows). The task also overlaps with the processes in two-chair dialogue for self-worrying (obsessions) and self-compulsions (discussed later).

The task can also be reflected on using the framework presented in Table 8.3. This framework may serve as a basis for "hot" teaching (psychoeducation), reflection at the end of session, or homework. For instance, the client may be invited to note during the week how they engage in worrying and what the function of that worrying might be (see Stages 2 and 5A in Table 8.2). They can also be invited to consolidate any positive experiences they had in the session by endeavoring to tap into these experiences during the week to stop worrying themselves or to stand up to the externalized Worrier (see Stage 5B in Table 8.2) or set a boundary to it (see Stage 6A in Table 8.2).

TWO-CHAIR DIALOGUE FOR SELF-WORRYING AND AN INTRUSIVE/PHOBIC OBJECT

A variant of the self-worrying task is the two-chair dialogue for self-worrying and an intrusive/phobic object (see Table 8.4). This task is suitable for presentations, such as specific phobia, panic disorder, some PTSD symptoms,

TABLE 8.3. A Framework for Reflecting on the Two-Chair Dialogue for Self-Worrying Task for Homework

Parts enacted in the Experiencer Chair	Parts enacted in the Interrupter Chair
	How do I worry myself? (Increasing awareness of the ways the person worries themself)
	What drives my worries? (Focusing on the underlying fears)
What impact does the worrying have on me? (Highlighting the emotional toll of the worry)	
What do I need in the face of the worry? (Articulating the need with regard to the worry)	
	What do I feel toward the impacted part of me? (Bringing a reminder of compassionate experiences that may help one let go of the worry)
How can I face the worry? (Reminding one of the resolve in the session to face and fight the worry)	

Note. From *Transforming Generalized Anxiety: An Emotion-Focused Approach* (p. 103), by L. Timulak and J. McElvaney, 2018. Routledge. Copyright 2018 by Routledge. Adapted with permission.

TABLE 8.4. Stages in the Two-Chair Dialogue for Self-Worrying and an Intrusive/Phobic Object

Stage	Experiencer Chair	Worrier Chair	Object Chair
1	Experiencing the marker: Worrying, feeling exhausted		
2		Enacting the worrying: The experiential quality	Enacting the intrusive/phobic object
3	Accessing and differentiating anxiety and tiredness (potentially also core pain)		
4	Articulating and expressing the need for a break in being scared		
5		Probing for compassion, seeing the impact/pain and need (highlighting the protective function of worry) Stage 5A–If no compassion is coming: Going with the increased worry (unable to control) Stage 5B–If compassion is coming: Savoring it experientially and expressing it	
6A	Building protective anger, setting a boundary to the worry or intrusive/phobic object		
6B	Letting compassion in, savoring it experientially but still insisting on a boundary		

and anxiety related to chronic debilitating illnesses. Although we are covering this task in the current chapter, which focuses on symptom-level experiential work, there are often strong links between this kind of worry and the core pain at the heart of client vulnerability. The main difference between this variant of the task and the generic self-worrying task is that it involves engagement with an intrusive object that evokes debilitating, chronic fear in the client. This intrusive object may be put into a third chair (hereafter called the Object Chair) and positioned next to the Worrier Chair. The client is asked to enact the intrusion (Stage 2) and, later in the task, is supported in standing up to the Intrusive Object (Stage 6A). (The stages in this task are outlined in Table 8.4 with the Object Chair occupying Column 4: Because compassion is not expected or invited from the Intrusive Object, there is no Stage 5 with regard to the object as there is with the Worrier).

The intrusive object may be a phobic object, a panic attack, or a life-threatening illness (see Connolly-Zubot et al., 2020). In the case of an illness, such as cancer, the client may worry about recurrence of the cancer, and this self-worrying is enacted in the Worrier Chair, as already outlined earlier in this chapter (see Stage 2, Column 3, in Table 8.4). The therapist, however, may also invite the client to enact the cancer and its intrusive qualities (see Stage 2, Column 4, in Table 8.4; e.g., "I am the threat to your health and life. I will take you away from those you are close to and from the things that are important to you in life") to build protective anger in the Experiencer Chair (see Stage 6A in Table 8.4; e.g., "I will not let you limit my life. I will face you"). We talk about the timing of such interventions shortly. As we have said, the intrusive object may be a phobic object (in case of specific phobia), panic (in case of panic disorder), or the attacker from a previously experienced trauma (in case of PTSD). In all instances, the intrusive object is experienced as an imminent or presently happening intrusion that invades/overtakes the client and elicits acute primary fear. Occasionally, the intrusive object may seem more superficial (e.g., needle phobia), perhaps having acquired its capacity to elicit fear as a result of displaced anxiety. At times, such as in the case of dominating panic attacks, it may be a combination of both symptom-level displaced threat and a real safety/integrity-related intrusion.

Whichever the case, the work in two-chair dialogues for self-worrying and an intrusive/phobic object is, broadly speaking, similar to the work with worry as already outlined in the self-worrying task and follows the stages highlighted in Table 8.2. After the client accesses and expresses protective anger (Stage 6A) toward the Worrier, though (e.g., "I won't let you continue to limit my life"), the therapist may also guide the client to express this anger toward the actual feared object (e.g., intrusive illness: "I won't let you limit my life"). To intensify the consolidation of this resolve to face the intrusive/phobic object, the client may be instructed by the therapist to enact that object in the Object Chair. Although a third chair can be introduced for this purpose, whether the client enacts the Intrusive Object in the same chair as the Worrier or in a third chair is not critical. In either instance, the therapist guides the client to enact the Intrusive Object (e.g., "Can you come over here . . . be that illness, be that panic attack, be that intruder . . .") and terrify the Self (". . . and terrify him/her right here and now?"). As we have said, this is done to facilitate a consolidation of the client's resolve as already expressed to the Worrier. After returning to the Experiencer Chair, the client is directed to face the object and attend to how they feel, particularly whether they still feel their resolve to not allow themselves be frightened or limited (e.g., "What is your response to this here and now? Will you let it [Object/Intruder] terrify you?").

Enactment of the intrusive (phobic) object is a form of exposure because by enacting/playing the feared or terrifying object, the client is in touch with what they dread. The appropriateness of enacting the Intrusive Object is always a clinical judgment on behalf of the therapist. For instance, it may not be appropriate to enact the intruder/abuser/assaulter in a case of PTSD. Instead, the client may engage the intruder/abuser/assaulter only from the Experiencer Chair and only when already present anger directed at the Worrier (Stage 6A) can be harnessed and directed toward that imagined person. Enacting of the Intrusive Object (see Stage 2, Column 4, Object Chair, in Table 8.4) or engaging the Intrusive Object via protective anger (Stage 6A) are therefore clinical decisions but, in all instances, are advised *only* after the client has already accessed protective anger within the task.

When we refer to enactment of the Intrusive Object as Stage 2, therefore, we do not mean this in a sequential sense; rather, we are referring to the logic of the task in which Stage 2 is enactment of the problematic self-treatment (i.e., worrying about the Intrusive Object; see Stage 2, Column 3, Worrier Chair, in Table 8.4) or Intrusive Object itself (see Stage 2, Column 4, in Table 8.4). To reiterate, the accessing and expression of protective anger (e.g., directed toward the Worrier; Stage 6A), in general, precedes the enactment of the Intrusive Object or engagement in the dialogue with the Intrusive Object. And to reiterate further, whether the Intrusive Object should be enacted at all is a clinical judgment related in the main to an assessment by the therapist as to how overwhelming such an intervention might be for the client at that particular moment as well as how respectful or appropriate it would be. (As we have suggested, it may be particularly inappropriate but also disrespectful to enact the Intrusive Object when the object in question is an actual perpetrator—that is, de facto an intrusive person.)

Experiential work in the two-chair dialogue for self-worrying and an intrusive/phobic object task can be reflected on by the therapist and the client using the framework presented in Table 8.5. Again, this framework can serve also as a basis for any potential homework. Such homework can be focused on bringing relevant processes into the client's awareness or on consolidating good processes achieved within the therapy session (e.g., "What could you do to support that protective anger-based resolve?").

TWO-CHAIR DIALOGUE FOR SELF-WORRYING, INTRUSIVE OBJECT, AND SELF-COMPULSION

Another variant of the self-worrying task is the two-chair dialogue for self-worrying, intrusive object, and self-compulsion (see Table 8.6). This task is suitable for presentations with features of OCD. Again, while this is a more symptom-level intervention addressing symptoms of OCD, in many instances, it can be closely linked to core painful feeling and core vulnerability. Usually, the intrusive object (e.g., a doorknob being contaminated) around which the client worries/obsesses (e.g., "I am getting infected") is a direct or displaced expression of core painful feelings (e.g., "I am unsafe"). Although primary fear (e.g., "I am unsafe") is often a common determinant, shame (e.g., "I will be found out as immoral") or associated loneliness/sadness (e.g., "I will then be abandoned and alone") may also be determinants.

In OCD, the term "obsession" is used to capture both an intrusive object/thought/image and the mental process that engages with it. To be consistent with the other described tasks and to avoid confusion, we use the term "worry" rather than "obsession" and thus talk about an intrusive object (a thought or an image) and the worry that the client engages in with regard to the intrusive object. Essentially, therefore, we are describing this process as one in which an intrusive object (e.g., in the form of a thought or image) worries the client to such an extent that the client seeks to neutralize or mitigate the thought/image by engaging in a compulsion or ritual. The two-chair dialogue for self-worrying (obsession), intrusive object, and self-compulsion, which we use to target this process, is similar to the already discussed two-chair dialogue for self-worrying and an intrusive object. However, here there is one additional level, which is captured in Table 8.6, and which we elaborate on here. In this task, we usually use three chairs: the Experiencer Chair, Worrier Chair (alternatively, this can be thought of as the "Obsessor" Chair) and Object Chair, which is placed alongside the Worrier/Obsessor Chair.

TABLE 8.5. A Framework for Reflecting on the Two-Chair Dialogue for Self-Worrying and an Intrusive/Phobic Object Task for Homework

Parts enacted in the Experiencer Chair	Parts enacted in the Worrier Chair	Parts enacted in the Object Chair
	How do I worry myself? (Increasing awareness of the ways the person worries themself)	What does it do to myself? (Increasing awareness of the most frightening parts of the object)
	What drives my worries? (Focusing on the underlying fears)	How does it want to take over myself? (Enacting dominating aspects of the object)
What impact does the worrying have on me? (Highlighting the emotional toll of the worry)		
What do I need in the face of the worry/object? (Articulating the need with regard to the worry)		
	What do I feel toward the impacted part of me? (Bringing a reminder of compassionate experiences that may help one let go of the worry)	
How can I face the worry/object? (Reminding one of the resolve in the session to face and fight the worry/object)		

TABLE 8.6. Stages in the Two-Chair Dialogue for Self-Worrying (Obsession), Intrusive Object, and Self-Compulsion

Stage	Experiencer Chair	Worrier/Obsessor Chair	Object Chair	Compulsor Chair
1	Experiencing the marker: Worrying, feeling exhaustion			
2		Enacting the worrying: The experiential quality	Enacting the intrusive/phobic object (thought, image)	Enacting the compulsion– experiential quality
3	Accessing and differentiating anxiety and tiredness (potentially also core pain)			
4	Articulating and expressing the need for a break (from the worry, from being frightened, from being controlled by the compulsion)			
5		Probing for compassion, seeing the impact/pain and unmet need (highlighting the protective function of worry) Stage 5A–If no compassion is coming (or Worrier is unable to stop): Going with the increased worry Stage 5B–If compassion is coming: Savoring it experientially and expressing it		Probing for compassion, seeing the impact/pain and unmet need (highlighting the protective function of compulsion) Stage 5A–If no compassion is coming (or Compulsor is unable to stop): Going with the increased compulsion Stage 5B–If compassion is coming: Savoring it experientially and expressing it
6A	Building protective anger, setting boundary to the worry/ intrusive object/compulsion			
6B	Letting compassion in, savoring it experientially but still insisting on the boundary			

The marker (Stage 1) for this task is the prototypical OCD presentation whereby the client is preoccupied with an unwanted thought or image and wants to neutralize or mitigate it by engaging in a compulsion or ritual. The client may report that this is what is preoccupying them currently within the session, or they may describe this as something currently dominant in their life that brings significant distress. After the marker is established, the therapist asks the client to sit in the Worrier/Obsessor Chair (see Stage 2, Column 3, in Table 8.6). The therapist points to the third chair, which is placed alongside the Worrier/Obsessor Chair, and describes the unwanted thought or image (e.g., bacteria, poison, inappropriate violent or sexual images) as being located there. The client is then instructed to worry themself in the Experiencer Chair about the intrusive object—for example, "So, tell him/her the bacteria is on your hand. It is dangerous." After the Worrier/Obsessor worries the Self in the Experiencer Chair, the client is asked to move back to the Experiencer Chair and attend to how they are impacted by this intrusive object–focused self-worrying (Stage 3)—for example, "What happens when [he/she] scares you like this?" Clients typically report feeling terrified, dirty, or ashamed (the latter may especially be the case if the content relates in some way to social/moral standards). As the effect is felt by the Self in the Experiencer Chair, the client is directed to express these feelings to the Worrier/Obsessor to see what they need from the Worrier/Obsessor and to again express this identified need to the Worrier/Obsessor (see Stage 4 in Table 8.6). While the actual need vis-à-vis the Worrier/Obsessor is for the Worrier/Obsessor to stop scaring them, the client may instead report feeling an overwhelming need to neutralize the threat because already, at this stage, the urge or tendency to engage in compulsion/ritual may come to the fore.

The client is asked by the therapist to move to the Worrier/Obsessor Chair, which, at this stage, typically becomes the "Compulsor" Chair. The client is instructed to make sure that the unpleasant anxiety/fear/shame goes away (see Stage 2, Column 5, Compulsor Chair, in Table 8.6). Again, reference is made to the Intrusive Object Chair: "How do you make sure that the threat coming from [the intrusive object] is neutralized? What do you do?" Typically, clients at this point begin to suggest rituals—for example, "You need to wash your hands repeatedly. You need to count to 10." The therapist prompts the client in the Compulsor Chair to compel the client to engage in these actions: "Tell him/her what to do. Make him/her do it." The therapist may also seek to highlight the function of the compulsion—for example, "What drives these suggestions?"—and clients typically report a protective function—for example, "to keep him/her safe." After the imperative urging to engage in ritualistic actions is expressed, the client is brought back to the Experiencer Chair and guided to attend to the effect of the compulsion. Initially, most clients typically report feeling calmed, that the compulsion/ritual has worked/helped. However, if asked to stay with the impact, they typically elaborate on an experiential cost to this process. For instance, they may say that the ritual/compulsion is tiring, that they are defined by it, or that they are unable to function without it. They are then asked what they need in the face of the compulsion and (bringing it back to the dialogue) what they need from the Compulsor that imposes these compulsions on them (see Stage 4 in Table 8.6). Most typically clients request a break.

The work then progresses to Stage 5 (see Table 8.6). The client is asked to move back to the Worrier/Obsessor Chair from which the therapist invites them to see the anxious Self in the Experiencer Chair and to notice how they feel toward the anxious part of the Self that wants the Worrier to stop worrying them—for example, "Now come here. Be that Worrier/Obsessing part of you. As you see him/her (*points to the Experiencer Chair*) here, so anxious, pleading with you not to flood him/her with these worries and obsessions, what do you feel toward him/her?" A variant of this may also take the form of inviting this same response, albeit with a slightly different instruction, from the Compulsor, that part of the self that urges the Experiencer to engage in ritualistic behavior to mitigate the anxiety: "Now be that part of you that pushes him/her to engage in the ritual," the therapist says. "What do you feel toward him/her (*points to the Experiencer Chair*) as you see how exhausted he/she is and hear him/her pleading with you to stop making him/her to do it." Here, again, there may be some softening or there may not. Often there is a mixture of softening and further worrying or insisting on the ritual. There also tends to be a development across a series of dialogues, with the client in the positions of Worrier/Obsessor and/or Compulsor likely to soften more in later compared with earlier dialogues.

During this stage (i.e., Stage 5; see Table 8.6), the client is guided to see what the response from inside actually is. Any hesitance to soften is acknowledged by the therapist, who also inquires about and highlights the function of the worry or insistence on rituals/compulsion—for example, "What makes it so difficult to see the impact you have on him/her and let go?" Essentially, the function of both worrying/obsessing and self-compulsion is to keep the Self safe. Specifically, the function of self-worrying/obsessing is to keep the client alert to threat while the function of urging the Self to engage in compulsions/rituals is to mitigate the impact of this threat. However, in the case of self-worrying/obsessing, this alertness inadvertently makes the client scared and anxious, whereas in the case of urging, the insistence on ritual exhausts the client and prevents them from experiencing that they can engage with the intrusive object more directly without it being defining of them. These functions of the Worrier/Obsessor and the Compulsor Chair are clearly highlighted alongside the cost or toll of these processes. If the client does not spontaneously report that they want to try to stop worrying/obsessing/insisting on the ritual, this is acknowledged by the therapist, who asks them to go with this process, essentially escalating the worrying/obsessing or insistence on performance of rituals.

The client is then asked to move back to the Experiencer Chair. If the client in the position of Worrier/Obsessor/Compulsor softened in Stage 5 (i.e., Stage 5B; see Table 8.6), the client in the Experiencer Chair is asked to see how it is to get this softening. Typically, this softening brings some sense of relief (see Stage 6B in Table 8.6). On the other hand, if the client in the position of Worrier/Obsessor/Compulsor either fully or partially indicates that they will continue to engage in the worrying/obsessing or insisting on performance of rituals, the client is invited to see from their impacted Self in the Experiencer Chair whether they are okay with it. Here, clients may begin to spontaneously assert themselves (see Stage 6A in Table 8.6). If this does not occur, or if self-assertion in the face of this self-treatment is difficult for the client, the therapist may facilitate the client to once again see the cost of this treatment or ask the client whether it is pleasurable or acceptable to be either scared or forced to engage in such rituals.

Alternatively, the therapist may invite the client to say what they would wish to say if they felt they had the power to face up to the Worrier/Obsessor or the Compulsor. Again, as in previous versions of this task, the expression of protective anger (Stage 6A) is more important than the softening in Stage 5 because this anger builds up the client, making them more resilient to face the threat (i.e., intrusive unwanted thought, image, object). If the client does report feeling some strength and stands up to the Worrier/Obsessor/Compulsor, the client may be invited to come to the Intrusive Object Chair (see Stage 2, Column 4, in Table 8.6) and terrify the Self in the Experiencer Chair directly by enacting the Intrusive Object (e.g., bacteria, unwanted image). The client is then asked to come back to the Experiencer Chair and see whether they will let the Intrusive Object terrify them and limit their life or whether they can stand up to it. In cases in which protective anger is fully accessed and expressed toward the Worrier/Obsessor or the Compulsor, clients are often capable of standing up to the actual Intrusive Object (e.g., bacteria, unwanted image).

As with other variations of this task, the process highlighted here is not linear, and stages can be iteratively engaged in. The sequence can also be creatively altered. Any therapy with OCD-type presentations usually contains a series of dialogues like this, and clients typically progress further through the model over multiple iterations of the task. Difficulties in the process also may exist, and, as with other tasks, a variety of therapeutic strategies may be used to facilitative constructive processes. We have provided examples of such strategies throughout our descriptions of the task. As with other variations of this task, the formalized structure given in Table 8.6 serves mainly didactic purposes, offering clarity for trainees and supervisees. And again, in Table 8.7, we provide a framework that can be used as a basis for reflection on this task and OCD-type processes as well as serve as a basis for homework.

The following excerpts from a two-chair dialogue for self-worrying, intrusive object, and compulsion task illustrate some of the processes we just described. The client, James, who presents with OCD symptoms and symptoms of depression, describes how he gets worried about images/thoughts of being unfaithful to his partner (in reality, he is very happy in the relationship and is afraid that he might destroy the relationship were he to do something he does not want to do). These images/thoughts are present in dreams he has, leading him to engage in the rituals to neutralize them. We now look at the therapeutic work across several of the stages outlined in Table 8.6.

Stage 2. In the Worrier/Obsessor Chair, Enacting the Worrier/Obsessor

THERAPIST: Okay. So, let's imagine that that's the dream there in that chair (*points to the third chair—the Object Chair—that is put next to the Worrier/Obsessor Chair*). So, this comes, the dream comes. Now post dream, or you wake up during the dream or after the dream. What's the worry then? Let's have a look: How would you worry yourself? What's so uncomfortable about the dream? Tell yourself (*points to the Experiencer Chair*) [asking James to enact his worries/obsessions about the dream].

CLIENT: You will mess up or, like, be—do something wrong in general . . . You will damage the relationship. The dream is a sign of it. The dream will make it happen.

THERAPIST: So, that's the worry that tells you that you can mess up—that you just get yourself into a situation like in a dream, that mess up in a way. So, my worry is that, somehow, if this is coming . . . [bringing to James's awareness what he does to himself].

TABLE 8.7. A Framework for Reflecting on the Worry/Intrusive Object/Compulsion Task or for Homework

Parts enacted in the Experiencer Chair	Parts enacted in the Worrier/Obsessor Chair	Parts enacted in the Object Chair	Parts enacted in the Compulsor Chair
	How do I worry myself? (Increasing awareness of the ways the person worries themself)	**What does it do to myself?** (Increasing awareness of the most frightening parts of the object)	**How will I make sure that the anxiety disappears?** (Increasing awareness of the rituals)
	What drives my worries? (Focusing on the underlying fears)	**How does it (object) want to take over myself?** (Enacting the dominating aspects of the object)	**What drives my compulsion?** (Focusing on the underlying fears of the phobic object)
What impact does the worrying/compulsion have on me? (Highlighting the emotional toll of the worry/compulsion)			

What do I need in the face of the worry/compulsion impulse? (Articulating the need with regard to the worry/compulsion)

What do I feel toward the impacted part of me? (Bringing a reminder of compassionate experiences that may help one let go of the worry)

How can I face the worry/object? (Reminding one of the resolve accessed in the session to face and fight the worry/object/drive for compulsion)

What do I feel toward the impacted part of me? (Bringing a reminder of compassionate experiences that may help one let go of the compulsion)

Stage 3. In the Experiencer Chair, Accessing the Impact of the Worrier/Obsessor

THERAPIST: What does it do to you, either of the things, either the worry or the dream itself. See what impact it leaves in you? Like, what does it bring inside [inviting James to see what impact the worries have]?

CLIENT: Scared, probably . . .

THERAPIST: Is it like, "I get infected by your worries," or "I get . . ." Do they bring anxiety in me and scare me, or . . .? Tell him. We'll try to put it to words.

CLIENT: You scare me . . . I don't feel like you're coming from a good, a rational place, really.

THERAPIST: Okay.

CLIENT: And then, you're not helping me in any way.

Stage 4. In the Experiencer Chair, Articulating and Expressing the Need Toward the Worrier/Obsessor

THERAPIST: What would you need from that worrier part, yes, 'cause this dream is involuntary, this happens, yes? You cannot control this, but what would you want from that worrier part that starts to picture all those scenarios that you'll mess up. What do you need from him [facilitating James to express the need toward the Worrier/Obsessor]?

CLIENT: Probably, like, um—um—like understanding that it's not real and, like . . .

THERAPIST: Okay. It's like, "I need you to calm down or something, or not to put it on me or something."

CLIENT: Or, like, I need you to take time to understand where they are coming from to an extent and then just let it—let it be, I guess.

THERAPIST: So, tell him: "Let it be and don't panic me," or something like this, yeah?

CLIENT: Yeah. Let it be and don't dwell so much on it.

THERAPIST: Yeah, it's like, "You're dwelling, that thing kind of infects me with anxiety inside, and I can't shift it or something," yeah?

CLIENT: Yeah . . .

Stage 6A. In the Experiencer Chair, Addressing the Object Chair and the Worrier/Obsessor Chair

THERAPIST: What would you say to that intrusion because that's not you, not in a way that . . . I know it brings doubt, but what would you say to the . . . it's like . . . [now guiding James to speak to the Intrusive Object; in this case, the dream].

CLIENT: You're not integral to me.

THERAPIST: Yes. Tell that dream: "You're not me, yes, you're not integral to me."

CLIENT: You're not me, you're not, you're just a product of worrying . . .

THERAPIST: Yeah . . .

CLIENT: . . . and anxiousness, and it's not . . . real . . .

THERAPIST: But it's like, you're uncomfortable. It's like, "I don't want you infecting me or bringing on me that heaviness because that's—I don't want to have it," yeah?

CLIENT: Mmm . . .

THERAPIST: And it's like, what would you do to it if you could. It's almost like, what would feel right for you. It's like . . . [prompting for protective boundary setting anger].

CLIENT: I will ignore you (*laughs*) . . .

Stage 2. In the Compulsor Chair, Enacting the Compulsion

THERAPIST: So, be that part that would want to make you to do the ritual. It's like what? Let's flesh it out: So, you better do this, this, this, and this, so the likelihood of this [cheating on the partner] is, you know, lower to happen. What do you do? We'll try to enact or put to words how you make yourself do those [rituals] things, right [asking the client to enact how he makes himself to do the rituals]?

CLIENT: [In the Compulsor Chair] Yeah, it's probably just like you can—you can gain control over this, or if there's a way for you to gain control over the thing, try.

THERAPIST: Okay, that's important—that's . . . So, it's like, "I'll help you to get control over it if you follow the procedure that I prescribe," yes? But let's try to flesh it out as an example. It may vary. Is it a thought that comes: "If you do this, it may work, or what happens?"

CLIENT: I think it's like . . . it probably comes from doing like, stuff that I like. Mmm . . . I just—I don't know . . . It's just giving me, like, some sense of control and sometimes . . .

THERAPIST: Yeah, I see, yeah, but that's fine. Yes, let's do that. Make him now do some ritual. How would you do it, yes, around sleeping [the client previously described that he engages in rituals around sleeping]? Tell him what you are going to make him do, yes?

CLIENT: Um, sleep on your front, one leg, your left leg up, right leg down.

THERAPIST: Okay, so left leg up like this, or . . .?

CLIENT: When your legs are curled.

THERAPIST: Okay, okay.

CLIENT: Like that.

THERAPIST: Okay, so you do that. What else, yeah?

CLIENT: Um—um—um . . . I always listen to the music . . .

THERAPIST: Okay, put the music on. What sort of music, and what else?

CLIENT: Or, there's so much like, yeah, so, I'm thinking about . . . the firmness. I think the firmness has been something as well, like, if I say something, so certainly, so many times, it has happened . . .

THERAPIST: Okay, yeah, it's like enhance the control by saying something so many times . . .

CLIENT: If I like move a certain way or breathe a certain way . . .

THERAPIST: Do it a little bit. Get the sense that I'm controlling you almost, yes. Do it little bit . . . [encouraging a full enactment of the how the client makes himself to do the rituals].

CLIENT: If you lie this certain way, then you will have . . . you will sleep. If you turn your head this way, it will be the best way you can, and then you will sleep. It'll be pure or better sleep . . .

Stage 3. In the Experiencer Chair, Checking for the Impact of the Compulsor Chair

THERAPIST: Okay, so let's swap. So, see what's the impact here now. What is the impact, what happens, or what does it leave you with when he kinda tries to control you or tries to order you around? What's the feeling here now when he does this to you . . .?

CLIENT: [In the Experiencer Chair, speaking to the Compulsor] Mmm, comforting, probably . . .

THERAPIST: Okay, so tell him: "So, that brings, like, comfort . . ."

CLIENT: It brings me a lot of comfort, um, guidance I guess, at this time.

THERAPIST: Okay, so guidance. So, "That's why I go along on side with that—that's why I go along, yeah, because somehow it's almost like I surrender to the ritual," right?

CLIENT: I find it really comforting to just follow along and have, um, no independence with my thoughts.

THERAPIST: Okay, and what's the sense as you're—as your saying this now here. What does it feel inside as you say this?

CLIENT: Overt comfort [a short-term relief of going along with the compulsion].

THERAPIST: Just so comforting. Tell him.

CLIENT: Yeah, this is very, very comforting. Following you brings comfort . . .

THERAPIST: . . . And you say it's calming, it's good, it narrows my mind or attention, and, somehow, how is it to be in that soothed feeling, right [rolling with the good aspects of compulsion]?

CLIENT: Honestly, I feel—I feel like it's all good because it still feels like he (*points at the Compulsor*) is a part of me. If it was coming from someone else, I wouldn't like it [starting to touch on the negative impact of compulsion]. . . .

THERAPIST: . . . Okay, yes, but it's only . . . "I go along because, on some level, I know you don't want me to get scared . . ."

CLIENT: Mm-hmm, yeah.

THERAPIST: But, "If you were somebody else, I wouldn't follow you." It would feel like what [stressing the boundary-setting response]?

CLIENT: Yeah, I don't have freedom . . . It takes away my playfulness.

THERAPIST: It's like, "You narrow me down," yes, or something.

CLIENT: Yeah, I've learned that's not good for me in the long term.

Stage 4. In the Experiencer Chair, Expressing the Need to the Compulsor

THERAPIST: Okay. So, it's like, "I need you what . . . to be . . ." What do you
               need from him? How . . . I need you to be with me like what . . .
               like . . . [asking the client to articulate the need directly to the
               Compulsor].

CLIENT: You know what I mean . . . I mean, like, that to like work in
               tandem or . . .

THERAPIST: Okay, so, it's like, "I need you almost not to dominate or some-
               thing (*Client: Yeah.*) to be more like . . . fair or more equal."
               (*Client: Yeah.*) So, "I would need you to be . . ." what?

CLIENT: To be—to be . . . like, considerate and (*Therapist: Okay.*) not as
               urgent (*Therapist: Okay.*), or, like (*Therapist: Okay, okay.*), not
               to be like . . . think about everything that's going on . . .

THERAPIST: Okay, so sometimes it's too much for you or something. "I would
               want you to be more considerate. (*Client: Mm-hmm.*) It's like,
               um . . . maybe we could find a better balance (*Client: Yeah.*) or
               something?"

CLIENT: Yeah, or just like . . . not like, rigid. Just move flexible, move.

THERAPIST: So, tell him: "I need you to be more flexible, less rigid."

CLIENT: I need you to move together with me.

THERAPIST: So, say it again: "I need you to move with me."

CLIENT: I need you to move with me together.

THERAPIST: What's the feeling as you say it here, now?

CLIENT: I want you to acknowledge that it's not good.

Stage 5. In the Compulsor Chair, Responding to the Experiencer Chair, Checking for Potential Letting Go and Self-Compassion

THERAPIST: So, this part (*points to the Compulsor Chair to which the therapist
               asked the client to swap*) kind of prescribes the rituals and what

to do. If James, yeah, says to you: "You know that feels good; it puts that at bay," as in, "I can somehow get rid of it if I comply (*Client: Mm-hmm.*) with you," and, somehow, it feels soothing or comforting or calm (*Client: Mm-hmm.*), but it also feels a like little bit constricting or narrowing, yes (*Client: Mm-hmm.*)? "I need you to be less demanding or somewhat more flexible," yes? What is your response to that from inside here and now [checking for possible letting go of the drive for compulsion]?

CLIENT: Um—I guess, yeah. I feel, uh . . . indifferent. Because I am used to . . . or I'd be used to just more, like, pushing on (*Therapist: Yeah.*) so then, like . . . [the client is unable to show any softening or letting go of the imperative to prescribe rituals].

THERAPIST: So, tell him: "I know just pushing on, I don't know anything else (*Client: Yeah.*). It's like I can't hear you or something." (*Client: Yeah.*) Tell him, yeah.

CLIENT: I don't really understand how you want me to . . .

THERAPIST: Yeah, so it's like, "I switch on make you to do those things." (*Client: Yeah.*) It is almost automatic, yeah. "And when I see you kind of appreciating it but also suggesting that you are missing out (*Client: Um.*), and it brings some sadness or missing out . . ." How is it to see that [pointing at the impact of following the rituals expressed in the Experiencer Chair]?

CLIENT: Yeah, it's like, maybe, more like interested to understand (*Therapist: Okay.*) but still not knowing how yet [showing some signs of softening but also an inability to let go of prescribing the rituals].

THERAPIST: Yeah, so it's—tell him: "I am listening, but I don't know if I know what to do with it."

CLIENT: I am listening to what you are figuring out that you need, but I still don't get it. But hopefully maybe [showing some further softening] . . . I don't have to go fully in one direction [insisting on rituals].

Stage 6. In the Experiencer Chair, Letting in the Compulsor's Effort to Relent and Setting a Boundary to the Compulsor

THERAPIST: (*Speaks to the client after asking him to move back to the Experiencer Chair*) So, what would you say to . . . I mean, first to . . . still . . . So, he is saying that firm part of you that prescribes rituals. (*Client: Mm-hmm.*) He is saying, "I see what you need, and I am listening (*Client: Mm-hmm.*). I don't know what to do with it," right? What's your response to that, right here, right now? What would you say to that? To him?

CLIENT: It probably feels good acknowledging that I am figuring out, trying figuring out what I need.

THERAPIST: Say: "It feels good that you are trying to listen" or something like that . . . (*Client: Yeah.*) So, tell him.

CLIENT: Yeah, it feels good that you are trying to listen and that there might be potential for change.

THERAPIST: Okay, "That's important to me. So, it sounds good that you are listening." What's the feeling inside as you are saying it to him?

CLIENT: Um, like nervous as well.

THERAPIST: What's the nervousness? Tell him, yes.

CLIENT: Independent thought.

THERAPIST: Yes, so it's like, "I normally just comply and go along with you, which robs me of freedom, but it saves something (*Client: Yeah.*), so standing up to you brings the anxiety of being on my own, facing the world or something."

CLIENT: I feel nervous to be alone in the world on this, but, yeah.

THERAPIST: It's like an unknown territory. "I am telling you I want you (*points to the Compulsor Chair*) to be a little bit less dominant, and it leaves me somehow unprotected . . ." [now shifting the focus back to the Intrusive Object]. What would you say to this dream thing (*points to the third chair in which the dream was imagined earlier in the dialogue*)?

CLIENT: You could be anything. You won't last forever [standing up to the Intrusive Object].

THERAPIST: Say it again: "You won't last forever."

CLIENT: You won't last forever.

Stages 2 and 6A. In the Object Chair, Client Is Asked to Enact the Intrusive Object/Thought/Image; in the Experiencer Chair, Client Is Encouraged to Set a Boundary to It

THERAPIST: Can I suggest something? Come here (*points to the third chair in which the dream was put initially*).

The client moves to the Object Chair.

THERAPIST: You will be this dreamlike thing, this dream in which you are cheating. So, it is like, "I will come in your dreams, and I will make you anxious" or what? "I will make you worried that I am real." Do it little bit—it's like a drama. Be that bad guy. What will you do to James?

CLIENT: (*Speaks from the Object Chair*) I'll make you worry.

THERAPIST: So, it's like, "I am a bad thing that is waiting for you."

CLIENT: I am a bad thing that is waiting for you and could happen.

THERAPIST: And it's like, "I want to . . . I am your threat. I'll scare you, and you can't stop me. I'll get under your skin. There is something, that it comes to your dream, so you can't stop me. I'm coming. You can't stop me." Come here (*points to the Experiencer Chair*).

THERAPIST: What's your response to it: "I'm coming. I'm your threat. You can't stop me." What's your response right there, right now [prompting for protective anger]?

CLIENT: (*In the Experiencer Chair*) You are not a part of me. You are just something that happened.

THERAPIST: If this was an unpleasant person in your life trying to be like this, to get under your skin, to do something to you, what would you say to him, to her.

CLIENT: (*Speaks firmly*) I don't want you in my life.

THERAPIST: Say it again [further affirming the boundary-setting].

CLIENT: I don't want you in my life.

THERAPIST: And what is the sense as you say it?

CLIENT: It's moving toward separating myself from it.

The example of James illustrates the work with symptoms of OCD. It involves addressing the worrying/obsessing process as well as addressing compulsions. The chair work is aimed at helping the client get a sense of their own agency in generating symptoms but also an appreciation of the function (protection) and cost (anxiety and various other costs associated with varied elaborated rituals).

TWO-CHAIR DIALOGUE FOR SELF-RUMINATION

A variant of the worry task is the two-chair dialogue for self-rumination. *Rumination*, as opposed to worrying, which focuses on future potential threat, is an internal psychological process in which the client goes over and over past events that they were unhappy with. The drive here is a sense that if I figure out what went wrong, I might be able to improve how I handle a similar event in the future or get a different perspective on what happened that might calm me. The marker for this task is either rumination present in the session or an in-session reference to rumination being a dominant and problematic (e.g., exhausting) process outside of therapy. As with worrying, ruminating can be seen as fulfilling an avoidance function (e.g., Watkins, 2018). In essence, when I ruminate, I do not fully have time to stay with the underlying painful feeling linked to the event that I am ruminating about. For instance, if I felt humiliated in a situation, rather than accepting, tolerating, or adaptively responding to the feeling of humiliation as experienced, going over and over what happened constitutes a process of trying to figure out what happened or seek reassurance about what happened in a way that takes me away from the sense of humiliation. It is as if the inability to stay with unbearable shame propels a frantic effort to constantly analyze the event, thereby constantly thinking about what happened rather than allowing oneself to feel the feeling of what happened.

The actual rumination task is similar to the self-worry task (see Table 8.2). In Stage 2, however, rather than enacting worrying, the client is instructed to enact ruminating (the Worrier Chair can be referred to as the Ruminator Chair), that is, to go over and over a specific past event. So, for example, the therapist might instruct the client in the position of Ruminator to tell and retell the Self in the Experiencer Chair what they should have done differently: "So, tell her (*points to the Experiencer Chair*), 'You should have done this, you should have done that, et cetera, et cetera.' Go on, do it to her." The impact of ruminating (Stage 3) is typically a brief calming (a sort of reassurance), mixed with underlying pain (e.g., the humiliation as felt in the original event) and an exhaustion brought on by the relentlessness of the rumination process. Need (Stage 4) is usually expressed as a need for a break from having to go over and over the same thing again and again. As with other variations of the worry dialogue, the setting of a boundary (Stage 6A) is perhaps more crucial than the softening of the ruminator (Stage 5B). Given that the function of ruminating (as with worrying, more generally) is to protect the vulnerable Self from feeling underlying pain, softening and expressed compassion are less of a guarantee that the client can desist from engaging in rumination than feelings of anger and the resolve to put in place a boundary to the Ruminator. In our clinical experience, this task may be indicated with some clients whose depression is marked by persistent rumination. As with other tasks, work on underlying core painful feelings and the transformation of problematic emotions schemes indirectly but often effectively addresses self-treatment processes, such as rumination.

THE RETELLING OF TRAUMATIC EMOTIONAL EXPERIENCES TASK

Another task that targets symptom-level distress while it also taps into underlying emotional vulnerability is the retelling of traumatic emotional experiences task. This task is specifically applicable to PTSD-like traumatic experiences (see Elliott et al., 2004). In some ways, retelling of traumatic emotional experiences is less a task per se and more a therapeutic strategy or set of strategies applicable to unbearable emotional experiences (e.g., memories of trauma, flashbacks, intrusive unwanted images in OCD) that were too traumatic for the client. Those experiences have given rise to emotional or behavioral avoidance, whereby, broadly speaking, deliberate but respectful engagement with the traumatic emotional experiences counters the avoidance tendency.

The marker for this task is the client's reference to unbearable experience within the session (e.g., flashbacks, traumatic memories) or the client's in-session reference to such experiences dominating their life outside of therapy. Given that such experiences are frightening for the client to touch on, they may be referenced earlier in therapy and bookmarked for later working with at such time as when the client feels ready to engage with them. The actual task/strategy consists of the therapist guiding the client to give a detailed (e.g., chronological) description of the traumatic event as experienced by them as well as an account of their own internal experience during the event or in relation to any other relevant aspect of the event.

For instance, the client may describe an assault, what preceded it, and what the sequela of it has been, all the time doing so in a manner that describes their own inner experience in relation to these various aspects. The therapist explicitly invites the client to narrate this detailed account of the experience and, as the client does so, tracks both the client's perceptual world and the client's internal experience. The therapist remains empathic throughout, both empathically exploring the client's experience and communicating empathic understanding regarding this internal experience.

At the symptom level, this task touches on the client's emotional and behavioral avoidance as well as the unbearableness of the client's experience. At a deeper level, this task touches on underlying fear, terror, and an unbearable sense of unsafety, feelings rooted in problematic emotion schemes developed as a result of the original traumatic experience. While the task is particularly relevant to PTSD presentations, it can also be of relevance in OCD cases (e.g., when the client describes the intrusive object) as well as other anxiety disorders when the client describes pivotal experiences that are difficult to go back to and that shaped the client's avoidance.

CONCLUSION

In this chapter, we focused on symptom-level work, presenting an outline of several experiential tasks targeting self-treatment processes that underlie symptomatic presentations. Specifically, we described the two-chair dialogue for self-worrying; two-chair dialogue for self-worrying and an intrusive/phobic object; and two-chair dialogue for self-worrying, intrusive object, and self-compulsion. We also discussed the two-chair dialogue for self-rumination and the retelling of traumatic emotional experiences tasks. For some clients, particularly those whom symptomatic presentations present a major obstacle to therapeutic process or those for whom symptomatic presentations represent a major focus of in-session or overall functioning, we argued that, in addition to the core therapeutic work of transforming underlying vulnerability, a parallel focus on treating symptoms may be required.

9 ACCESSING AND TRANSFORMING CORE EMOTIONAL PAIN

This chapter presents two major transdiagnostic emotion-focused therapy (EFT-T) tasks: (a) the self–self two-chair dialogue for problematic (self-evaluative) self-treatment (classically referred to as a self-evaluative or self-critical split, or, simply, self-critic; Elliott et al., 2004; Greenberg at al., 1993; see also Chapter 2, this volume) and (b) the self–other (empty-chair) task for an interpersonal emotional injury (classically referred to as "unfinished business"; Elliott et al., 2004; Greenberg at al., 1993; see also Chapter 2, this volume). These tasks are at the core of emotion-focused therapy (EFT). Both originally come from gestalt therapy, and Les Greenberg, himself a trained gestalt therapist, has dedicated a significant portion of his research career to further developing them (e.g., by studying the tasks to distinguish productive from unproductive processes within them; see Greenberg, 1979, 1980, 1983; Greenberg & Dompierre, 1981; Greenberg & Foerster, 1996; Greenberg & Higgins, 1980; Greenberg & Malcolm, 2002; Greenberg & Webster, 1982). We refer to these two tasks as *transformational tasks* (Timulak & McElvaney, 2018) because it is in these tasks that we hope the client will not only access core painful feelings and the unmet needs associated with them but also

https://doi.org/10.1037/0000253-010
Transdiagnostic Emotion-Focused Therapy: A Clinical Guide for Transforming Emotional Pain, by L. Timulak and D. Keogh

transform those core painful feelings by generating self-compassion and healthy boundary-setting protective anger. It is also often in the context of these tasks that the therapist, through their relational presence and communication, most powerfully offers compassionate responses toward the client's pain and affirmative validation of the client's needs.

It is in these two tasks that the client accesses and transforms the core painful feelings and core vulnerability that underpin their symptomatic presentation. These tasks are at the core of a transdiagnostic approach because they target an idiosyncratic underlying emotional vulnerability that may only be loosely connected to the actual symptomatic presentation. Indeed, this underlying vulnerability may be similar across clients from different diagnostic groups (symptom clusters) and dissimilar among clients within the same diagnostic group. One person may feel unloved and rejected, and develop symptoms of social anxiety, whereas another person may feel unloved and rejected, and develop symptoms of depression. It is the underlying vulnerability of being prone to feeling unloved and rejected that we target in these two major transformational tasks.

These two major EFT-T tasks focus on two central psychological processes: One, the two-chair dialogue for problematic self-treatment, focuses on self–self processes; the other, the empty-chair dialogue for an interpersonal emotional injury focuses on self–other processes. Thus, these tasks correspond with two major pillars of EFT work: work with (a) problematic self-treatment processes (specifically self-criticism, self-contempt, self-judgments) and (b) interpersonal emotional injury processes (e.g., being neglected, rejected, overlooked, judged, attacked, unsupported). The two tasks also relate to the case conceptualization framework we have discussed in which many historical and current triggers of emotional pain (see Figure 3.1 in Chapter 3) are addressed through use of the empty-chair dialogue for an interpersonal emotional injury and the self-defining problematic self-treatment addressed in the two-chair dialogue for problematic self-treatment. These two tasks are also typically intertwined because problematic self-treatment often develops in the context of painful interpersonal triggers (see Chapter 3). This is reflected in experiential work in which the process often moves between tasks (i.e., beginning in one dialogue, moving to another, and perhaps returning to the first, often within the same session; see the discussion later).

The two tasks have several commonalities. First, both have the potential to be highly evocative. Given that both tasks use imaginary dialogues (whether between parts of the self or with an imagined other), they can access both painful and transformational emotions in a powerful and vivid way. Second, these tasks share similar goals: (a) to increase client awareness (e.g., of own problematic self-treatment, of the perceived problematic behavior of the Other); (b) to access the underlying core pain in an aroused manner (thus activating problematic emotions schemes); (c) to access, identify, and articulate unmet needs as embedded in core painful emotions; and (d) to generate transformational compassion or protective anger-based experiences in response to the core pain and unmet needs. The use of a dialogue (between parts of self or between the self and an enacted other) facilitates emotions to be accessed, named, and expressed in a seamless flow that ensures a live and vivid experiential process. The therapist is present to facilitate empathic exploration and to communicate empathic understanding but also to offer process guidance that propels dialogues so that core pain can be accessed and eventually transformed through corrective emotional experiences (Greenberg & Elliott, 2012). Throughout this process of accessing pain, articulating unmet needs, and generating transformational experiences, the therapist's empathic presence also enriches the client's experience through the offering of a healing and corrective interpersonal-relational experience (Timulak, 2014).

The two tasks are also central to EFT-T for depression, anxiety, and anxiety-related disorders insofar as the majority of time in therapy is spent in these two tasks. It is our experience that in 16 to 20 sessions of therapy, there may be around five of each of these dialogues. Particularly in the middle part of therapy (Sessions 4–15), one or other of these tasks may be present in every single session. In some sessions, both may be present because the processes targeted by these tasks are intertwined, so the work may flow from one task to another and even back again. In other sessions, one or other of these tasks may combine with a more symptom-level focused task (see the previous chapter) as the client moves from symptom-level work to work on the attendant underlying vulnerability within the same session. We spend the rest of this chapter describing the processes involved in these two tasks. Our description is a variant on the original descriptions in Greenberg et al. (1993) and Elliott et al. (2004).

SELF-SELF TWO-CHAIR DIALOGUE FOR PROBLEMATIC (SELF-EVALUATIVE) SELF-TREATMENT

This task, variously referred to in the literature as the two-chair dialogue for self-criticism (Greenberg et al., 1993) or two-chair dialogue for self-evaluative and/or conflict split (Elliott et al., 2004), is an experiential task initiated at a marker of self-criticism (or variants, e.g., self-devaluation, self-contempt, self-attack, self-judgment). As we have outlined elsewhere (Timulak & McElvaney, 2018), self-harming behavior may also be an expression of self-criticism, although this is not necessarily always the case. At times, it may predominantly serve a self-numbing function and thus more appropriately be seen as a form of self-interruption or emotional avoidance. An important consideration with this marker is that it typically involves a characterological judgment of the self. In other words, it constitutes a judgment with regard to one's own essential essence (e.g., "I am stupid," "I am flawed," "I am at my core a bad person"). It is also typically accompanied by a harsh experiential treatment of the self—for example, expressed self-contempt, coldness toward the self, a relentlessness of self-attack, and so forth. It is distinguished from a more "superficial" blaming of the self in which the client judges some specific behavior or state but is not necessarily attacking the self characterologically (e.g., "I should know how to park my car"). This more superficial blaming is termed a *coach split* within EFT (Greenberg, 2015) with one part of the self chastising another part as if to coach the self into performing more optimally. Similarly, blaming oneself for having mental health or other difficulties (e.g., "I should not be depressed") can be seen as a superficial coach–critic form of self-criticism and, in and of itself, is not a marker for this task. However, even in these more superficial forms, such self-criticisms may often be an expression of a more fundamental dissatisfaction with the self. Empathic exploration will thus often unfold this harsher self-criticism, and it is this harsher, characterological criticism that we try to focus on in therapy.

The judgment of the self, and the accompanying harsh treatment of the self that is the focus of the two-chair dialogue for problematic self-treatment, is thus a *self-defining* judgment. The judgment is typically perceived by the client as "true." That this is how they are is seen as a "reality," and thus the harsh self-treatment that can accompany this judgement typically "feels" deserved. This is why such self-treatment is linked to underlying emotional vulnerability. The judgment is unshakeable. It is not an evaluation regarding something the person has done in error, but, rather, what they have done is merely an illustration of who they are at their core. It is simply who they are, and nothing can be done about it. It constitutes a form of essential non–self-acceptance accompanied by an experientially self-punitive stance.

The specific manner of this problematic self-treatment is explored in this task. The emotional impact of the self-treatment is accessed, and the needs embedded in the core pain are articulated. Transformation of the self-criticism is typically brought about in the form of a softening of the self-criticism by facilitating the client to witness the painful impact of the self-criticism or by building boundary-setting protective anger that sets limits to the power of the critic. The task is often linked to the unfinished business task (described later) because problematic self-treatment often develops in the context of interpersonal relationships either as some sort of internalization of the Other's stance (e.g., "My father sees me as lazy; he must see something that is in me") or as a response to the Other's stance (e.g., in the context of a mother who is depressed and thus does not pay attention to me: "It is something in me that is responsible for it, and, therefore, I should be better to deserve her attention"). The process of therapeutic work in the task is described in Table 9.1. Again, as we have emphasized with other tasks, the table does not mean to imply that the process is a linear one; rather, it serves as a didactic tool that can facilitate learning and supervision.

TABLE 9.1. Stages in the Self–Self Two-Chair Dialogue for Problematic (Self-Evaluative) Self-Treatment

Stage	Experiencer Chair	Critic Chair
1	Experiencing the marker: Feeling self-contempt, having negative self-treatment present	
2		Enacting the criticism: Harsh, poignant, main message; experiential quality
3	Accessing and differentiating core pain	
4	Articulating and expressing unmet needs	
5		Probing for compassion, seeing the pain and unmet needs
		Stage 5A—If no compassion is coming: Highlighting rejection (message and mistreatment in it, function of it)
		Stage 5B—If compassion is coming: Savoring it experientially and expressing it
6A	Building protective anger, setting a boundary to the self-criticism	
6B	Letting compassion in, savoring it experientially	

Note. From *Transforming Generalized Anxiety: An Emotion-Focused Approach* (p. 128), by L. Timulak and J. McElvaney, 2018, Routledge. Copyright 2018 by Routledge. Adapted with permission. The original source also cited Elliott et al. (2004).

Stage 1. Seeing That the Marker of Problematic Self-Evaluative Self-Treatment Is Present

For the task to be introduced, a marker of problematic self-evaluative self-treatment needs to be freshly present in the session. The client may either talk about how self-judgmental or self-critical they are outside the session, or they may actually be self-critical within the session (e.g., "I shouldn't have done that. Typical me"). EFT therapists develop a sensitivity to hearing such self-criticism and differentiate between, on the one hand, self-criticism in which the client judges themselves regarding some action or behavior (e.g., something they regret saying to another person) or state (e.g., I don't like the me who is so depressed), and on the other hand, criticisms or expressions that imply some characterological self-nonacceptance (e.g., "I'm weak/ stupid/selfish"); see our earlier discussion of the distinction. At times, clients may present with what is referred to in the literature as an *attributional split* (Greenberg et al., 1993), whereby a criticism described as coming from another person (e.g., "He saw how inept I am"), actually reflects a judgment the client holds against themselves (e.g., "I am inept").

When a potential marker of self-criticism is noticed, the therapist confirms the marker by clarifying with the client what their internal experience is— for example, "So, you were saying you made a mistake. . . . How does it feel inside when you say that to yourself?" or, "It sounds like there is this part of you that says those harsh things about you. How does it feel when this part is saying that?" Les Greenberg's EFT for depression demonstration video by the American Psychological Association (Greenberg & Carlson, 2007) shows a good example of this process when the client blames herself for uprooting her son. The therapist checks with the client how it feels when she blames herself. She states that it is horrible, that she cannot forgive herself, and that she feels guilty. Exploring around this marker allows the therapist both to clearly establish the suitability of introducing the task but also to reflect the client's experience in such a way that, once introduced, both the task and the dialogue central to the task intuitively make sense to the client. The therapist establishes with the client that there is a part of the client's self that blames the client (the Critic) and another part that is affected by the criticism (the Experiencer). Without the therapist actually using technical or theoretical terms like "Critic" or "Experiencer," the client can begin a dialogue with an intuitive understanding of both parts of self in the dialogue and in their respective chairs.

The marker for this task is thus self-judgment, or self-contempt, or similarly harsh self-treatment. It should be freshly present and bring significant pain in the client. It should refer to some characterological traitlike feature of the self (or at least the therapist should have a sense that it does). Work with it in the session should be relevant for the client at that point in the session. When these criteria are met, the therapist seeks agreement with the client that it is indeed an appropriate marker and that the client would be willing and interested to explore what is happening, what impact it has on them, and what needs to happen with the process so that it will not be so painful. The therapist also proposes the dialogue: "Could we have a look at this process? It sounds like there is a part of you that judges yourself and a part of you that is impacted by it? I suggest that we could look at this in a dialogue."

Stage 2. Enacting the Problematic Self-Treatment (Self-Criticism)

After introducing the task, the therapist asks the client to move from the chair they are sitting in (the Experiencer Chair) and sit in the other chair facing it (hereinafter called the Critic Chair; see Table 9.1). Once in the Critic Chair, the client is asked by the therapist to enact the criticism (Stage 2 in Table 9.1): "How do you criticize yourself? You were saying you say to yourself, 'You are stupid?' Let's do it. Imagine yourself in the [Experiencer] chair. . . . Criticize her/him." Here, the therapist wants to ensure that the client engages as fully as possible in experientially enacting the critic. At times, particularly when it is their first time engaging in a chair dialogue, some clients find it strange or difficult to enact their critical Self. Understandably, they may perceive the therapist's suggestion to enact their critic as peculiar and may experience their initial efforts to comply with this request as forced or artificial. Overly anxious clients, especially those presenting with social anxiety, may become especially self-conscious regarding their "performance." It is important in such instances that the therapist normalizes client hesitancy but nonetheless gently guides the client to engage in the enactment process to the extent that they are capable of.

When enacting the criticism, the therapist encourages the client to express specific, and in particular, characterological or traitlike criticism. The enacted flow of criticism is verbally mirrored by the therapist ("Yeah, this is what you say: 'You are stupid'"), who selectively captures and reflects these more personal and characterological attacks. The therapist further emphasizes the personalized and characterological aspects of these attacks by asking the client to repeat those that are most salient or attacking (e.g., "Say it again: 'you are stupid'"). The therapist may also share their own observations of the client's manner of delivering the criticism, particularly those aspects of delivery that contribute to what is hurtful about the judgment (e.g., "And you say it with such a contempt . . . Do it again: Criticize him/her"). The enactment of the critical self-treatment is optimally achieved when the client expresses characterological self-defining judgment of the self and does so in a fresh and vivid experiential manner (e.g., with a harsh or contemptuous tone). Once the critical self-treatment is enacted in this way, the therapist brings both the criticism and the manner in which it is conveyed to the client's awareness (e.g., "So this is how you criticize yourself: 'You are stupid,' and you do it with such contempt" [the therapist's facial expression mirrors the client's contemptuous expression]). The therapist then asks the client to move back to the Experiencer Chair.

An example of Stage 2 can be seen in the following transcript coming from client Paul, who presents with depression and generalized anxiety[1]:

THERAPIST: Can you be that part that criticizes you? . . . You are saying, "You can't even do that!" What is it that you don't like about him?

CLIENT: [In the Critic chair, speaking to the Experiencer Chair] It's like you've no backbone. You're not a man. You're not strong. You're not able to fight your corner.

THERAPIST: "You are not a man, you have no backbone." What else do you say to yourself, to him?

CLIENT: People can see you're pushed over and taken advantage of. You're weak. You're not capable!

THERAPIST: What else do you not like about him?

CLIENT: Just stand up for yourself!

THERAPIST: And what's the attitude toward him?

CLIENT: The shakiness and all. Yeah, I despise it. I don't like it. You are weak. And I don't like it.

THERAPIST: And you show all this contempt (*facially mimics the contempt expressed by the client*): "I despise it." So, this is how you criticize yourself—with all that contempt: "You're weak, shaky. I despise you" [summarizing characterological attack on the Self].

Stage 3. Accessing and Differentiating the Core Pain

Once the self-defining and condemning problematic self-treatment is clearly enacted and the manner of this self-treatment is brought to the client's

---

[1]Chapters 5 through 9 include several case studies. Some are based on real clients, and others are composite sketches. Permission to use client data is on file with the authors.

awareness, the client is asked to sit back in the Experiencer Chair (Stage 3 in Table 9.1). The client is instructed to check inside for the impact of the particular criticism or attack: "What happens inside when you get this 'You are stupid'?" Again, in repeating the client's self-criticism, the therapist also mirrors the manner in which the critic communicated the criticism (e.g., dismissive verbal tone or contemptuous facial expression). The major task here for the therapist is to help the client access and feel the experiential/emotional effect of the Critic's attack. The therapist uses empathic exploration and a gentle, caring voice that invites the client to focus on, notice/see, and feel the hurt the Critic brings. The client is encouraged to name these feelings and to communicate them to the Critic. At all times, the therapist endeavors to keep this dance alive by encouraging the client to pay attention inward, name the feelings (which the therapist empathizes with), and express these feelings to the Critic (Greenberg, 2015). Throughout, the therapist seeks to maintain a dialogue between the Experiencer and the Critic as if there were actually two people present having an exchange during which one attacks the other, and the other expresses the impact this attack has on them. The exchange may look as follows in this hypothetical example:

THERAPIST: What happens inside as you get this "You are stupid"? When she attacks you like this (*points at the Critic*).

CLIENT: [In the Experiencer Chair, speaking to the Critic Chair] It hurts so much when she says this to me.

THERAPIST: It hurts so much [empathic affirmation]. Tell her—tell her how it hurts [instruction to express the feeling].

CLIENT: It hurts so much when you say this to me.

THERAPIST: And how does this make you feel. Tell her.

CLIENT: I feel so worthless [core pain, shame].

THERAPIST: "I just feel so, so worthless." Tell her.

In this exchange, the client goes directly to the hurt and pain. This does not always happen with clients frequently either collapsing—"She is right. I am stupid" (such responses illustrate how defining the Critic's voice can be of the Self)—or defending themselves—"I don't want to hear you" (secondary anger). The therapist always acknowledges the client's response, whatever it might be, but refocuses the client on the underlying painful feeling that the attack inevitably brings—for example, "So, you say, 'You are right' . . . but how does it feel inside when she is like this with you?" The underlying painful feeling is usually accessible even if it initially might appear as if the client is struggling to get in touch with it. The freshness of the marker that led to the task points to the proximity of the underlying pain. The therapist therefore simply needs to be patient, gently focusing the client on the emotional impact of the criticism. It is important here that the therapist keeps the client in dialogue with the Critic because it is actually the dance between accessing feelings and expressing them directly to the Critic that maintains emotional arousal and the freshness of the experience. It is freshly accessed emotional experience that activates the underlying vulnerability (problematic emotion schemes), and, in turn, it is the freshness of the felt and expressed pain that, later in the dialogue, has the potential to elicit compassion (see Stage 5B). It is therefore crucial that, at this stage, the therapist succeeds in accessing the pain and differentiating it through the twin processes of exploration of internal experience and subsequent expression to the Critic, all of which is accompanied by the therapist's empathic support and guidance.

Theoretically speaking, the underlying pain typically elicited by self-judgment and nonacceptance is shame based. This feeling of shame may be accompanied by the sadness of being condemned and thus rejected and excluded: "You are not worthy of my presence." Although it is a self–self process, self-criticism may be felt as a truly interpersonal rejection; hence, sadness and a sense of exclusion or loneliness can often be present ("Nobody understands me, not even my own self [i.e., Critic]"). In this stage (Stage 3), the work may digress to work with unfinished business (e.g., empty-chair dialogue for an interpersonal emotional injury) because problematic self-treatment in the form of self-criticism is often either internalized criticism from emotionally important others or is a form of self-adjustment to get some needed interpersonal response from important others (e.g., being perfect so that my success/achievement brings the attention from parents that I crave).

An example of Stage 3 in Paul's case looked as follows:

THERAPIST: What happens inside when you get that "You're weak. I despise you"? How is it to hear that inside?

CLIENT: [In the Experiencer Chair, speaking to the Critic Chair] (*Pauses*) I feel sad. I am sad. I'd love to be the way you'd want me to be, but I just can't seem to manage.

THERAPIST: But what does it do to you? Inside. You are saying it brings that sadness.

CLIENT: You don't care. It's . . . I'm an easy target.

THERAPIST: "I feel like I can't protect myself against you"?

CLIENT: Yeah. I feel quite open and vulnerable.

THERAPIST: So, tell him: "I feel sad and unprotected when you talk to me like this."

CLIENT: I am sad, unprotected. I feel so small and inadequate when you talk to me like this.

Stage 4. Articulating and Expressing Unmet Need(s)

As the client touches on the core pain evoked by the harsh criticism, explores (differentiates) it, and expresses it to the Critic, the therapist asks the client to check inside and articulate what it is they need from the Critic in the context of the felt pain (Stage 4, Table 9.1). This may look as follows in this hypothetical example:

CLIENT: I feel so worthless [core pain, shame].

THERAPIST: "I just feel so, so worthless." I can imagine it must really bring a lot of pain. Tell her . . .

CLIENT: It hurts so much when you do this to. I feel like a small girl that has no voice and no right to talk.

THERAPIST: Tell her: "I feel so much pain. I feel so small."

CLIENT: It hurts so much. I feel so small.

THERAPIST: What is it that you need from her?

CLIENT: I need her to understand . . .

THERAPIST: Tell her: "I need you to understand . . ."

CLIENT: I need you to understand that I am trying so much. I need you to be gentler with me.

THERAPIST: "I need you to be gentler with me." Say it again.

Clients are only able to articulate the unmet need when they are in touch with the underlying pain. In the preceding example, it was only when the client was feeling the hurt that she was, with relative ease, able to articulate what she needed from the Critic. At times, EFT therapists have difficulty facilitating their clients to articulate need, usually because the client is not in touch with the core painful feeling or those painful feelings are not present in an aroused manner (Stage 3). When clients do not feel the pain, they do not know what they need. The ease with which the client identifies need at this point is therefore a function of the therapist's success in facilitating the client to focus on and access the underlying emotional pain in Stage 3.

Clients may also have difficulty articulating and expressing need because they fall into hopelessness and do not believe that the need could be responded to. (More often this is an issue in unfinished business dialogues, but it can also occur in the context of self-critic dialogues.) In such cases, the therapist validates the hopelessness (e.g., "Tell her: 'There is no point telling you what I need because you won't hear me'") but then encourages the client to nonetheless articulate and express the need (e.g., the therapist says, "There is no point telling you what I need . . . tell her what the need is that she would not respond to"). If the client is able to articulate the need, the expressed need often takes the form of asking for acceptance from the Critic, to be treated in a gentler manner, or for a break from the attacking judgment.

An example of Stage 4 can be seen in the following transcript taken from Paul's case:

THERAPIST: "And now, when I feel so sad and inadequate, I need what from you?"

CLIENT: [In the Experiencer Chair] Genuine concern.

THERAPIST: "I need you to care about me when I'm actually struggling."

CLIENT: When you see me vulnerable, don't attack. Show some concern! I need your support.

Stage 5. Probing for Compassion

Once the client accesses and expresses the core painful feelings linked to the criticism and articulates what they need from the Critic, the therapist asks them to move back to the Critic Chair. The therapist then invites the client, as Critic, to see what their response is to the pain and need as expressed by the vulnerable Self (Stage 5 in Table 9.1). The main focus here is on what the client as Critic feels toward the client in pain (i.e., in the Experiencer Chair) and on asking the Critic for a response to the expressed need. The therapist may say something like this in this hypothetical example:

THERAPIST: So, if you could come back here (*points to the Critic Chair*). So, she is saying (*points to the Experiencer Chair*), "I am aching. I feel so, so worthless." And she is so distressed. She is saying, "I need you to be gentler with me." What is your response to that? Can you see her pain? What do you feel toward her here and now as she is expressing this to you?

Here, the therapist is essentially checking whether the client's pain and unmet need elicits any softening or compassion in the critical Self (hence the name of this stage: Probing for compassion). The therapist wants to see whether the expressed pain and need moved the client (the Critic) enough that they might respond in a more considerate or caring way. Essentially, there are two main types of responses here. The client either softens and expresses compassion (e.g., "I do not want you to be hurting. I feel caring toward you"; Stage 5B in Table 9.1) or escalates the attack (e.g., "Look at you moaning again. You're pathetic" [accompanied by contempt]; Stage 5A in Table 9.1). At times, therapists see a mixture of these responses (e.g., "I see how you suffer, but if I don't push you, you won't amount to anything and you will not be happy. Therefore, I have to do it. I have to push you"). From an assessment and case conceptualization perspective, difficulty softening in early dialogues, which is common in clients with depression, anxiety, and related disorders, is an indicator of the chronicity of self-judgment, self-rejection, and self-nonacceptance. The more difficult it is for the Critic to soften, the more likely there will be a chronic problematic self-defining self-treatment and corresponding chronic emotional pain (which is typically a variant of shame). We have seen in our studies (Timulak & McElvaney, 2018; Timulak et al., 2017) that it usually takes a sequence of dialogues before many clients can easily access softening and self-compassion. That said, although early softening of the Critic may indicate a potential for change, on its own, it is not totally predictive; equally important is that clients can access protective anger, and some clients who readily access self-compassion struggle to generate healthy self-protecting anger.

If there is no softening in the Critic and thus no expression of compassion toward the Self in the Experiencer Chair at this stage, the therapist acknowledges this and asks the client to express where they are in terms of self-treatment (e.g., "So, you are saying I do not see your pain. So, tell her: 'I don't see your pain. I feel cold toward you'"; Stage 5A in Table 9.1). This further escalation in the Critic will be used in Stage 6A as a challenge for the Experiencer to stand up to the Critic and set a boundary to him/her. The therapist acknowledges the client's (in the position of the Critic) rejection of the vulnerable Self's plea for compassion, amplifies it by inviting its expression, and moves the intervention further by inquiring after the function of the criticism/escalation. In this hypothetical example, this may look as follows:

CLIENT: I don't know what you are talking about. I don't see your pain. If I don't push, nobody will.

THERAPIST: So, tell her (*points at the Experiencer*): "I don't see your pain. I will keep on pushing you and being harsh on you" [acknowledgment and amplification of the Critic's rigid and harsh position].

CLIENT: I will keep pushing you (*shakes head in disapproval, expressing coldness*). I don't know what you are talking about.

THERAPIST: What drives it? What drives your harsh position? What is so difficult about softening toward her, responding to her need for you to be gentler [asking after the function of the Critic]?

CLIENT: If I soften, she won't do anything. She will be even worse. Not amounting to anything. I make her do all she does [the function here is that, without the pushing, without the Critic, the client would be even unhappier because they would not achieve anything].

The function of the Critic is often of a protective nature. In the preceding example, it is rooted in a sense that without the Critic pushing her, the client would be even less happy than she currently is. Clients often report at this stage that the Critic functions to prevent the judgment of others. There can be a fear that if the Critic steps back from doing what it does, the client will not meet standards set by the Self or important others. The function of problematic self-treatment may take many other idiosyncratic forms. In general, though, from the perspective of case conceptualization (see Chapters 3 and 5), problematic self-treatment is seen as the client's self-adjustment in the context of painful triggers that are typically of an interpersonal nature (e.g., to get recognition from an emotionally important other; to push oneself to become independent when there is no support from another). Such self-treatment is likely to have been functional at some point but can become problematic over time, in and of itself becoming a trigger of chronic pain. The Critic can also, in some instances, represent their own standards (e.g., "I should be an excellent professional") perhaps forged through interactions with others (Greenberg et al., 1993). In any case, the function of the Critic is often protective, albeit looking after the interests of the self in a nonadaptive way. Thus, even when the client expresses a rigidly harsh and invalidating position, highlighting the function of that harshness points to implicitly self-protective (and thus inherently compassionate) aspects of the self-treatment.

In some instances, however, it may be impossible to discern any self-protecting function behind the Critic's attack on the Self. The criticism may constitute what is seen by the Critic as a deserved punishment. Such harsh positions may be internalized from rejecting others, but they may also be executed on the basis of own values and harsh standards (although these are also likely forged through interactions with others). When neither the client nor therapist can see any adaptive aspect to this type of position, the transformative work of therapy is likely to occur mainly from the position of the Experiencer Chair in which the client can be facilitated to set a boundary to the Critic (Stage 6A).

Relatively common in dialogues is a position that represents a mixture of Stages 5A and 5B—that is, some softening and compassion as well as an elaborated version of the criticism: "I see how you suffer, and I feel caring toward you, but I have to keep pushing you because, otherwise, you will end up in a bad place." In this type of mixed position, the therapist works with both parts. The softening (Stage 5B) is expressed and savored, and the client in the Experiencer Chair (Stage 6B in Table 9.1) is asked to let this expressed compassion in. Further criticism (Stage 5A) is used as a challenge to probe for protective, boundary-setting anger in the Experiencer Chair (Stage 6A). Overall, the process in Stage 5 is fluid, and the therapist uses a mixture of exploration and facilitation of client enactment to move the dialogue along. The crux of this stage is, however, in seeing whether the client can see and respond to the pain (Stage 3 in Table 9.1) and corresponding unmet need (Stage 4 in Table 9.1) expressed in the Experiencer Chair.

Returning to excerpts from Paul's dialogue, we can see that his initial reaction at this stage is not to soften toward the vulnerable Self but, instead, to escalate the attack (Stage 5A):

THERAPIST: So, how do you respond to that as the Critic? "I feel so sad, inadequate, I need your support"?

CLIENT: [In the Critic Chair, speaking to the Experiencer] (*Pauses a long time*) You're just whining.

THERAPIST: Okay, it's like, "I don't actually care. You're just whining."

CLIENT: Up your game! Get into the ring! It's no point in your moaning.

THERAPIST: It's like, "When you tell me to support me, it's like, 'I can't do that.' It's like—almost like it has a function because if I would stop, what would happen?"

CLIENT: (*Pauses a long time*) I'd have to listen . . .

THERAPIST: "And I don't want that."

CLIENT: School of hard knocks. Actions beat louder than words! [Actions speak louder than words!]

THERAPIST: So, "I will build you up by attacking you, and that's why I will keep doing it" [highlighting the function of the Critic].

Later in the dialogue, when Paul in the Experiencer Chair accessed and expressed to the Critic the deep hurt he felt (feeling like a small boy who is being bullied), he actually then showed some softening in the Critic Chair (Stage 5B):

THERAPIST: Can you see his pain? Can you see it? Can you see the little boy? He is asking you to understand and support him?

CLIENT: [In the Critic Chair] Yeah. Yeah. I do. I see it: He's crippled, yeah.

THERAPIST: How do you feel toward him?

CLIENT: (*Pauses, eyes fill with tears*) I'm sorry for being so hard.

THERAPIST: I didn't know I crippled you that much.

CLIENT: (*Pauses, is quiet, eyes fill with tears*)

THERAPIST: What happens, Paul [responding to seeing the client emotional]?

CLIENT: I'm feeling—I'm feeling a sadness for both.

THERAPIST: Tell him! "I feel sadness when I see you so . . ."

CLIENT: It fills me with sadness when I see you so down . . . I see how much you struggle. It must be hard.

THERAPIST: And he is saying, "I need your support." How do you respond to that?

CLIENT: That's a tough one. No other than I will support you.

THERAPIST: It is like, "I want to support you"?

CLIENT: Definitely.

THERAPIST: So, tell him.

CLIENT: Tell me how I can support you.

THERAPIST: And what is the feeling as you are saying this to him?

CLIENT: Caring.

Stage 6A. Building Protective Anger, Setting a Boundary

An escalation or partial escalation of the criticism (Stage 5A in Table 9.1) or the nonsoftening of the Critic toward the expressed pain (Stage 3) and expressed need (Stage 4) is used to build protective anger in the Experiencer Chair toward the Critic (Stage 6A in Table 9.1). After the Critic's response to the expressed need and pain is articulated, the therapist asks the client to move back to the Experiencer Chair and see what their response is to the Critic's escalated attack, as in this hypothetical example:

THERAPIST: If you come back (*points to the Experiencer Chair*), what is your response to that . . . she is saying, "I will keep pushing you." What is your response to that . . . here and now?

In contrast to Stage 3 in which the client is invited to focus on the impact of the Critic ("What happens inside when you get that?"), here, the client is guided to focus on how they respond to the Critic's nonresponsiveness or continuing attack ("What is your response to how she treats you? Is it okay with you that she treats you this way?"). Thus, the therapist slightly nudges the client toward a more protective, boundary-setting stance.

Of course, many clients will struggle to set such a boundary. Indeed, if it were easy to do so, they most likely would not have a problem with problematic self-defining self-criticism. The client at this point is thus likely to oscillate between collapsing (a variant of Stage 3) and attempting to stand up for themselves. If the client collapses, the therapist empathically acknowledges the client's inability to protect themself by standing up to the Critic. At the same time, however, the therapist offers, on a trial-and-error basis, various suggestions that might help the client generate boundary-setting anger. The process is somewhat like a seesaw: The client collapses and the therapist acknowledges the collapse but suggests trying to set a boundary. For instance, in this hypothetical example, the process may look like the following:

CLIENT: It is not okay that she [the Critic] pushes me, but I cannot do anything about it.

THERAPIST: You are unable to stand up to her. So, tell her: . . . "I am unable to put you in your place" (*points at the Critic*).

CLIENT: I am unable to stop you.

THERAPIST: And how does it feel as you say that?

CLIENT: It feels horrible.

THERAPIST: So, tell her: "It feels really horrible" . . .

CLIENT: It feels really horrible.

THERAPIST: And what is it you really want?

CLIENT: I feel horrible, and I need you to stop.

THERAPIST: Okay, say it again.

CLIENT: I need you to stop.

THERAPIST: And if she does not stop?

CLIENT: Then I will not listen to her.

THERAPIST: So, tell her: "I won't listen to you."

CLIENT: I will not listen to you.

THERAPIST: How does it feel to say this?

CLIENT: It feels good, as if I had some power.

THERAPIST: So, tell her: "I can sense that power . . . right here, right now."

The therapist thus acknowledges the client's inability to stand up for the Self but does not give up on the client and continues to explore whether it is possible to ignite the flame of self-protection. While self-compassion (softening of the Critic; Stage 5B) is elicited by seeing the pain (i.e., as expressed in Stage 3) and unmet need (as expressed in Stage 4), protective anger is elicited by highlighting the Critic's mistreatment of the Self (i.e., as seen in Stage 2 but even more so as amplified in Stage 5A).

In our previous writings, we highlighted several strategies for or tips on facilitating the emergence of protective anger (Timulak, 2015; Timulak & McElvaney, 2018). For instance, the therapist might confront the client in the face of the Critic's challenge—for example, "Will you let the Critic treat you like this?" Alternatively, the therapist may roll with the collapse until the client protests and fights back, as in this hypothetical example:

CLIENT: I am unable to face her.

THERAPIST: Tell her: "I am unable to face you. You can do whatever you want to me. I will be your slave forever."

CLIENT: I won't say it.

THERAPIST: So, tell her: "I will not say it. I am not your slave."

CLIENT: I am not your slave.

THERAPIST: And how does it feel as you say it?

CLIENT: It feels good.

THERAPIST: So, say it again to her.

The therapist may invite the client to consider what they would do if they did have the ability to stand up for themselves—while also acknowledging that the client does not have that power now:

THERAPIST: "You're saying I am unable to stand up to you." So, tell her that.

CLIENT: I am unable to stand up to you.

THERAPIST: "And if I had the power to stand up to her?" What would you do?

CLIENT: I would shut you up.

THERAPIST: Say it again.

CLIENT: I would shut you up.

THERAPIST: And again . . .

CLIENT: I would shut you up.

THERAPIST: And how does it feel as you say it?

CLIENT: It feels good.

THERAPIST: So, tell her it feels good to say it to you.

In general, the process in the critic task is nonlinear and idiosyncratic. Despite these idiosyncrasies, all dialogues share one common feature: While the therapist always acknowledges and empathizes with where the client is, they do not give up on the client but, instead, seek to recalibrate suggestions in such a way that the client could use those suggestions to access, experience, and express protective anger. Again, the goal is experiential: The focus is on helping the client generate anger, feel that anger, and express that anger. Only in the context of a new experience truly felt, enacted, and expressed, can problematic emotion schemes be restructured.

In the case of Paul, when his Critic did not soften at first and instead escalated its attack, Paul responded as follows (Stage 6A):

THERAPIST: So, he (*points at the Critic*) is saying, "You're not a man. Stop whining." What is your response to that?

CLIENT: [In the Experiencer Chair] Ouch!

THERAPIST: What happens now?

CLIENT: I'm angry. I'm saying, "Hang on. Who gives you the bleeding authority to say what's what?"

Stage 6B. Letting Compassion In

While in Stage 6A, the therapist facilitated the client to stand up to the escalated criticism in Stage 5A. Stage 6B corresponds to Stage 5B in that it follows from the expression of compassion from a softening Critic (see Table 9.1). When the Critic softens and expresses compassion (e.g., "I see your pain, and I care about you. I will try to be gentler with you"), the therapist asks the client to move back to the Experiencer Chair and see how it is to receive this compassion: "Come back here [to the Experiencer Chair]. How is it to hear, 'I care about you?' How does it feel inside? Can you let it in?" Although one might assume it is a relatively straightforward process to let in such compassion expressed toward the Self, in reality, problems with letting compassion in often occur. The client's self-criticism may manifest in the Experiencer Chair (e.g., "I do not deserve for you to be so nice with me"). The expressed compassion may feel too new or alien. The client may not want to trust that the compassion is genuine for fear that, in their naivety, they would only get hurt even more next time (e.g., "I don't trust you. You will come and attack me again").

Whatever the block to letting in compassion, it is important that is explored, named, and expressed by the client and acknowledged by the therapist. As should be evident, cautiousness on the part of the client about letting in such compassion may serve a protective function (e.g., "I do not want to fool myself by letting your [the Critic's] care in and then getting more hurt"). At the same time as acknowledging the client's hesitation to let in the expressed compassion, the therapist gently persists with asking the client to refocus on how it feels to receive such compassion. This is very important because irrespective of why the client struggles to let such compassion in (e.g., whether chronic self-criticism and a sense of undeservedness or protective cautiousness), this difficulty deprives the client of the transformative experience of feeling the soothing care, love, or validation. This difficulty can extend beyond a chair dialogue with the critical Self: Clients often struggle to really let in compassion from anywhere or anyone. The dance between acknowledging the block to receiving the compassion while also gently prompting for it to be allowed in can look something like the following in this hypothetical example:

THERAPIST: Come back here [to the Experiencer Chair]. How is it to hear it, "I care about you?" How does it feel inside? Can you let it in?

CLIENT: I don't know whether I can trust her . . . that she wouldn't attack me again.

THERAPIST: Okay, so it is, "I cannot trust you." Can you tell her that?

CLIENT: I cannot trust you. You will come and attack me again.

THERAPIST: Okay, so it is like, "I cannot trust" . . . But how is it when she says this . . . here and now. How does it feel to hear it here?

CLIENT: It feels nice.

THERAPIST: Okay, so, tell her: "It feels nice, but I have to be cautious with you."

CLIENT: It feels nice.

THERAPIST: And what is the feeling?

CLIENT: Really nice. It is a sense of warmth and relief.

THERAPIST: So, tell her: "I feel that warmth and relief."

Self-compassion is most fully felt when both its offering (Stage 5B) and reception (Stage 6B) are experienced and expressed. So, for example, in the Critic Chair, the client might offer compassion by saying, "I want to be there for you" while also being prompted to notice and articulate "and it feels good to say this to you." Equally in the Experiencer Chair, the client can receive this compassion but also notice and articulate that "it feels calming to hear this from you." We like to describe this process as analogous to the client *bathing*, or immersing themselves, in the experience of compassion. As with protective anger, it is important that the experience is real, vivid, and moving; that it allows the client in one chair to feel real caring toward the Self; and that, in the other chair, it allows in this compassion. Only then can problematic emotion schemes be restructured such that the client develops new, more self-supportive self-organizations. Again, the essence of the transformation process is in the vividness of the experience.

An example of Stage 6B in Paul's dialogue looked like this:

THERAPIST: Can you let that in, what he (*points at the Critic*) just said? "I feel caring. I want to support you."

CLIENT: [In the Experiencer Chair] Really? Well, I'm asking the question, um, because if you're going to give me support, I need to know if it's genuine.

THERAPIST: It's like, "I am a bit hesitant. I don't trust you that you actually want to be there with me."

CLIENT: Yeah, it's kind of . . . But I do appreciate the effort and the words.

THERAPIST: What was is like when he said, "I feel caring toward you. I want to support you."

CLIENT: Yeah. Yeah. It does. It did feel genuine. Yeah. It's a start.

THERAPIST: Can you let that in, what happens inside?

CLIENT: Having the strength and support as well would be nice. Yeah. It's like having my vulnerabilities and your strength.

THERAPIST: Because you can sense his strength?

CLIENT: Yeah, and I feel it.

THERAPIST: "I would like to have you on my side. It would be lovely."

CLIENT: Yeah, no better person to have on my side!

THERAPIST: What happens in your body. Check in with your body—just for a second.

CLIENT: It's not like somebody pulling me down. That dread is gone.

PROCESSES IN THE TWO-CHAIR DIALOGUE FOR PROBLEMATIC SELF-TREATMENT: REFLECTION POINTS

Although the stages and processes outlined in Table 9.1 and in the preceding section appear to be linear, in reality, they are not. For example, both Stages 6A and 6B as well as both Stages 5A and 5B tend to overlap with clients experiencing blocks to expressing compassion, letting compassion in, and standing up for the Self. As we have stated in relation to previous tasks, the structure of the task as outlined in Table 9.1 has utility primarily as a didactic tool in teaching and supervision and as a heuristic to guide the therapist's thinking. The process within sessions is much messier, and clients may move between stages in a nonlinear manner. The process also differs across sessions: Well-progressing therapies show movement across therapy in the client's ability to be more easily self-compassionate or more quickly capable of generating protective anger. Equally, the process in an individual dialogue may get stuck, and the therapist needs to acknowledge this, summarizing what the issue is and marking this out as something important for the client and therapist to work on (e.g., "So, it sounds like this critic is so harsh and contemptuous, and it brings a lot of pain in you." The therapist continues: "And, at the same time, it is difficult for you to feel for yourself in that pain or to stand up to that critical voice. It looks like something we might focus on in therapy").

The task can overlap with other tasks, and the therapist and client may move from one task to another (see the next chapter). For instance, a client with social anxiety may worry about being judged and may, at first, engage in a worry task (e.g., "I am worried that they may judge me"). However, the implicit self-judgment and attendant sense of shame (e.g., "They will judge me because they will see how flawed I am") may quickly emerge as more central to the client's here-and-now experiencing than the worry itself. Thus, the work may shift from a worry to a critic task. Equally, the self-critical process may, in turn, be intertwined with an interpersonal relationship (e.g., "My father always said how flawed I was"), and, so, the work may shift to an unfinished business task. The process is fluid, and we talk about some of the principles of this fluidity in the next chapter. This fluidity notwithstanding, the therapist does not forget about the critic task; even if the work shifts to other tasks, the therapist can eventually bring the client back to the critic dialogue either to continue with that work or to acknowledge and bookmark where it is.

As with other tasks already discussed, the framework outlined in Table 9.2 can be used to support work on problematic self-treatment by facilitating client and therapist reflection on the work. The framework can serve as a basis for possible homework (Greenberg & Warwar, 2006; Warwar & Ellison, 2019), stimulating reflection and awareness regarding the processes explored in therapy as well as inspiring activities that might consolidate any progress or change experienced in therapy—for example, by supporting self-compassionate or self-protecting stances vis-à-vis the self. Although we have developed psychoeducational materials based on this framework that could be used for homework or in the context of low-intensity (e.g., internet) interventions (Kwatra et al., in press), we are not prescriptive in any way regarding how therapists may choose to use or not use this framework.

SELF-OTHER (EMPTY-CHAIR) TASK FOR AN INTERPERSONAL EMOTIONAL INJURY (UNFINISHED BUSINESS)

The principal transformational experiential task used in EFT and, therefore, also in EFT-T is the self–other (empty-chair) task for an interpersonal emotional injury (unfinished business), traditionally referred to as the "unfinished business task" or "empty-chair work for unfinished business" (Elliott et al., 2004; Greenberg et al., 1993). As with the two-chair task for self-criticism,

TABLE 9.2. A Framework for Reflecting on the Self–Self Two-Chair Dialogue for Problematic (Self-Evaluative) Self-Treatment for Homework

Parts enacted in the Experiencer Chair	Parts enacted in the Critic Chair
	How do I criticize (attack) myself? (Increasing awareness of the ways the client treats—e.g., criticizes, attacks, devalues—themself)
	What drives my criticism? (Examples: Wish to improve; wish to avoid interpersonal judgment and rejection; wish to earn recognition, respect, love; a sense that I deserve to be punished; see Chapters 3 and 5 on case conceptualization)
How do I feel when I am being criticized (treated badly)? (Highlighting the emotional impact—often variations of shame—that, at times, are linked to other painful emotions)	
What do I need in the face of the criticism? (Articulating the need stemming from the hurt feelings)	
	What do I feel toward the hurt, shamed, put-down, vulnerable part of me? (Bringing a reminder of compassionate experiences that may respond to the unmet needs in the vulnerable experience accessed in the Experiencer Chair)
How can I face the critic? (Reminding one of the resolve experienced in session to face and fight the Critic)	

Note. The work of Serine Warwar served as an inspiration for the development of this framework. From *Transforming Generalized Anxiety: An Emotion-Focused Approach* (p. 140), by L. Timulak and J. McElvaney, 2018, Routledge. Copyright 2018 by Routledge. Adapted with permission.

this task originates in gestalt therapy, but its use in EFT has been informed by decades of process research studies investigating the task's application (e.g., Greenberg & Foerster, 1996; Greenberg & Malcolm, 2002). The task originally was formulated as an intervention to be used in response to chronic unresolved emotional feelings in relation to a significant other; working with those feelings required them to be present in the session in an evoked manner, and there could be signs of self-interruption regarding those feelings (Elliott et al., 2004; Greenberg et al., 1993). In our conceptualization, it is used in this context but also is used more broadly in relation to past and current interpersonal triggers that bring emotional pain. Although, typically, levels of emotion arousal indicate that a client is experiencing upset in relation to another individual, in some instances, this distress may be less visible because of emotional avoidance/interruption processes (e.g., a client might say in an emotionally flat voice, "My parents are not important. I have not spoken to them for 20 years"). Thus, markers for this task can emerge in the client's narrative even in the absence of observable emotional arousal within the session.

From a transdiagnostic perspective, chronic emotional pain that has interpersonal connotations (see examples in Chapters 3 and 5) appears to be at the heart of the problem for nearly all clients irrespective of symptomatic presentation or diagnosis. In some cases, the link between interpersonal context and symptomatic presentation seems clear (e.g., "I was given the message from a significant other that I am a disappointment; so, I feel worthless and am inclined to feel down and depressed"); at other times, it may not be so clear (e.g., "I was neglected and unprotected by significant others and thus developed rituals to shield myself from scary thoughts, dangers, or images"). There are infinite idiosyncratic variants of unfinished business experiences that shape underlying emotional vulnerability.

Often, the most impactful interpersonal experiences giving rise to problematic emotion schemes are those experienced over time, particularly during developmentally pivotal times. Experiences with parents or caregivers can be especially formative, and experiences, such as feeling disproved of, being seen as a disappointment, feeling unsupported, or experiencing parents as not there or as fragile, overly anxious, terrifying, violent, or intrusive, are all frequently seen determinants of underlying emotional vulnerability. Other interpersonal experiences that may lead to the development of emotional vulnerability include those involving painful interactions with siblings, teachers, or peers in developmentally formative years (e.g., experiences of being bullied, excluded, shamed, assaulted). Painful experiences in past, recent, or even current relationships, particularly romantic relationships but also work relationships, friendships, or relationships with other family members, such as one's own children, can shape client vulnerabilities.

Although many of these experiences are historical, some may be current. Often, current interpersonal triggers of emotional pain in current relationships overlap with historical interpersonal triggers of pain rooted in early relationships. It is also possible, particularly with posttraumatic stress disorder–like traumatic difficulties, that these experiences involve relative or total strangers (e.g., perpetrators of an assault on the client, vicarious trauma resulting from witnessing another's suffering). What all these deeply painful interpersonal experiences have in common, however, is that they shape maladaptive emotion schemes centered around the emotional injury (or injuries), thus making clients susceptible/vulnerable to experiencing chronic emotional pain. This is why the empty-chair task for an interpersonal emotional injury is pivotal to EFT and to EFT-T. Indeed, in terms of case conceptualization, it is here in the context of pivotal interpersonal experiences that symptom-level presentation, problematic self-treatment, emotional avoidance, and core pain meet (see Chapters 3 and 5).

We introduce this task using the structure presented in Table 9.3. It can be seen as a variant on the original EFT formulations (Elliott et al., 2004; Greenberg et al., 1993). We emphasize that this structure primarily serves didactic purposes. Perhaps even more so than in any other task, work in this task is deeply idiosyncratic for individual clients. We try to discuss some of those variants as we outline the general structure.

Stage 1. Seeing That the Marker of Unfinished Business Is Present

The therapist introduces the empty-chair task when an appropriate marker emerges in the session that indicates that painful feelings linked to the Other are evoked. As explained earlier, this introduction can, at times, be tricky because clients may not always be clearly emotionally activated at such moments. The absence of strong feelings at moments when the client is talking about something clearly salient in relation to a significant other is one form the marker for this task takes. In such instances, the client may instead show signs of emotional interruption and constriction. The marker for this task can therefore be either the presence of distress linked to a significant other or a narrative that implies that such feelings should be present. The therapist tracks the perception of the Other through empathic exploration and invites the client to check inside as to how they feel about the described actions of the Other: "So, you are saying your mother was never there . . . How did it make you feel inside, not having her there for you?"

TABLE 9.3. Stages in the Self-Other (Empty-Chair) Task for an Interpersonal Emotional Injury (Unfinished Business)

Stage	Self Chair	Other Chair
1	Experiencing the marker: Having unfinished business, feeling hurt	
2A	Expressing pain, hurt, and anger	
2B		Enacting hurtful Other; getting core message from them
3	Accessing and differentiating core pain: Loneliness, shame, primary fear, and perhaps protective anger, if it comes	
4	Articulating and expressing unmet needs	
5		Probing for compassion, seeing the pain and unmet needs
		Stage 5A–If no compassion is coming: Highlighting rejection (message and mistreatment contained in it, highlighting the function of it)
		Stage 5B–If compassion is coming: Savoring it experientially and expressing it
6A	Building protective anger, setting a boundary to the hurtful behavior of the Other	
6B	Letting compassion in, savoring it experientially	

Note. From *Transforming Generalized Anxiety: An Emotion-Focused Approach* (p. 142), by L. Timulak and J. McElvaney, 2018, Routledge. Copyright 2018 by Routledge. Adapted with permission. The original source also cited Elliott et al. (2004).

The therapist thus spends time before initiating the dialogue to track both the client's perceptions of the Other and their actions and the client's internal emotional reactions to those perceived actions of the Other. In doing so, the therapist is, in a way, seeking to establish (a) this is how you saw the Other and (b) this is how you felt. Only once both have been established does the therapist propose the task: "So, it sounds like it left you with so much pain, not having your mom there. Could we have a look at it in an imaginary dialogue? It sounds important—as if it left you with this wound inside?"

At times, clients may hesitate to engage in such a dialogue because the subject may be incredibly painful for them. It is important that the therapist validates both the pain and the hesitation but still proposes the task. The task is an opportunity to heal the wound and restructure attendant emotion schemes or vulnerability. The therapist may recalibrate the task, checking with the client what might help them to engage in the dialogue (e.g., moving farther back in the room the chair of the Other whom the client is invited to imagine sitting there). If the dialogue involves an abuser, that person may not be brought into the dialogue until late in the process (discussed later in Stage 6A); instead, the main body of the dialogue involves another person who might have but did not protect the client (e.g., a potentially protective Other who was unavailable at the time of abuse). This is all by way of saying that the task is a fluid process with the client and therapist developing their own way of working with it. As therapy progresses, even those clients who were initially hesitant generally get used to being involved in such imaginary dialogues and, in general, engage more easily with the process.

Stage 2A. Expressing Pain, Hurt, and Anger

The unfinished business dialogue begins in the client's own chair (hereinafter called the Self Chair; see Stage 2A in Table 9.3). The therapist, as in the following hypothetical example, asks the client to imagine the person that the unfinished business relates to in the chair facing them (hereinafter called the Other Chair) and asks the client to check inside to see how they feel as they imagine the Other sitting there:

THERAPIST: Can you picture your father there (*points to the Other Chair*)? Can you see him there?

CLIENT: Yeah.

THERAPIST: So, what happens inside as you picture him there?

It is important that the therapist asks the client to picture the Other and then immediately focuses the client internally to see what feelings it brings. From our perspective, it is not that important to spend too much time picturing the Other. Once the client confirms that they see the Other, the therapist quickly redirects the client to check inside to notice how they feel. This type of quick start to the dialogue is done to clearly establish that it is an experiential activity that is happening, not something abstract or conceptual; rather, it is something that is happening in the here and now.

For this same reason, the therapist typically does not direct the client to begin saying the specific things to the imagined Other that a few minutes previously they were saying to the therapist (i.e., at the marker stage). Rather, the therapist goes for freshness: "What is happening inside, as you see him here, right now?" As the client names the feelings that are brought up by picturing the Other, the therapist invites them to express these feelings directly to the imagined Other in the Other Chair:

CLIENT: I feel uncomfortable.

THERAPIST: "I feel uncomfortable" [mirroring empathy]. So, could you tell him, "Dad, I feel uncomfortable when I picture you here."

The therapist thus facilitates the dance already described: focusing the client inside, naming aspects of the internal experience (feelings), empathizing with these feelings, and asking the client to express them. This dance heightens emotional arousal. To further facilitate emotional arousal, the therapist may ask the client to repeat statements that are particularly poignant—for instance, "Say it again: 'I have never felt heard by you.'" Overall, the therapist facilitates an unfolding of the painful experience, facilitates the client's exploration of that painful experience, and facilitates the client's expression of that painful experience to the Other. The process is underpinned by the quality of the therapist's explorative empathy, empathic affirmation, and communication of empathic understanding. At this stage in the process, clients often oscillate between expressing their inner feelings and describing what it was in the Other's behavior that was so hurtful. As the client describes the behavior of the Other that they experienced as hurtful—for example, "You never came to see me when I played football"—the therapist may ask the client to swap chairs and move to the Other Chair.

An example Stage 2A can be seen in the following transcript taken from an unfinished business dialogue between client Petra, who presented with depression and a history of trauma, and her imagined mother with whom she had most of her unfinished business dialogues:

THERAPIST: Is it okay to picture her here? (*Therapist motions toward an empty chair.*) What happens just now as you see her here?

CLIENT: I feel really small.

THERAPIST: Yeah. Tell her: "I feel . . ."

CLIENT: I feel small when I see—I feel vulnerable and scared. You scare me.

THERAPIST: Yeah, "I'm frightened of you." Tell her what you're frightened of.

CLIENT: I don't know what goes on in your head. You want to know everything about me.

THERAPIST: "And it frightens me."

CLIENT: I feel unsafe. I want boundaries. . . . And, yet, I see you at the same time, and I feel empathy and pity for you . . .

THERAPIST: "And the way you don't respect any boundary," or "I've no space for me to be myself." Can you come here, please (*points to the Other Chair*)?

Stage 2B. Enacting the Hurtful Other

In Stage 2A, clients spontaneously describe their inner feelings as well as the behavior of the Other that triggered those feelings. As the client describes the hurtful behavior of the Other, the therapist asks the client to swap to the Other Chair and enact the hurtful behavior of the Other (Stage 2B in Table 9.3)—for example, "Come here. Be your dad, the dad that never showed interest, that never came to see you at the football game. Let's do it." This step is often forgotten by trainee therapists, who swap the client to the Other Chair and instruct the client to speak as the Other (something like, "What do you say back?") without specifying that the client should actually enact the problematic behavior of the Other as just described by the client in the Self Chair. At this stage in the task, we want the client to enact what they saw as problematic in the Other both to get clarity regarding what is painful and because a vivid enactment of what is painful is likely to activate fresh pain (and thus maladaptive emotion schemes) within the session (Stage 3 in Table 9.3). The enactment of the perceived problematic aspect of the Other thus conceptually corresponds with Stage 2 in the Critic dialogue (see Table 9.1) in which the client is asked to enact the problematic self-treatment. Again, this is done to freshly activate and allow access to the painful impact of the Critic.

At this stage in the unfinished business dialogue, the therapist asks the client not only to enact the perceived problematic behavior of the Other but also to elaborate on it so that there is an idiosyncratic sense as to what actual message the perceived Other is giving to the client. For instance, in Les Greenberg's EFT for depression video (Session 2 in Greenberg & Carlson, 2007) the client, enacting her mother, elaborates on the mother's criticism of her, thereby revealing that the mother's criticism was rooted in the mother's hurt at feeling rejected by her daughter when her daughter became a teenager. Having protected her daughter in her early years, it was painful for the mother when she felt her daughter turned her back on her to go her own way. This hurt and the anger it gave rise to fueled the mother's disapproval of the client. All of this was embedded in what initially appeared to simply be the mother's disapproving judgment, and it is a good example of an idio-syncratic elaboration on the message the Other is giving to the client. In a sense, this process is about perceptual differentiation of the hurtful trigger, and it is a process that requires attunement and skill on behalf of the therapist. The therapist needs to spend time at this stage in the task helping the client both to enact the Other's behavior and to identify what message is actually being communicated to the client. With both the behavior of the Other enacted and the implicit message captured, the therapist summarizes both aspects and asks the client to move back to the Self Chair (Stage 3 in Table 9.3).

Some clients may struggle with this stage of the task because it can be difficult for them to get a sense of the Other. The therapist therefore needs to encourage the client to play with the material, reassuring the client that it is not necessary to be correct. Again, this is more about exploring the client's perceptual field rather than ascertaining what actually happened or happens in reality. For some clients, it may be too painful to enact the Hurtful Other, and here again, the therapist can reassure the client that it is more about exploring their own perceptual field than about the Other. Enacting the Other can actually serve an exposure function because it involves the client engaging with perceived hurtful aspects of the Other's behavior that they might otherwise avoid. In some situations, however (e.g., if the Other were a stranger who committed an assault), it is not appropriate to enact the Other, and we talk about these contexts later in this chapter in the section The Process of Self–Other (Empty-Chair) Task [Dialogue] for an Interpersonal Emotional Injury (Unfinished Business).

An example of Stage 2A can be seen in the following transcript from one of Petra's dialogues with her mother:

THERAPIST: Be the mom who is so transgressive, or so disrespectful of, or intrusive. Be that mom who does that.

CLIENT: [In the Other Mother's Chair] I am your mother, and I should be the most important person in your life. I feel entitled to this information and knowledge. And I don't understand why you don't want to give it to me.

THERAPIST: "And so I'm going to . . ." what? "I'm going to . . ."

CLIENT: I'll follow you. I will ask all your friends about you. You don't have anything separate to me.

THERAPIST: Right, tell her again: "You don't have anything separate to me."

CLIENT: You don't have anything separate to me.

THERAPIST: Yeah . . . "and I am doing it because"?

CLIENT: You are just an extension of me, and I know what is best for you. You do not have your own judgment. I know what your limits are and how you can be in life. You are an extension of me, and you owe me, and you should look after me.

THERAPIST: So, this is a message you are getting: "You are an extension of me, and I know your place. You should be grateful and respect me." And it is like, "If you went your way, I would feel abandoned, so you should be looking after me."

Stage 3. Accessing and Differentiating Core Pain

Once the client enacts the perceived behavior and message from the Other in the Other Chair (Stage 2B), the therapist summarizes and asks the client to move back to the Self Chair. Here, in this hypothetical example, the therapist asks the client to focus inside and see what impact the message from the Other has in the here and now (Stage 3 in Table 9.3): "Come here to your . . . own chair, see what happens . . . right now as you get that: 'You're a disappointment. I was unhappy in my life. I wanted a son to be proud of, and you turned out to be a disappointment.'" The therapist asks, "How is it to hear this right here and now?" The therapist then facilitates the client's exploration and expression of various aspects of the pain activated by the hurtful behavior of the Other. This is essentially a further elaboration on Stage 2A. At times, the client may access and express either secondary, defensive anger (e.g., "You are such a horrible father") or, even at this stage, the adaptive boundary-setting anger more typically accessed at Stage 6A. The therapist validates such anger but ensures that it does not serve the function of avoiding vulnerability and underlying hurt. The therapist therefore ensures that any such anger is expressed in the context of the hurt and the pain that the Other's actions (or nonactions) bring.

In some contexts—for example, when the Other is especially unresponsive—clients may be unable to express their hurt to the Other. In such instances, the therapist needs to improvise—for example, by asking the client to imagine a more receptive Other and express the painful feelings to them (e.g., "It hurts so much when she treats me that way. It makes me feel like I'm nothing to her") while simultaneously encouraging the client to express to the original unresponsive Other where things are (e.g., "I cannot show you my pain"). Alternatively, the pain (Stage 3) may be articulated from the position of a caring Other, or even a caring or protective Self (e.g., "I see the pain that you are going through. When she treats you this way, I see how worthless it makes you feel"). Here, the therapist might invite the client over to the Other Chair and guide them to enact a caring Other or a caring Self who describes what they see the client in the Self Chair going through. Although this aspect of the enactment is more typically characteristic of Stage 5B (see Table 9.3), here in Stage 3, it facilitates the accessing and expression of pain. For some clients, it can be easier to express the pain when that pain is looked at as if from the position of a receptive Other. Ultimately, however, it is still the client accessing and expressing the pain evoked in the here and now by the Other's treatment of them.

Overall, the therapist creatively facilitates the client to get in touch with painful feelings (variations on loneliness/sadness, shame, and fear), describe them, and express them. Throughout, the therapist seeks to remain empathically attuned while also appropriately guiding the client so that the client remains in dialogue with the Other. The constant dance between focusing inward, naming feelings, and expressing those feelings to the Other brings optimal levels of emotional arousal (see Chapter 2). Only when the client's emotions are aroused is the whole schematic structure of the core vulnerability activated and thus ready for potential transformation. To maintain productive levels of emotional arousal, the therapist remains creative—for instance, asking the client to repeatedly express the most poignant feelings and narrative. The therapist may also ask about pivotal, episodic memories that would illustrate and make vivid the hurt the client talks about (e.g., the therapist may say, "Does any memory comes to mind of when you particularly missed your dad?"). When the client volunteers a particular memory, the therapist may ask the client to reenact that memory—for example, "Be that boy on the pitch when you played that cup final . . . everybody had their father there, but your dad was not there. How does it feel inside? . . . Can you tell him, can you tell your dad, how it feels?"

An example of Stage 3 in Petra's dialogue can be seen in the following excerpts:

THERAPIST: What happens? Just check, right here right now. As she (*points to the Other Chair*) says, "You are an extension of me, and I know your place. You should be grateful and respect me. I would be upset if you resisted."

CLIENT: [In the Self Chair] I feel weak.

THERAPIST: Yeah.

CLIENT: I feel weak when you speak to me like that. I feel like you control me . . . and that I don't matter.

THERAPIST: Hmm, "I feel so . . ."

CLIENT: Insignificant (*cries*).

THERAPIST: "And it brings this sadness inside."

CLIENT: Feels so sad. It hurts so, so much.

THERAPIST: "It hurts so much. Somewhere inside, I miss . . ."

CLIENT: I miss your understanding, I miss you trusting me and giving me the freedom to make my choices, I miss you being there when I would want and in the way I would want . . .

Stage 4. Articulating and Expressing Unmet Needs

As the client expresses the core painful feelings related to the perceived actions or nonactions of the Other, the therapist asks the client to articulate what it is that they need from the Other and to express that need to the Other (Stage 4 in Table 9.3): "So, you feel so lonely on the pitch, so much missing your dad. What is it that you need from him?" It is important that this need is expressed in the context of freshly felt pain (a heartfelt need; Timulak, 2015; Timulak & McElvaney, 2018), so the right time to focus the client on articulating and expressing need is when the client's vulnerability is activated—the wound open, the pain vividly present. Typically, unmet needs are expressed directly to the Other within the dialogue, although there may be exceptions to this. For instance, if the Other were too abusive or remains too terrifying for the client, then the need—coming as it does from a very vulnerable place—may be expressed to an imagined Other who would have the potential to hear it. The client can be asked to nominate such a person (e.g., "Who would have heard what you would need? Who would see your pain?"), imagine them in the chair facing them, and express the need to them (e.g., "So, tell her how it feels inside. Tell her what you need when you feel this pain").

Typically, these needs are idiosyncratic expressions of longing for connection, recognition, or safety (O'Brien et al., 2019; see also Chapters 3 and 5, this volume). The articulation of such needs, accessed and articulated in the context of freshly felt pain, is at the core of the transition to potentially transformative experiences, such as protective anger, compassion, or grieving (A. Pascual-Leone, 2009; A. Pascual-Leone & Greenberg, 2007a). Although they may refer to past experiences (e.g., "I needed you to be there for me"), they are experienced in the here-and-now context of the fresh pain activated within the dialogue. While the client may express need in terms of the past and even in the past tense, the therapist emphasizes experience in the here and now. So, for example, the past event and the pain and attendant needs related to that past event can be brought into the here and now and experienced in the here and now, and the need, felt in the here and now, can be articulated (e.g., "Be that boy. Tell him what you need" or "I needed you, and I still need you to . . .").

An example of Stage 4 can be seen in the following excerpt from Petra's dialogue:

THERAPIST: Yeah. Yeah. What do you want to say to mom right now in this sadness? It's like . . . what is it that you need from her?

CLIENT: I wish you could love me.

THERAPIST: Right. Tell her again.

CLIENT: I need you to love me for who I am. I need you to comfort me when I am hurting.

Stage 5. Probing for Compassion: Seeing the Pain and Unmet Needs

Once the client has accessed the freshly felt pain and expressed both this pain and the need implicit in the pain to the Other, the therapist asks the client to move back to the Other Chair. At this stage, the client is asked to enact the Other—not as the client normally sees them (Stage 2B) but as the Other sitting here now, seeing and hearing the pain and need expressed in the Self Chair. The prototypical instruction in Stage 5 (see Table 9.3) is something along the following lines in this hypothetical example: "Come back here" [*points to the Other Chair*]. "Be your dad. What do you feel toward that little boy, missing you, wanting you to be there for him [the client in the Self Chair]? What do you feel toward him now? What is your response to him?" In essence, the therapist is inviting the client to be the Other, check inside, and respond to their own pain as expressed in the Self Chair only a few moments previously. The client thus does not enact the known and seen Other but, rather, a mixture of the known/seen Other and the Self in the face of the Self's own pain and unmet need. If the Other, in reality, was seen by the client as, at times, capable of being at least somewhat responsive, the likelihood of this experience of the Other coming to the fore at this point in the enactment (i.e., after witnessing the Self's freshly expressed raw pain and need) is higher (we speak more about this later). Speculatively, this may occur, in part, because perceptions or memories or the Other as caring (and not only hurtful) have been forgotten or are not readily available, and they come to the fore only in the context of the freshly witnessed pain or in the context of the unfolding dialogue, which also names difficult aspects of the relationship.

In any case, the response of the Other can come in either one of two forms (again, Stages 5A and 5B) or in a mixture of these two forms (a mixture of Stages 5A and 5B). If the client-enacted Other is nonresponsive to the pain and unmet needs (Stage 5A in Table 9.3), the therapist goes with this rejection (as in the critic dialogue) and asks the client to express this nonresponsiveness from the Other Chair: "So tell him: 'I don't see your pain. I do not know what you are talking about.'" As with the critic dialogue, this is coupled with an inquiry about what it is that blocks a compassionate response or what the function of the nonresponsiveness is: "What makes it so difficult to see his pain?" The therapist can use this delineation of the block or explication of the function of nonresponsiveness to move the dialogue onto different ground. For instance, if the client as the Other expresses that it is the Other's own vulnerability that blocks their being responsive (e.g., "I am too damaged to see what you need"), then this creates clarity for the client that the problem is with the Other and not them, and this clarity, in turn, may allow for a stronger sense of the Self as okay and thus able to stand up to the Other (Stage 6A). Indeed, the original work of Greenberg and his colleagues when researching this task (Greenberg & Foerster, 1996; Greenberg & Malcolm, 2002; Greenberg et al., 1993) pointed out that, at times, the view of the Other can change at this point in the task. In any case, the nonresponsiveness of the Other is used in Stage 6A to build protective anger toward the Other, thereby validating unmet needs from within (consolidated by affirmation from the therapist).

If the client in the position of the Other softens toward the pain and unmet needs expressed in the Self Chair (Stage 5B in Table 9.3), the therapist encourages the client to express this compassionate and caring response, as is shown in this hypothetical example:

CLIENT: [In the Other Chair, enacting the father] I did not know you missed me.

THERAPIST: And what do you feel towards him (*points to the Self Chair*), toward your son here and now?

CLIENT: I love him.

THERAPIST: Could you tell him: "I love you"?

CLIENT: I love you.

THERAPIST: And what do you feel as you are saying it?

CLIENT: I feel a lot of love, but I am also sad that I did not know, that I was not there for you.

THERAPIST: So, there is this love but also sadness. So, tell him: "I love you, and I am also sad for the time we lost and for the loss you felt, and still feel."

It is important here that the client not only expresses or offers compassion to the vulnerable Self but also savors the experience of offering it. The therapist thus invites the client to see how it feels to express compassion. The therapist wants the client to be aware of how it feels when they feel compassionate toward the Self. Although clients typically report that it feels good to express this compassion to the Self, the expression of compassion can also frequently bring sadness (as in the preceding example; see also Stage 6B). It is as if the expression of compassion invites more vulnerability but also sadness and grief for the pain that had to be endured (Stage 6B).

Clients may struggle with accessing and expressing compassion for several reasons. At times, this can be a function of suboptimal in-session processes. For instance, if the therapist does not adequately facilitate the client's accessing and expression of freshly experienced core pain (Stage 3), then there is no pain for the client in the position of Other to witness and thus nothing to elicit the client's compassion. At other times, client factors related to the nature of their injury or emotional processing style may impede the accessing or expression of compassion. Some clients may have few positive experiences of the Other in reality and thus no sense of the Other than might serve as a foundation for such compassion. Such clients may feel that it is genuinely impossible to feel any shift as the Other either because it simply does not happen experientially or because to "perform this" in the position of the Other would invalidate their perception of reality.

At other times, compassion may not be forthcoming because the client collapses into hopelessness that the Other isn't there or because avoidance tendencies make it hard for the client to truly witness the Self's pain as expressed in the Self Chair. It is important to remember that the eliciting of compassion is a process. Even if the potential for softening in the enacted Other exists, it usually takes a number of dialogues before such a shift in the enacted Other occurs (Hughes et al., 2014). The therapist and the client's work is exploratory, looking to see if the enactment of the Other in the context of felt and expressed pain and unmet needs brings a different experience of the Other. While we can speculate as to the specific processes by which such shifts occur (see Greenberg, 2015), in general, it seems to be the case that acknowledging and processing different aspects of emotional experience allow for the emergence of a more flexible picture of the Other and an openness of the memory process (that we hypothesize to be one of the potential sources of the enactment) to more differentiated recollections.

All that said, it is important to note that it is not always necessary that the response to expressed pain and unmet needs come through the client's enactment of the Other who caused the emotional injury. In many cases of assault or abuse, it would be inappropriate to even expose the client's vulnerability to the Other, let alone seek a compassionate response. In such instances, the caring response can come through the enactment of another caring person in the client's life. Whether to pursue this route is a judgment call for the therapist. While there is nothing more therapeutic than if the compassionate response comes through the enactment of the Other who caused the injury (because, experientially, this is so unexpected for the client), this may not always be possible either because it simply does not happen (i.e., the Other does not soften) or because, for reasons specific to the client's personal story, it is inappropriate to seek this.

In these instances, the softening and compassionate response can come from the enactment of some other person whom the client has experienced as caring for them. This is similar to the self-soothing dialogue discussed in Chapter 6 (the global distress soothing through an imaginary dialogue task). However, here, the soothing is directed not at symptom-level global distress but toward the underlying core pain. In other words, the caring Other enacted from the Other Chair is invited to respond not at the level of dysregulation or symptoms but instead to the freshly expressed core pain and unmet needs expressed in the Self Chair and experienced in the context of the emotional injury with the unresponsive Other. As to how this looks in practice, in the context of an Other who does not soften or from whom softening cannot or should not be invited, the therapist may ask the client (irrespective of what chair they sit in), "Was there anybody who could see your pain? Was there ever anybody who had those qualities . . . anybody you assume could understand what you feel?" As the client nominates the person, the therapist asks them to enact that person in the Other Chair, to see the client in pain in the Self Chair, and to respond to that pain—for example, "So come here, be that teacher as he sees this boy feeling so sad, missing his dad. What is his response to the boy?" If the client struggles to nominate a person from their life, they may be prompted to nominate an idealized person (e.g., an ideal parent; the therapist may suggest this collaboratively) or a nonhuman subject (e.g., a loved pet; God). In the case of God, Robert Elliott and his colleagues have written about a particularly poignant example of a client nominating God and then spontaneously enacting God's unconditional love and care for her (MacLeod et al., 2012).

A common variant of the responsive Other in the self-soothing part of this dialogue is a compassionate response from the adult Self in the Other Chair to the younger vulnerable Self in the Self Chair. In dialogues in which the client, as part of Stage 3, has enacted a younger, vulnerable Self, this variant of the enactment makes intuitive sense. In the example given earlier of the boy on the pitch who missed his absent father (Stage 3), the therapist may ask the client later in the dialogue (Stage 5) to be their adult Self now, to look at the younger Self (the boy), and to see what they feel toward the younger Self and that younger Self's pain: "So come here, be yourself as you are now, an adult. Can you see that boy? What do you feel toward him right here, right now? Can you see his pain? What would you say to him?" Many clients will be able to spontaneously access self-compassion at this point. However, even here, others may encounter a block, whether in the form of self-criticism (e.g., "I am not deserving"), a sense of hopelessness (e.g., that it would be too easy to be responsive to their younger Self from their adult's position, and that this somehow would invalidate the suffering), or some other form. The therapist acknowledges this but does not give up and may, in a creative effort to acknowledge but bypass the block, ask the client to imagine not themselves as a little boy but simply another boy of a similar age. This might be a child the client knows well (e.g., a niece), a child they know only from seeing them playing on the street, or even a universal child (e.g., "Can you look at that boy from your neighborhood who so much wants his dad to be there for him? What do you feel toward him as you see him here?"). Whatever creative path the therapist pursues, the point is to facilitate the client to look at their own pain and to explore whether doing so elicits a caring response. The process is inevitably a complex one and may hit many impasses that the therapist addresses bit by bit, both within individual dialogues but also across dialogues over the course of therapy (see the discussion later).

An example of Stage 5 can be seen in the following excerpts from one of Petra's dialogues with her mom:

THERAPIST: Be mom for a moment, and you see Petra's pain. She is saying, "I wish I could show you this pain. I wish I could be comforted by you." Be mom for a moment . . . How do you feel toward her when you see her in this pain, needing your comfort?

CLIENT: [In the Other Chair] I don't understand why you feel that way [Stage 5A, no compassion coming].

THERAPIST: Right. Tell her again: "I don't understand . . ."

CLIENT: *(speaks in a measured and detached tone)* I don't understand why you feel that way. I think you might need some professional help.

THERAPIST: And this detachment comes . . . and being dismissive, right. It's like, "I cannot see your pain. It makes me feel uncomfortable. I am almost threatened by it"?

CLIENT: [Still speaking as her mom] Yeah, I feel like you attack me and try to make me look bad and feel bad when it's not my fault.

THERAPIST: "And in my defensiveness, I then dismiss, but, in a way, it is difficult to hear that how I am with you is hurting you."

CLIENT: I do not want to hear that.

THERAPIST: And how is it to see her saying, "I want you to love me for who I am"?

CLIENT: [Still speaking as mom] I do not know how to respond.

THERAPIST: And the sense is? You sound sad.

CLIENT: I would want it to be different between us but do not know how.

THERAPIST: And what do you feel toward Petra here and now?

CLIENT: I would want to be with her [some softening coming].

THERAPIST: Can you tell her?

CLIENT: I would want to be with you, but I am not sure how I should be with you.

THERAPIST: Do you feel like judging her?

CLIENT: [Still speaking as mom] Not really.

An example of a responsive compassionate presence (Stage 5B) was present in one of Paul's dialogues (the client whose critic dialogue we tracked earlier in this chapter). The dialogue first started as a critic dialogue but then turned into a dialogue with his mother, who also was critical of him. In the dialogue, Paul revealed his hurt to his mother and set a boundary. When he enacted his mother, she eventually softened as well.

In the excerpt that follows, the therapist then returns Paul to the experience that he felt as a little boy (sad and inadequate, feelings he often now also feels) and asks him to speak to the boy from his adult Self (enacted in the Other Chair speaking to the Self Chair):

THERAPIST: I'm going to ask you as adult Paul now, okay? Can you see little Paul there (*points to the Self Chair*)? Okay, what's happening inside?

CLIENT: [In the Other Chair, speaking to the Self Chair] (*speaks in a clear voice*) Yeah, he needs support. I know you need support, and I'll give you support. Absolutely.

THERAPIST: Because when the Critic gets so loud and tells him that he does things wrong that he is deserving . . .

CLIENT: I'll protect you. I'll look after you. You're an innocent little chap, a little boy.

THERAPIST: "An innocent little chap."

CLIENT: And a lot of things happened, and you didn't deserve it. Yeah, I'll still support you.

THERAPIST: And how do you feel toward him . . .?

CLIENT: Yeah, I can support you, and I can love you. And I can help you.

THERAPIST: And do you love him?

CLIENT: I do love you. Yeah.

THERAPIST: And it's almost like I need to park that critical part . . .

CLIENT: Yeah.

THERAPIST: So, what do you like about him as a person, as a man?

CLIENT: Um (*pauses*)—you have integrity. No matter what is thrown at you, you still come back. Well done. And I am proud of you.

THERAPIST: Say it again.

CLIENT: Yeah. I am proud of you. Yeah. I love you.

Stage 6A. Building Protective Anger: Setting a Boundary

When the client-enacted Other is nonresponsive to the client's pain and need, the therapist uses this nonresponsiveness to facilitate the client's accessing and expression of boundary-setting anger. The therapist asks the client to come back to the Self Chair and see what their response is to the non-responsive Other (Stage 6A in Table 9.3). Again, this resembles the process in Stage 6A of the critic dialogue. Rather than directing the client inward (e.g., "What happens inside when he says he does not know what you are talking about?"), the therapist directs the client to respond to the nonrespon-siveness (e.g., "What is your response to 'I don't know what you are talking about'?"). Here, the therapist probes for a capacity in the client to stand up for the Self and to face the nonresponsive Other. The highlighting of the Other's nonresponsiveness is purposely used to mobilize the client's response (e.g., "Will you let him to talk to you like this?").

Again, as with the Critic, clients may have difficulty generating protec-tive anger (see Timulak, 2015). Indeed, a limited ability to access protective anger (together with a limited ability to generate self-compassion) is hypoth-esized to be a primary contributing factor behind painful feelings becoming chronic and painful feelings developing into emotional vulnerability. The inability to enact healthy boundary-setting anger is also noted for case con-ceptualization purposes: Some clients have more difficulty generating self-compassion, whereas others struggle more accessing anger. For instance, a client may become resigned to the possibility of standing up for themselves as a result of formative distressing experiences with the Other, whereby stand-ing up for the Self simply led to terrifying retaliation. Alternatively, a client may struggle to express anger to the Other as a consequence of not wanting to hurt the Other, thus remaining overly respectful and deferential in the face of mistreatment.

As with other tasks, the therapist validates every such block, naming it, empathizing with it, and asking the client to express it, while nevertheless siding with any emergent or potential capacity for self-assertion or boundary-setting. So, for example, although the therapist acknowledges the client's difficulty generating healthy anger or acknowledges what is blocking such anger, they nonetheless direct the client to identify what they really need and to express this need to the Other. If the client feels powerless to express a boundary-setting stance, the therapist may recalibrate, asking the client to express any assertiveness that they are able to express or asking the client what they would like to be able to say or do if they had the power, as this hypothetical example illustrates:

THERAPIST: You're saying, "I am unable to tell you what I deserved from you." So, tell him that.

CLIENT: I am unable to tell you what I deserved from you.

THERAPIST: "And if I had the power to tell you?" What would you say?

CLIENT: I would tell him that I deserved for him to be there for me like every son deserves it from his dad.

THERAPIST: So, tell him that.

CLIENT: I deserved for you to be there. That little boy deserved it.

As with the Critic dialogue, paradoxical interventions may occasionally be productive:

CLIENT: I am unable to face you. I am unable to tell you what I deserved.

THERAPIST: So, tell him: "I will never allow myself to feel or express that I deserved for you to be there for me. You can ignore me as you wish."

CLIENT: I won't say it.

THERAPIST: So, tell him: "I will not say it. It is not okay for me that you treat me like this."

CLIENT: It is not okay for me how you are with me.

THERAPIST: And how does it feel as you say it?

CLIENT: It feels good.

THERAPIST: So, tell him.

Facilitation of protective anger is important as a response not only when the enacted Other does not soften or respond but even in those instances in which there is softening or partial softening. Often, the enacted Other may offer a mixture of softening and nonresponsiveness (Stages 5A and 5B present together). In such instances, the therapist focuses the client not only on letting in the softer response (see Stage 6B that follows; e.g., "So, he did not know that you missed him. How is it to hear that?") but also on responding to the nonresponsive aspects of the Other (e.g., "But he is still saying that it is not a big deal. What is your response to that?"). Indeed, even when the enacted Other moves relatively quickly to a compassionate stance, it is important to acknowledge the hurtful behavior of the Other, to name it, and to set a boundary to it. Thus, work on Stage 6A is important even in the context of an enacted Other who is responsive to the Self's pain and unmet need.

An important form of Stage 6A is its enactment in the context of a perpetrator of abuse or assault. Even when the transgressing, violent, or abusive Other has not been enacted in the dialogue (and as suggested already, it is often inappropriate to enact such an individual before this point in the dialogue, i.e., at Stages 2A or 5A), self-assertion and protective anger directed at the Other can still be facilitated in its own right. The therapist, noting the client's emerging strength and assessing the client's capacity to do so, may invite the client to picture the Other in the Other Chair and express their protecting anger from a position of strength and self-esteem. This can facilitate the buildup of resolve but also can help take power away from the abuser/assaulter. When there is a just anger, there is less room for being terrified and at the mercy of a terrifying Other. Work on protective anger is thus a central and pivotal process in building the Self and in building resilience and a capacity for freedom.

Stage 6B. Letting Compassion In

If the client-enacted Other (Stage 5B) spontaneously expresses a compassionate response toward the Self, or if that response comes from the client enacting a responsive Other (including the client's current Self responding to a younger Self), the therapist asks the client to move back to the Self Chair and instructs them to see whether they can let in the compassionate response directed at them (Stage 6B in Table 9.3): "How is it to hear it, here and now, when he says, 'I love you, and I am sorry'. How is it to hear it from him here? Can you let that in?" If the client is able to let in the compassion, the therapist instructs the client to stay with the feeling. At this point, the therapist's aim is that the client not only stays with the feeling but also can savor it, noticing experientially how it feels, and bathing in it as if relaxing into it and allowing the Self be warmed or soothed by it. The exchange may look as follows:

THERAPIST: How is it to hear it, here and now, when he says, "I love you, and I am sorry." How is it to hear it from him here? Can you let that in?

CLIENT: It feels nice.

THERAPIST: So, tell him: "It feels nice."

CLIENT: It feels nice. I really appreciate it.

THERAPIST: And how does it feel inside?

CLIENT: I feel warmth.

THERAPIST: Can you tell him? "I feel such a warmth inside."

Letting in the expressed compassion deepens the experience of being compassionate toward the Self (even when this is in the context of an enacted Other). Allowing oneself to bathe in the compassion directed at the Self is also in and of itself a further act of self-compassion. Frequently, these experiences can constitute experiences of connection and closeness because the caring response of the Other is often a bid for connection and closeness. The therapist may, for instance, check in with the client: "Is he now closer to you, or how is it?" Or the therapist may facilitate an exchange, such as the following:

THERAPIST: Can you sense his presence?

CLIENT: Yeah, I feel it.

THERAPIST: Can you say it to him? "I have a sense you are really here, and it feels so nice."

Experiences such as these—of being cared for, of having a sense of the Other's loving or supporting presence, of a sense of connection—are antidotes to experiences of loneliness, rejection, or fear. This is their healing potential. Interestingly, such experiences often lead to a spontaneous grieving: "It is a pity we did not have it before." This grieving, while still a form of sadness, is an expression of adaptive sadness (A. Pascual-Leone, 2009; A. Pascual-Leone & Greenberg, 2007a) and tends to have a letting-go quality that stands in marked contrast to the overbearingly painful experiences of loss and loneliness previously expressed. The therapist can support an adaptive grieving process by facilitating and encouraging its expression while simultaneously validating the healing experience of being cared for that just happened in the session.

As with Stage 6B in the critic dialogue, clients frequently struggle to let compassion in (see Timulak, 2015). Self-criticism, a sense of undeservedness, or apprehension that it would be naive to believe the Other, may emerge as blocks to the letting in of compassion. It is important that the therapist acknowledges such blocks, explores their function with the client, names them, and encourages the client to express them while simultaneously inviting the client to see how being an object of compassion feels inside. A delicate balance is required because the therapist does not want to invalidate the client's suffering and difficulty (for some clients, the very idea that an imaginary dialogue could heal their suffering might feel invalidating of the suffering they went through in life). The balancing exchange may look as follows:

THERAPIST: How is it to hear it, here and now, when he says, "I love you, and I am sorry." How is it to hear it from him here? Can you let that in?

CLIENT: Not really. It is too late for you to be saying this.

THERAPIST: He just came too late. So tell him: "You came too late."

CLIENT: It is too late for you. It is too late for us.

THERAPIST: It is too late, nothing can be done . . . (*pauses*) But how is it to hear it, here and now: "I love you." How is it to hear?

CLIENT: It feels nice.

THERAPIST: Okay, so tell him: "It feels nice, but I also feel a lot of hopelessness for what we lost."

CLIENT: It feels nice, but it is a pity that we lost so much, and I am also angry about that.

The preceding example also shows that Stage 6B is often accompanied by Stage 6A. The client may let in compassion and express grieving, but they may also express boundary-setting anger. It is important that the therapist facilitates all of these aspects of the process, which, as with all aspects of this work, varies significantly and in highly idiosyncratic ways from individual to individual.

In the example with Petra, we see some elements of both Stages 6A and 6B in the following excerpts:

THERAPIST: [Speaking to the client who is now seated in the Self Chair] So, she does not understand but does not want to judge you and would want for you to get on. What happens with this here and now? What's your response?

CLIENT: [In the Self Chair] I know deep down that you hurt just as much I do. And that makes me sad because I don't want you to hurt . . .

THERAPIST: "I see you are lost and don't know . . ."

CLIENT: I think maybe the things that makes me so sad is that you don't understand.

THERAPIST: And when she says that she does not judge you here and that she would want you to be closer . . .

CLIENT: It is new to hear that, but it makes me sad (*cries*). I am also not sure what to do with it.

THERAPIST: It is new.

CLIENT: It is sad to see you sad, but I know I need to look after myself.

THERAPIST: "So, there is that loss, but also that I carry on."

CLIENT: I want to be me.

THERAPIST: Right. Tell her: "I want to be."

CLIENT: I want to be. I want to have a sense of identity separate to you, separate to your opinion of me.

THERAPIST: What does it feel like as you say this to her?

CLIENT: Very sad but, also, I feel some strength.

THERAPIST: Right, so tell her it brings this sadness but also some strength.

CLIENT: It brings this sadness to have to say this to you. I am me, and I'm separate to you. I don't want to be defined by what you think I should be.

THERAPIST: Yeah. Tell her what you are.

CLIENT: I'm a grown woman with her own life and her own marriage that doesn't rely on your opinion . . . I would like you to respect me . . . And I would like you to find a way to make yourself happier.

THE PROCESS OF THE SELF-OTHER (EMPTY-CHAIR) TASK FOR AN INTERPERSONAL EMOTIONAL INJURY (UNFINISHED BUSINESS)

As with other tasks, the description of the self–other (empty-chair) task for an interpersonal emotional injury (unfinished business) outlined earlier (and in Table 9.3) is a simplification of a fluid process. Again, it is outlined in this manner primarily for didactic purposes, and its presentation in the form of a sequence of stages should not be taken as implying that the process is either straightforward or linear. There will be lots that the therapist will need to consider. For example, it may not always be appropriate to engage in all stages. Some processes may be more about pure grieving (i.e., Stages 3, 4, 5B, and 6B), whereas others may be more about confronting the Other (e.g., in the case of a perpetrator of assault; see Stage 6A). At times, one dialogue may be embedded in another. For example, an empty-chair dialogue may involve exploration of the pain of being unsupported by an otherwise caring Other in the context of confronting an assaulter with the process moving between these two dialogues. Similarly, a dialogue may begin with another whom the client currently feels hurt by before transforming into a dialogue with a past Other whom the client experienced as similarly hurtful. Typically, there is also a link between the self-critic (e.g., "I am not doing anything right") dialogue and unfinished business (e.g., "I disappointed my mother").

As with the critic task, the unfinished business task is fundamental to the core therapeutic work with chronic pain and emotional vulnerability. Inevitably, therefore, many symptom-level tasks (see Chapters 6–8) are in some way linked to either or both the self-critic and unfinished business tasks. For instance, the worry of social or interpersonal judgement (e.g., "I will be ridiculed") in social anxiety may be linked to an underlying self-criticism (e.g., "I am flawed") that, in turn, may be linked to unfinished business (e.g., "My father saw me as a disappointment"). Therefore, irrespective of where the process of therapeutic exploration starts, it inevitably will come to some variant of an underlying self–self or self–other process that is defining of the client and their emotional vulnerability.

Individual unfinished business dialogues pertaining to central interpersonal relationships (e.g., parents) typically also constitute part of a series of dialogues that take place across the course of therapy. The progression toward more adaptive experiences (e.g., protective anger in the face of mistreatment, or compassion directed at the wounded Self), therefore, take time, and any one particular dialogue may end up in what is experienced as an impasse or a partial impasse. When this occurs, it is important that the therapist acknowledges where the client is, validates this, and communicates that they see (or witness; Timulak, 2014) the client's suffering. The therapist acknowledges what still needs to be worked on and points to any adaptive processes that were present in the dialogue. Transforming vulnerability is a process, not a one-stop shop.

In Table 9.4, we outline a framework that the therapist and client can use to reflect on the task. This framework can also be used as a basis for homework aimed at building awareness or consolidating progress made in therapy. Again, we do not prescribe in what format this framework should be used, but it can help clients to be aware of aspects of the Other's behavior that they found hurtful, to better know their own vulnerability, to reflect on how to seek and let in the support they need, and to plan for how to support themselves so they can set desired boundaries.

CONCLUSION

In this chapter, we looked at the process of working with core client emotional vulnerability and described the two main tasks involved in this work: (a) the self–self two-chair dialogue for problematic (self-evaluative)

TABLE 9.4. A Framework for Reflecting on the Self-Other (Empty-Chair) Task for an Interpersonal Emotional Injury (Unfinished Business) for Homework

Parts enacted in the Self Chair	Parts enacted in the Other Chair
	What was hurtful in the Other's behavior? (Increasing awareness of the things that hurt)
	What was the implied message? (Example: Hypotheses about the Other's motivations)
How do I feel when I am being treated like this? (Highlighting the emotional impact of the Other's behavior—e.g., loneliness/sadness, shame, fear)	
What do I need (what had I needed) when I am (when I was) treated like this? (Articulating the need stemming from the hurt feelings, identifying to whom need could be expressed)	
	What do I or the Other (caring or caring part of the Other) feel toward the hurt, vulnerable part of me? (Bringing a reminder of compassionate experiences that may respond to the unmet needs in the vulnerable experience accessed in the Self Chair)
How can I protect myself when I am treated in a way that hurts? (Reminding one of the resolve in the session to face and fight the perceived mistreatment)	

Note. From *Transforming Generalized Anxiety: An Emotion-Focused Approach* (p. 158), by L. Timulak and J. McElvaney, 2018, Routledge. Copyright 2018 by Routledge. Adapted with permission.

self-treatment and (b) the self–other (empty-chair) task for an interpersonal emotional injury (unfinished business). These two tasks are at the core of EFT, and they are, therefore, also at the core of EFT-T. It is in these tasks, and in the fluid movement between these and other tasks both within sessions and across therapy as a whole, that the therapist aims to facilitate the accessing and transformation of those core chronic painful feelings underpinning client distress and symptomatic presentations.

10

ADAPTING THERAPEUTIC STRATEGY AND CONSOLIDATING CHANGES

Emotion-focused therapy (EFT) is an exploratory—not a prescriptive—therapy. This means there is no linear protocol for how therapy should unfold, and this contrasts with cognitive behavior therapy (CBT) approaches (e.g., Barlow, Farchione, Sauer-Zavala, et al., 2017). Although EFT itself is exploratory in nature and, in practice, is open-ended, most empirical studies examining it have done so in the context of 16- to 20-session interventions. On the basis of our clinical experience, we recommend EFT (or for that matter, any psychotherapeutic intervention) lasting for up to a year. In some ways, this can be considered an optimal period of treatment because it allows for the gradual integration of in-session processes into everyday life while also allowing the opportunity to work with a client during different annual tasks and events (e.g., Christmas, holidays, school year).

In this chapter, we try to outline an overall therapeutic strategy and give examples of how treatment may unfold over the course of a brief format (up to eight sessions), short-term format (up to 20 sessions), and a year-long or longer format (40-plus sessions). We address common difficulties the therapist encounters in the therapeutic process. We already covered some

https://doi.org/10.1037/0000253-011
Transdiagnostic Emotion-Focused Therapy: A Clinical Guide for Transforming Emotional Pain, by L. Timulak and D. Keogh

of those difficulties in previous chapters, so here we provide only a short summary. We also address common issues therapists may encounter when providing transdiagnostic emotion-focused therapy (EFT-T). And we discuss the delivery of EFT in different formats and as a part of comprehensive health care and psychological provision.

OVERALL THERAPY PROCESS: INTERPLAY BETWEEN SYMPTOMS AND CORE PAIN

The overall process of EFT-T marries the client's presenting issues with the EFT-T theory of symptom-level distress and underlying vulnerability. It is critical that the therapist forges an alliance with the client early on. An important part of this alliance-building process is the successful matching of the client's understanding of their own difficulties with the therapist's offered rationale for EFT-T. The therapist's conceptualization therefore has to be relevant to the client, and the treatment rationale needs to sound both relevant to the client's presenting issues and credible (see Chapters 4 and 5). As we have stated many times, all the work of therapy, including such alliance formation, takes place within the context of a caring and safety-promoting relationship. This genuine, caring, and validating relationship is transformative in and of itself but also underpins the therapist's skillful endeavors to help the client engage in emotion-focused work. This relationship thus constitutes a core aspect of the treatment across therapy, and any alliance ruptures need to be attended to accordingly. One of the main features of emotion-focused work is the therapist's skillful interweaving of exploration of client narrative and activation of the chronically painful experiences that pertain to those narratives and that represent the client's core underlying emotional vulnerability (or core pain). As we have already elaborated on, these core chronic painful emotions are the source of suffering and symptomatic presentation.

Work on underlying emotional vulnerability is only possible if the client has resources that allow them to touch on the painful aspects of emotional experiences without being overwhelmed by them. For this purpose, the therapist ensures that the client is able to regulate their emotional experiences to the extent that they do not feel overwhelmed and dysregulated. In the case of more emotionally fragile clients, more regulation-focused work may be required (see Chapter 6). Overall, however, the therapist is trying to facilitate a focus on, and an activation of, core painful chronic emotions (emotional vulnerability; see Chapter 9). Therapeutic effort may then need to focus on helping the client access chronic painful feelings and overcome any emotional avoidance that may be part of their emotional processing style (see Chapter 7). This includes facilitating the client to acknowledge and respect the self-protective role and function of avoidance while also freeing their capacity to not be so restricted by it.

Major obstacles to transformational work targeting core vulnerability are symptoms that typically involve some form of self-protection (often avoidance or the dampening of painful, or potentially painful, emotional experiences; see Chapter 8) and alliance ruptures in the therapeutic relationship (see Chapter 4). It is important that alliance ruptures are attended to, and successfully doing so can in and of itself constitute a corrective emotional experience as well as facilitate a productive refocusing on client core pain and its transformation (we discuss this process in Chapter 4). Work with symptoms involves bringing their nature and function to the client's awareness while simultaneously allowing the client to experience their impact and emotional cost. This process typically leads to the client's letting go of costly self-protective processes (e.g., self-rumination, worry) or setting a boundary to experientially burdening self-processes (e.g., setting a boundary to rumination, to worry). In terms of relational processes, this may mean increasing awareness regarding the self-protective nature of relational behavior (e.g., seeking reassurance) and its interpersonal effect on and cost to the clients' relationships (e.g., the impact of a client's overly protective behavior involving constantly checking on and seeking reassurance from independence-seeking teenage children). This awareness typically facilitates the client to be self-accepting and self-affirming regarding the adaptive aspects of emotional vulnerability and interpersonal need-based relational stances while they also are self-compassionate and self-protective in a more adaptive way (e.g., being open about what they are actually anxious about while recognizing the limits of other's reassurance).

The main transformational work targets underlying vulnerability. It is focused on helping the client to stay with their chronic painful feelings, differentiate them, and articulate the unmet needs embedded in them. This work then is closely followed with the generation of compassionate responses to underlying vulnerability and unmet needs as well as the setting of adaptive anger-based boundaries to any pain bringing mistreatment by the self or others. Most of this transformational work in EFT-T happens in imaginary (chair) dialogues with problematic parts of the Self or with imagined Others in which the perceived, pain-eliciting behavior of the Other is enacted (see Chapter 9).

The therapist's strategy throughout the course of treatment is thus informed by a series of interrelated aims: (a) establishing the relational safety and collaboration necessary to allow painful emotions to surface in the session; (b) overcoming emotional dysregulation, overregulation (emotional processing), and problematic/unproductive symptoms; and (c) transforming underlying emotional vulnerability (problematic emotion schemes) by the generation of adaptive emotional experiences. Although the transformation of core pain is the main focus of therapy, the establishment of a therapeutic relationship and the working through of emotional processing difficulties and problematic symptoms are prerequisite to that core work but also continue to constitute a central aspect of that core work (e.g., emotional processing/symptom-level work contains within it relational work, and both emotional processing/symptom-level and relational work are embedded in the transformation of underlying vulnerability).

Thus, although a therapist may favor a relatively early focus on transformational work, this type of work is possible only if relational safety exists and if emotion processing (avoidance, dysregulation) or symptom-related issues are not in the way. When such issues do exist, they become the immediate focus of therapeutic work. These simple strategic guidelines can be embedded into the work of an EFT therapist. The exploratory and experiential nature of EFT also facilitates an evolution in the clients' and therapists' understanding (case conceptualization) of the client's emotional, intrapersonal, and interpersonal difficulties, and the therapist can thus readjust their therapeutic strategies throughout the course of therapy. While each client's therapy is idiosyncratic in nature and follows an idiosyncratic course, there are also certain commonalities that can be seen across sequential phases of therapy, to which we now turn our attention, doing so in the context of short-term, long-term, and brief therapy.

SHORT-TERM THERAPY

EFT has primarily been studied in the context of a short-term format (up to about 20–25 sessions; Timulak et al., 2019). This has been the case primarily for pragmatic reasons because this time frame corresponds more closely with the time frame adopted by many (public, in our context) services offering therapy; thus, it lends itself to the process of seeking research funding for the purposes of conducting randomized controlled trials. It also corresponds with intervention norms established by pivotal (often CBT) empirical studies. Given that sessions are typically weekly, 20 to 25 sessions amounts to 4 to 6 months of therapy. This is a sufficient period for both the therapist and the client to have a sense of how experiences in therapy interact with life events happening outside the therapy room. It allows experiences in therapy to inform the actions of the client in their everyday life and allows for ensuing reflection and processing to take place in therapy. For these reasons, we suggest that, in general, this is an optimal time frame for a meaningful therapeutic experience within EFT-T.

Beginning (Sessions 1 and 2)

The EFT-T therapist, as with any other EFT therapist, starts with seeking to forge a therapeutic alliance. The therapist attempts to reach agreement on the goals and tasks of therapy while also seeking to develop an emotional bond with the client (see Chapter 4; Bordin, 1979). The EFT therapist tries to meet the client's conceptualization of their presenting issues with the therapist's own conceptualization and corresponding treatment rationale, which the therapist offers the client in the context of a caring and validating relationship. In Chapter 4, we present examples of relationship-building strategies involving the provision of treatment rationale and transdiagnostic conceptualization. Here, the therapist often needs to acknowledge the symptomatic presentation and the suffering it brings albeit while focusing on those underlying emotional vulnerabilities that fuel the symptom presentation. The art of building a working relationship is in the balance of focusing on symptom-level work that respects and builds on the client's own understandings while also focusing on more in-depth work attending to core vulnerability.

The initial sessions are focused on empathic exploration that allows the client to describe the nature of their difficulties. While the client does so, the therapist follows the client's narrative, endeavoring to facilitate the latter's elaboration, unpack nuances, and share their own emerging understanding with the client. The therapist also focuses on the interplay between client perceptions and internal feelings, particularly those that are most painful. Here, the therapist may, somewhat uncharacteristically for EFT, also gather some relevant information about the client's current close, or otherwise important, relationships; the client's perceptions and experiences of these relationships; and information on intrapersonal processes (self-treatment and its impact) in the context of those relationships. The therapist may also inquire about the client's life projects and about any major events or interpersonal experiences (e.g., traumas) that may have played a pivotal emotional role in the past. The therapist observes the client's idiosyncratic emotional processing style and may metacommunicate and check their understanding of it (e.g., "So, you are saying you can easily get very upset").

Some clients offer a narrative of their experience in a way that balances their experience of symptoms with an appreciation of core vulnerabilities and insight into both inter- and intrapersonal aspects of their lives. However, not all client narratives inform the therapist in such an EFT-compatible way, and the therapist may need to be more inquisitive or may need to prompt the client to change pace or focus. In any case, the therapist has the freedom to collaboratively, and in a caring and validating way, explore for triggers of pain, nature of problematic self-treatment, and nature of emotional processing style (e.g., dysregulated, avoidant).

Although this assessment may occur in the context of a referral or as part of an initial intake screening conducted by the agency in which the therapist works, an important goal at this very early stage of therapy is to assess whether the client can benefit from EFT-T for depression, anxiety, and related disorders, and that interventions for other problems, such as addiction or psychosis, are not instead indicated. The initial part of therapy is typically accomplished when both the client and the therapist agree that they will work together. The client has an initial sense as to what EFT involves, and the therapist has a sense as to whether EFT is an appropriate therapy and whether individual EFT (and not, e.g., couples therapy) is the appropriate format. The potential focus of therapy (i.e., the underlying vulnerability) may also have begun to emerge. For clients who first attend in a state of crisis or who are very fragile, this initial phase may also constitute a form of support and containment.

Middle (Session 3 to About Three to Five Sessions Before Therapy Ends)

Traditionally, EFT was conceptualized as client-centered relational conditions supplemented with experiential work, with the recommendation that experiential work, such as chair tasks, be used from Session 4 onward (Greenberg et al., 1993). This recommendation was made with a view to the necessity of building a therapeutic relationship and alliance that could sustain the more evocative work that would take place across the course of therapy. This principle applies to all stages of therapy, and, thus, a sustained focus on the quality of the alliance is defining the entire working phase of therapy. The relationship is not something that is established once and for all at the beginning of therapy. The therapist constantly monitors whether the client feels interpersonally okay with them, whether any ruptures need to be focused on, and that experiential work does not become intolerable for the client (see Chapter 5). Nothing productive can happen in therapy without a solid relationship, and if the relationship is in any way under threat, attempts to mitigate those threats or repair any ruptures that have occurred need to become the focus. All regulating and transformational work occur in a relational context, and it is imperative that the client has a real experience of being cared for with compassion by their therapist as well as feeling validated, recognized, acknowledged, and affirmed by their therapist.

That said, in our experience with clients who are not too emotionally fragile or easily emotionally dysregulated, the therapist may, as early as Session 2—although more typically from Session 3—at an appropriate marker, initiate experiential work. This gives the client a sense relatively early on of what therapy will actually entail. With clients who are more dysregulated or emotionally fragile, experiential work may take the form of regulating tasks, such as clearing a space or symptom-level Soothing (see Chapter 6). With clients who are able to tolerate their emotional experiences and are not distressed to the level of dysregulation, the therapist, again at an appropriate marker, may initiate either symptom-level (e.g., worry task) tasks or tasks focused on underlying vulnerability (critic or unfinished business task).

The actual task that becomes the focus of a given session always depends on the in-session presentation and the presence of an appropriate marker. In many cases, early on in therapy, markers for symptom-level tasks may predominate because this is often the focus of the client's attention as well as the reason for their presenting to therapy. When the therapist initiates a symptom-level task, it is important that they shift focus from symptoms to any underlying emotional vulnerability should the client reach a juncture that signals the presence of such underlying emotional vulnerability (e.g., self-criticism, unfinished business emerging in the context of a worry dialogue), This is particularly important in early dialogues because this symptom-to-underlying vulnerability shift early on in therapy informs both the therapist's and client's conceptualization of the client's difficulties. As therapy progresses, the primary focus remains on underlying vulnerability. However, if symptoms serve as a barrier to working on underlying vulnerability or they remain strongly present in the client's life despite therapeutic progress regarding underlying vulnerability, it is important that attention is also paid to them. From early on, the therapist thus maintains a primary focus on underlying vulnerability but also keeps tracks of symptomatic difficulties.

Theoretically, we initially thought that the transformation of core chronic painful feelings (core emotional vulnerability) would perhaps automatically also bring symptomatic change, but in our clinical experience, this is only partially the case, and symptom-level work may therefore need to be present to a certain extent, even in the later stages of therapy (Timulak & McElvaney, 2016, 2018). That said, we are aware that a focus on symptoms can also have an avoidance function, so a finely balanced and thinly sliced approach is required that focuses primarily on chronic painful feelings (underlying vulnerability) but includes periodic checking on and working with symptom-level presentation when appropriate in-session markers indicate this is warranted. Given that symptoms often serve an avoidance function, it is important that the therapist does not only stay at the level of working with symptoms, thus inadvertently staying in an avoidance loop with the client (e.g., looking at the worry process in everyday situations rather than attending to the specific pain the worry seeks to mitigate).

Some clients with anxiety difficulties (e.g., generalized anxiety, social anxiety) may have a tendency to be preoccupied with their symptoms without awareness of the avoidance function of this preoccupation. Special attention needs to also be paid to openly avoidant processes, such as self-interruption (see Chapter 7), particularly in the case of chronically emotionally constricted clients. While it is particularly important with this type of client to focus on the interruption/avoidance process, it is also important that related tasks (i.e., self-interruption dialogue) are not the first experiential tasks initiated by the therapist. As we explain in Chapter 7, the self-interruption dialogue requires a sophisticated intrapsychological awareness, and thus it is better, at first, to try by alternate means to at least partially bypass the interruption/avoidance. At some stage, the remaining or dominating constriction is likely to become the focus of therapy and may even become a central focus of therapy as the therapist seeks to try to broaden the client's ability to access, experience, and express an inner emotional world.

The main, or middle, phase of therapy typically contains a chair dialogue almost every single session. In our experience (Timulak et al., 2020; Timulak & McElvaney, 2018), each major process, whether self-critic, unfinished business, or main symptom-level difficulty, requires three to five chair dialogues per course of therapy. This may mean that more than one type of dialogue occurs in a given session (e.g., a worry dialogue combined with a self-critical dialogue, or a critic dialogue combined with an unfinished business dialogue). In general, we promote the flexible movement from one type of dialogue to another because it maps onto the real interplay of symptom-level processes with underlying intrapersonal and interpersonal dynamics. We also see that productive processes in the context of one type of process (e.g., standing up to one's own worrying) positively influence other processes (e.g., standing up to the unresponsive Other). At times, this can also be used strategically by the therapist so that, for example, the client who is able to stand up to the imagined Other can be asked within a short period to stand up to their own Critic, something they may have previously been unable to do (see Chapter 9).

Depending on the length of therapy, there is often time to focus on other difficulties besides the main symptom or core intrapersonal/interpersonal issue that clients experience (even here, though, such issues tend to be linked to underlying core vulnerability). Thus, the therapist and client may spend time looking at less central processes (e.g., a less dominant symptom, a less dominant interpersonal injury) in a more limited time frame (one to two dialogues). As the therapy approaches its end, the therapist also checks in with the client regarding what they need to focus on in the remaining time available to them. Work on increasing awareness and supporting the consolidation of transformational experiences (e.g., through homework; see reflective frameworks offered in previous chapters) may come to the fore at this point.

The Ending of Therapy

The ending of therapy is embedded in its beginning. The available time frame defines the nature and scope of the work (see the next sections on long-term therapy and brief therapy). In short-term therapy, the ultimate ending is brought to the client's awareness early on: five to six sessions before the planned ending. It is thematized in the context of accomplishments in therapy as well as outstanding issues. The work may then focus on reflecting on accomplishments and learning as well as on the consolidation of these developments in the client's life outside of therapy. The future and the potential scenarios or difficulties it may bring are discussed, and the client's prospective use of resources in the context of possible future crises can be considered.

Some clients may have difficulty ending therapy because they get anxious about losing the therapist and the therapist's support. Similarly, clients who have endured a lot of, or major, losses in life may also be wary of ending. We recommend focusing explicitly on this anxiety, recognizing the anxiety, affirming the freedom of individuation, and facilitating and processing grieving. We also acknowledge here that therapist flexibility around ending may be appreciated by some clients, so we are open to staggered sessions toward the end or even the possibility, in some contexts, of offering booster sessions. In any case, we strongly advise that this is explicitly framed as a staggered ending or set of booster sessions so that boundaries are clear and respected. Endings can thus also be concretely worked with as real-life examples of triggers of the client's vulnerability.

LONG-TERM THERAPY

While the type of EFT we describe in this book has been studied mainly in the context of a short-term format of up to 20 to 25 sessions, in private clinical practice it is routinely offered in a more open-ended format. We see yearlong therapy as a particularly good time frame for the course of therapy. Within the year, the client experiences many typical triggers of their pain and can also integrate any transformational experiences from sessions into their everyday life. A yearlong therapy facilitates therapeutic engagement with the different personal and professional tasks and challenges that arise in the course of a calendar year (e.g., summer holidays, winter holidays, birthdays, anniversaries) and also allows the client to approach these situations in an experiential manner supported by their continuing attendance at therapy. These tasks, challenges, and times of year thus interplay with the in-session therapeutic process. That said, a yearlong therapy does not need to have the same intensity and frequency across its duration. In our experience, we tend to have weekly sessions at the beginning (to forge an alliance and build momentum) and in the main working phase of therapy. Later on, let's say, after 6 to 8 months, sessions may become staggered so that they occur biweekly or every third week with perhaps a 4-week checkup for the last session. Obviously, therapy may also continue on a more intensive (weekly) basis and last across several years, but, from our perspective, it then becomes a more supportive than highly experiential EFT type of therapy.

In terms of the actual course of long-term therapy, we do tend to start with the experiential work (chair work) as early as in short-term therapy. We also tend to do a lot of experientially focused work, like chair tasks, in the first 20 to 30 sessions of therapy. After that, the work becomes more reflective, albeit remaining exploratory and emotion-focused and with episodic use of experiential tasks and dialogues. The initial course of experiential work usually focuses on core emotional vulnerability and symptoms. Hopefully, the client, as a result of that work, has transformational experiences. The reflective/exploratory work in the later phase of therapy then looks at the interplay of core emotional vulnerabilities with everyday triggers, incorporating experiences of different feelings with these familiar contexts or trying to do something different in these contexts. Further experiential work often targets the painful experiences that come along familiar lines. These can be conceptualized as known and expected challenges or, in some cases, as setbacks. We do not expect clients to become totally emotionally resilient. We assume that emotional vulnerabilities remain and clients remain susceptible to feeling core chronic painful feelings. We, however, hope that clients are more capable of generating balancing feelings of compassion, grieving, and healthy boundary-setting anger. In long-term therapy, we thus offer further assistance to support clients in their pain and vulnerability as well as further attempts to generate and consolidate adaptive emotional experiences in the context of vulnerability.

BRIEF EFT-T

We now have the experience of studying EFT-T delivered in a brief format of up to eight sessions. This brief format has been delivered in a student counseling context primarily focused on anxiety presentations (O'Connell Kent et al., 2021). The work in this format does not differ dramatically from short-term work, although it can be considered more episodic with more emphasis on reflection, homework, or the use of supplemental materials. In this format, the appropriateness of referrals is central. Clients have to be sufficiently functional, and depression, anxiety, or related disorder presentations should not be at the more severe end of the spectrum. Experiential chair work begins earlier, typically in Session 2. There is also an explicit focus on working with symptoms (see Chapters 6–8) early on because this is what typically brings clients to therapy.

The therapist focuses as early as possible on underlying vulnerability and any problematic self-treatment or interpersonal emotional injuries that arise. Chair work is present in virtually every single session, and particular care is taken to ensure that before the sessions ends, there is ample time left for reflecting on experiential work and for devising any potential homework. The in-session experiential work is thought of as islands of experience that the client is then invited to reflect on and devise plans in relation to. Such plans are aimed at supporting further awareness outside the session of processes explored in the session and at supporting and consolidating any transformational experiences that may have happened in the session. From the beginning, the work focuses on preparing for the ending of therapy and preparing for future crises. Psychoeducational materials (Kwatra et al., in press) can be used and supports that may be relevant to the client in the future identified.

CHALLENGES IN THE THERAPEUTIC PROCESS

Our previous publications (Timulak, 2015; Timulak & McElvaney, 2018) devoted sections to working with challenges in the therapeutic process. In writing this book, we aimed, as we went along, to address difficulties that might arise. Thus, in the corresponding chapters, we present specific strategies as they relate to forging a therapeutic alliance, fostering emotional regulation, overcoming emotional avoidance, addressing symptomatic presentation, and accessing and transforming underlying emotional vulnerability. Indeed, the work as a whole assumes that there are difficulties in the therapeutic process. These difficulties are actually defining of the therapeutic process. Clients are stuck and seek targeted help in the form of psychotherapy precisely because their usual emotional processing strategies are not working. Challenges in the therapeutic process are therefore best conceptualized as a natural part of the process of trying to help clients overcome their presenting issues.

The most fundamental challenge in EFT-T, as in any other psychotherapy, is strain on the collaborative nature of the therapeutic relationship (see Chapter 4). Such difficulty has the potential to be present in any therapeutic relationship because client vulnerability has interpersonal connotations. It can be further compounded by the therapist's lack of awareness and potential insensitivity to the client's background, identity, or cultural references (Levitt et al., 2019; see also Chapter 4, this volume). The actions or non-actions of the therapist may then trigger emotional pain for the client. The therapist's capability to reach out and offer an interactional stance that goes authentically beyond what may constitute a trigger for the client is important in facilitating the client's access to underlying core pain and unmet needs embedded in it. This in itself constitutes a corrective interpersonal experience that is further broadened and solidified as the client, in the context of their relationship with the therapist, processes underlying pain and unmet needs, and generates new and adaptive internal emotional responses to that underlying vulnerability.

One aspect of the therapist's skill set that facilitates client engagement in the therapeutic process is the ability to optimally use experiential tasks. Given that these tasks are highly evocative, it is necessary that the therapist be able to scaffold them in such a way that the client can engage in the therapeutic process on a level that they can benefit from. This is a complex process within which the therapist eases the client into the task while also coaching (Greenberg, 2015) the client to immerse themself in the experiential process such that healing or transformational experiences can be accessed. We described the details of such work in Chapters 6 through 9.

For more emotionally fragile clients, the main difficulty may be a propensity to feel emotionally overwhelmed or become emotionally dysregulated, particularly early on in the therapeutic process. Work on emotion regulation (see Chapter 6) then becomes the focus with tasks, such as clearing a space, and experiential soothing strategies, including breathing and symptom-level/ emotion-dysregulation–focused self-soothing, being typically used. Their use may not be without difficulty, as we outline in Chapter 6. These more containment-based strategies are, however, typically coupled early on in therapy with more underlying vulnerability-focused work (e.g., self-critic, unfinished business), and an increased capacity to stay with core pain or to access boundary-setting anger or self-compassion also tends to have an emotionally regulating impact.

Inaccessibility of emotional experiences and restricted emotional expressivity are major obstacles to therapeutic progress and need to be focused on if they present a difficulty in accessing those underlying core painful emotions that need to be transformed. In Chapter 7, we outline strategies for trying to overcome these difficulties. We also devote space to describing the two-chair dialogue for self-interruption, a task that specifically targets interruption/restriction and that can be used when such processes constitute a chronic restriction or present a major obstacle to any other work. We highlight the importance of bringing the interruption process to awareness, of validating the protective function of interruption, and of highlighting its experiential cost (e.g., physical symptoms, behavioral withdrawal, and the missing out on being active or connected). Broadly speaking, the difficulty with such processes lies in balancing protection with cost. In Chapter 7, we discuss the nuances of this type of work together with difficulties that the therapist may encounter.

The therapist also needs to be aware of varying clients' baselines regarding how emotionally accessible they are. What can be significant progress in one client's access to emotions and their expression may for another simply constitute an entry point to getting in touch with emotion (Warwar & Greenberg, 1999). Therapists thus need to calibrate their expectations in that regard and not forget that each client is their own benchmark in terms of emotion accessibility and expression. Broader societal contexts and culturally sanctioned or dominant rules regarding emotional awareness and expression may impact the client's emotional awareness and expression in the session. Stereotypic gendered socialization may affect client comfort with, awareness of, and expression of emotion in the session with the manner in which these processes manifest also depending on who their therapist is. Work roles (e.g., being a soldier, being a pilot) may emphasize (for good reasons) control and restriction of emotional experience and expression. In addition, particular family cultures may powerfully socialize clients in how they are with their emotions. All of these potentialities need to be considered by the therapist, the developmental sociocultural context negotiated, and the work scaffolded to optimally allow the client to engage in emotion-focused work to the degree that they are capable of while still pursuing the principles outlined in this and other EFT writings.

Chapter 8 covers various types of work with symptoms, such as worry, ruminations, obsessions, and compulsions, as well as interventions to address symptoms of trauma. Symptomatic presentations bring their own challenges. First, symptoms tend to be well ingrained. Despite the cost they bring, they constitute some form of self-protection that is difficult for the client to let go of. The therapist has to validate this self-protective function, bringing it more fully into awareness while helping the client experience the toll or cost of the problematic self-treatment. The process is truly two steps forward, one step back; avoidance is often central (as we have already elaborated on, a focus on symptoms may in and of itself constitute a form of emotional avoidance, preventing as it does a focus on those underlying chronic painful feelings central to the client's self-definition—for example, "I am socially anxious" is less painful than "I am fundamentally flawed"). Symptom work therefore needs to be supplemented, right from the beginning, with a focus on underlying vulnerability and central self–self and self–other processes.

Symptom-level task difficulties often center on client inability to let go of the process (e.g., self-worry) that brings the emotional toll (e.g., anxiety). Validating the function of this process while simultaneously bringing to the fore the experienced emotional toll constitutes a dialectical process central to this type of work. Desistance or softening on behalf of the part of the self that causes symptoms (e.g., Worrier, Obsessor) typically only comes about as a consequence of experiencing the full impact of this treatment on the experiencing self. Furthermore, such softening is frequently brought about not only by witnessing the pain wrought on the self but also by the expression of boundary-setting protective anger from the experiencing self, anger that, in turn, is often only activated by the intransigent refusal on behalf of the symptom initiating part of the self to soften. Well-developed awareness of these processes provides a holding that can help the client reconcile these types of dialectical-emotional processes (protection vs. cost: self-worrying vs. the anxiety it brings).

The major difficulties in EFT-T work are those that arise in the process of seeking to address and (hopefully) transform core chronic painful feelings (emotional vulnerability). By definition, core chronic emotional pain is chronic precisely because it is difficult to shift. As such, the therapist and client will inevitably struggle to achieve productive and adaptive movement in the therapeutic process (reworking/restructuring of problematic emotional schemes). As already touched on, the process is complicated by difficulties with emotional dysregulation, avoidance, and symptomatic distress. Clients may collapse into secondary hopelessness, helplessness, irritability, or anxiety. Facilitating the client in the face of these challenges to stay with core pain, tolerate it, and articulate unmet needs, as well as creatively staging enactments such that adaptive experiences of self-compassion, grieving, or protective anger can be activated are at the core of EFT-T (and any EFT for that matter).

Facilitating these processes is thus the main challenge for the therapist, and these processes are, in turn, challenging to facilitate. The therapist needs to remain hopeful, be creative, and work hard to ensure that there is a balance between validation of the client's pain and the proposition of enactments that might activate adaptive emotional responses to that pain. The therapist calibrates their interventions to scaffold client emotional processes and must, at all times, remain attuned both to where the client is and what they are capable of. To help clients access core painful emotions and, in turn, adaptive emotional processes, such as self-compassion, grieving, and protective anger, the therapist needs to creatively draw on a wide range of strategies, an overview of which we offer in Chapter 9. All the time, these creative strategies must be immersed in the therapist's validating and compassionate relationship and offering of a corrective emotional experience.

PERSONALITY DIFFICULTIES

Although we present EFT-T as an approach for working with depression, anxiety, and related disorders, such as obsessive-compulsive disorder and trauma, in our studies we also routinely assess participants to ascertain whether they meet diagnostic criteria for personality disorders (e.g., Timulak, et al., 2017, 2018, 2020). As a result, we know that the outpatient population targeted in our studies has a high prevalence of comorbid personality disorders, most commonly those traditionally grouped as Cluster C personality disorders in the American Psychiatric Association's (2013) *Diagnostic and Statistical Manual of Mental Disorders* (fifth ed.) that are particularly characteristic of anxiety disorders: avoidant, obsessive-compulsive, and dependent. The presence of these difficulties usually indicates more ingrained patterns of symptomatic difficulties, often of an interpersonal nature—for example, avoidant or controlling behavior. While, in essence, the work with clients who meet criteria for a diagnosis of comorbid personality disorders does not differ from the descriptions we provide for short-term work in general, it is likely that because of the chronicity and ingrained nature of their difficulties, such clients would particularly benefit from longer term therapy. In this context, short-term work may be conceptualized as an episodic experience with the potential to motivate the client to seek new horizons.

Our samples also include many clients who met criteria for other personality disorders (i.e., those traditionally grouped as Clusters A and B), such as borderline or paranoid. In the case of borderline difficulties, the major issue can be the level of dysregulation clients may experience, and thus a focus on explicit soothing (e.g., self-soothing task, clearing a space) is important. Homework focused on identifying and practicing soothing activities outside the therapy session have been helpful. Both presentations may potentially evince greater interpersonal sensitivity, thereby putting increased pressure on the therapeutic relationship and increasing the potential for ruptures in the alliance. Although within our studies, therapists were required to adhere to the research study framework of up to 20 to 25 sessions of therapy, the aforementioned factors indicate that longer term work will likely be more optimal for such clients than short-term work. Overall, though, the presence of personality difficulties does not mean a dramatic change to therapeutic strategy. Rather, it is more likely a predictor of chronicity of client difficulties and a predictor of the degree of challenge the therapeutic process may encounter.

The reader must be mindful that we refer here to presentations common to mainstream outpatient settings. The presence of other comorbidities, such as (but not limited to) psychosis, bipolar disorder, eating disorders, or substance abuse, may require multidisciplinary team engagement and, in some cases, inpatient treatment. These comorbidities are not the focus of our formulation as presented in this book. The reader may find useful information in the recent *Clinical Handbook of Emotion-Focused Therapy* edited by Les Greenberg and Rhonda Goldman (2019).

MEDICATION

A proportion of the clients seen in our studies were on psychotropic medication, most typically some form of antidepressant. In general, this is not an obstacle for EFT. Although the client's use of medication may not be of particular relevance to therapy per se, some clients bring up the theme of medication within therapy. For example, clients may talk about whether to phase out medication, or they may express uncertainty about whether it is medication, therapy, or both that is helping them feel better. Obviously, decisions regarding the phasing out of medication need to be referred to and deferred to the prescribing physician, but the therapist needs to acknowledge such wonderings, and it may be important that the client experiences the therapy room as a safe space within which to sound out their thinking.

With regard to uncertainty as to whether it is therapy or medication that is responsible for any improvements in the client's feelings and functioning, this is something that is quite typical of the reassurance-seeking behavior that comes with many anxiety disorders. Again, this uncertainty and wondering are to be acknowledged by the therapist; however, it is equally important that the therapist does not allow the client's self-critical or self-doubting/ worrying process to undermine their own therapeutic work and their own accomplishments. This is central to the consolidation of those adaptive therapeutic experiences generated in therapy. The therapist validates the client, pointing out that regardless of the presence/absence of medication (which may or may not have helped on some physiological level), it was the client who worked on letting go of hindering symptomatic processes and behavior, it was the client who developed the capacity to stay with painful emotions, and it was the client who generated new adaptive emotional experiences. It is important to reflect on, and to support the client in reflecting on, these achievements.

LIFE EVENTS AND THERAPY

In our experience running psychotherapy trials within the public health primary care service in Ireland, participating therapists whom we have trained in EFT often express the concern that a very niche, clearly defined therapeutic approach does not leave space for them to venture off the manualized course. In their experience, clients experience a wide variety of "real-life issues," such as work disputes, legal battles, health issues, and bereavements, that need to be discussed in therapy. We frequently therefore have had recourse to reassure therapists that there is always space to bring a commonsense therapeutic perspective to bear on the work and to meet individual clients where they are, attending to whatever needs to be attended to.

On the other hand, we encourage therapists to see how current life events serve as triggers of emotional pain, so although there may be a commonsense or generic therapeutic approach to everyday life events (e.g., a job loss), and that commonsense approach may include discussing the particularities of what happened, the client's plans to address the situation, and so on, there is also an EFT perspective that will explore what emotional vulnerability, core painful feelings, or problematic self-treatment may have been activated by the event. An important distinction needs to be made between those real-life events, when the client needs to pragmatically tease something out, and those times when such a focus might constitute avoidance of underlying emotional pain.

CONSOLIDATION OF CHANGES: HOMEWORK

While we do not explicitly focus on the use of homework, we provide a framework with each task in this book that may be used for reflection and for devising potential homework (see also Timulak & McElvaney, 2018). We suggest two types of homework (Greenberg & Warwar, 2006; Warwar & Ellison, 2019): *awareness-based homework* in which the therapist and the client creatively think of ways the client could develop their awareness of the processes noticed in session (e.g., self-criticism, self-worrying) and *consolidation-based homework* that focuses on supporting adaptive processes that happened in the session. For instance, the therapist and the client could think of ways the client might support experiences of protective anger in real life (e.g., by expressing boundaries to a colleague). In reality, clients naturally and spontaneously experiment with what they learn in therapy, bringing such experimentations to subsequent sessions for further exploration. The same process can apply to any proposed homework with the client debriefing with the therapist as to how the experience went and reflecting on how it might inform the client's functioning (or further homework).

Because we see EFT-T as an exploratory therapy, we therefore do not prescribe the use of homework. Even though we offer frameworks that reflect the scaffolding of both symptom-level and underlying vulnerability tasks, and we encourage therapists to use those frameworks to devise any potential homework as they see fit, we have learned that the inclination to use or not use homework in EFT is a function of the therapist's preferences. Some are inclined to use homework; some are less so. Similarly, in our experience, some clients like this type of supplementation of what is happening in session, whereas others do not and instead prefer and appreciate the more typically exploratory nature of EFT.

There is an inherent fear among EFT theoreticians that the use of homework could lead to EFT's losing some of its experiential, discovery-oriented, and (authentically validating and compassionate) relationship-anchored nature. We share those fears and also believe that mandated homework could quickly turn into a chore for both the client and therapist. We thus see homework not as something to be prescribed but, rather, as something that may fit for some clients and some therapists, and that ultimately is at the individual therapist's discretion to reflect on and devise. The work and writing of Serine Warwar (Greenberg & Warwar, 2006; Warwar, 2015; Warwar & Ellison, 2019) offers inspiration here. The use of homework is second nature to how Warwar works and comes across as a natural expression and extension of her therapeutic presence and interventions. In our lab, we have developed a manual that can be used for psychoeducational interventions as well as for homework (Kwatra et al., in press). For readers interested in incorporating homework into their EFT skills repertoire, we recommend checking those sources for inspiration. We are also ourselves very much looking at the future use of these types of interventions.

STEPPED-CARE, GROUP THERAPY, AND OTHER FORMATS OF DELIVERY

The focus of the research endeavors of our research group has been on how to adapt EFT-T so it can become a part of the mainstream public health provision in countries, such as Ireland and the United Kingdom, that operate a centralized national health service. In those contexts, stepped-care provision is a necessity. *Stepped-care* means that traditional face-to-face therapy is provided only when the client (referral) meets a certain threshold of severity; for lower levels of distress, other interventions, such as group psychoeducation, bibliotherapy, or automated internet-delivered interventions with human support (e.g., internet-delivered CBT), are offered. This means that high-intensity therapeutic interventions, described in this book, are necessarily supplemented with low-intensity interventions that are theoretically compatible but differ in the mode of delivery.

To make EFT-T of interest to stakeholders in these types of contexts, it is critical that it be supplemented with psychoeducational materials that could potentially be delivered online (similar requirements can be found in student counseling services). That need for supplemental materials led our research group to develop a psychoeducational program to serve this purpose (Kwatra et al., in press). The program consists of modules, psychoeducational material, and instructions for experiential exercises, copying all the major tasks described in this book. The material will soon be available in a book format and hopefully also as an internet-based intervention. While we tried to capture the spirit of EFT when developing this material, it remains to be answered whether it is possible to adapt experiential therapy into these types of low-intensity formats without losing its essence as an authentic human experience that happens in the context of a caring and validating therapeutic relationship.

The COVID-19 pandemic crisis has taught all therapists that there is room for mental health interventions that can be delivered remotely. This was our experience with delivering EFT-T through videoconferencing or phone. Although we do not have the space to go through the details of this type of delivery, we must confess that our experience with it was more positive than expected. Yes, it is possible to conduct EFT-T through video or audio channels. Doing so requires the same precautions that would apply to any other therapy delivered remotely. To ensure privacy, it also requires good technology and increased scaffolding compared with face-to-face therapy. Specific to EFT are issues pertaining to room setup and audio/video coordination to allow for smooth chair dialogues. Once these issues are considered, there is no real boundary to delivering a high-quality EFT-T through these media in a manner that can be truly transformative and relational (for some perspectives on delivering EFT or other experiential therapies using imaginary chair dialogues in a telehealth context, see Pugh et al., 2021).

A further development in the form of delivery is in the modality of group therapy, the first manualized deliveries of which are now documented (e.g., Lafrance Robinson et al., 2014; Thompson & Girz, 2020; Wnuk et al., 2015). While we do not describe this modality of working in this book, it is an area of interest to us and is one of the areas that we would like to pursue empirically. The documented experiences of others serve as an example and inspiration for us (e.g., Thompson & Girz, 2018).

COUPLES THERAPY

EFT is particularly strong in its couples therapy format (Greenberg & Goldman, 2008; Greenberg & Johnson, 1988; Johnson, 2004). Emotion-focused therapy for couples (EFT-C) was developed for relational difficulties in couples. In many cases, either one or both partners also suffer from depression, anxiety, or related disorders. Depression and anxiety are often directly triggered by relational disputes. Equally, depression and anxiety may compound relational difficulties or complicate those constructive interactions that could prevent relational difficulties. While EFT for couples is empirically well established, only a few studies have examined it in the context of comorbid depression (e.g., Denton et al., 2012; Dessaulles et al., 2003; Wittenborn et al., 2019) or anxiety and related difficulties (e.g., posttraumatic stress disorder; Weissman et al., 2018).

It is one of our own areas of interest to adapt EFT-C as a transdiagnostic treatment for relational difficulties with comorbid depression, anxiety, and related disorders. In our conceptualization, the underlying emotional vulnerability at the core of depression, anxiety, and related symptomatology is often triggered by partners' interactional stances, and symptomatic distress, in turn, often contributes to an escalation of problematic relational interactions (problematic interactional cycles). Work on each partner's underlying emotional vulnerability and its symptomatic expression can thus reduce that emotional reactivity that is triggered by the way relational stances of the other activate core pain in the self. Similarly, work on one partner's constructive soothing and validating responses helps to transform the other partner's underlying emotional vulnerability. In EFT-C, we are thus trying to work relationally and interactionally so that partners know each other's emotional vulnerabilities and are thus capable of responding to the other partner's vulnerability in a corrective manner. Interactional patterns that are an expression of symptomatic distress (e.g., the controlling behavior of an anxious partner) have a specific role to play here. At the same time, we are trying to work intrapsychologically on each partner's vulnerability and emotional flexibility and resilience so that nonoptimal interactional stances from the other can better be tolerated, thus not giving rise to such chronically painful self-organizations or symptomatic distress that might not only bring individual suffering but also might further compound problematic aspects of the couple's interactional life.

CONCLUSION

This chapter closes our outline of EFT-T. It presents thoughts on the course of therapy and on clinical issues that need to be considered. We talked briefly about the many practical issues that pertain to the delivery of EFT-T and touched on various formats of delivery, including those areas that we predict will undergo much development in the near future.

Each book has its own limitations and needs to finish somewhere. We see this as a good point at which to end, and we look forward to the discussions we will doubtless have with colleagues, both from within the ever-growing EFT community and from beyond it in the broader field of mental health professionals working with depression, anxiety, and related presentations.

References

American Psychiatric Association. (1994). *Diagnostic and statistical manual of mental disorders* (4th ed.).

American Psychiatric Association. (2013). *Diagnostic and statistical manual of mental disorders* (5th ed.). American Psychiatric Association Publishing.

Angus, L., Watson, J. C., Elliott, R., Schneider, K., & Timulak, L. (2015). Humanistic psychotherapy research 1990–2015: From methodological innovation to evidence-supported treatment outcomes and beyond. *Psychotherapy Research, 25*(3), 330–347. https://doi.org/10.1080/10503307.2014.989290

Angus, L. E., & Greenberg, L. S. (2011). *Working with narrative in emotion-focused therapy: Changing stories, healing lives.* American Psychological Association. https://doi.org/10.1037/12325-000

Arseneault, L., Bowes, L., & Shakoor, S. (2010). Bullying victimization in youths and mental health problems: "Much ado about nothing"? *Psychological Medicine, 40*(5), 717–729. https://doi.org/10.1017/S0033291709991383

Asher, S. R., & Paquette, J. A. (2003). Loneliness and peer relations in childhood. *Current Directions in Psychological Science, 12*(3), 75–78. https://doi.org/10.1111/1467-8721.01233

Auszra, L., & Greenberg, L. S. (2007). Client emotional productivity. *European Psychotherapy, 7*(1), 137–152.

Auszra, L., Greenberg, L. S., & Herrmann, I. R. (2010). *Client Emotional Productivity Scale–Revised (CEPS-R)*. York Psychotherapy Research Clinic.

Barlow, D. H., & Farchione, T. J. (Eds.). (2018). *Applications of the Unified Protocol for Transdiagnostic Treatment of Emotional Disorders*. Oxford University Press.

Barlow, D. H., Farchione, T. J., Bullis, J. R., Gallagher, M. W., Murray-Latin, H., Sauer-Zavala, S., Bentley, K. H., Thompson-Hollands, J., Conklin, L. R., Boswell, J. F., Ametaj, A., Carl, J. R., Boettcher, H. T., & Cassiello-Robbins, C. (2017). The Unified Protocol for Transdiagnostic Treatment of Emotional Disorders compared with diagnosis-specific protocols for anxiety disorders: A randomized clinical trial. *JAMA Psychiatry, 74*(9), 875–884. https://doi.org/10.1001/jamapsychiatry.2017.2164

Barlow, D. H., Farchione, T. J., Sauer-Zavala, S., Latin, H., Ellard, K. K., Bullis, J. R., Bentley, K. H., Boettcher, H. T., & Cassiello-Robbins, C. (2017). *Unified Protocol for Transdiagnostic Treatment of Emotional Disorders: Therapist guide* (2nd ed.). Oxford University Press.

Barrett, L. F., Wilson-Mendenhall, C. D., & Barsalou, L. W. (2014). A psychological construction account of emotion regulation and dysregulation: The role of situated conceptualizations. In J. J. Gross (Ed.), *Handbook of emotion regulation* (pp. 447–465). Guilford Press.

Baumeister, R. F., Twenge, J. M., & Nuss, C. K. (2002). Effects of social exclusion on cognitive processes: Anticipated aloneness reduces intelligent thought. *Journal of Personality and Social Psychology, 83*(4), 817–827. https://doi.org/10.1037/0022-3514.83.4.817

Boettcher, H., & Conklin, L. R. (2018). Transdiagnostic assessment and case formulation: Rationale and application with the Unified Protocol. In D. H. Barlow & T. J. Farchione (Eds.), *Applications of the Unified Protocol for Transdiagnostic Treatment of Emotional Disorders* (pp. 17–37). Oxford University Press.

Bond, L., Carlin, J. B., Thomas, L., Rubin, K., & Patton, G. (2001). Does bullying cause emotional problems? A prospective study of young teenagers. *BMJ, 323*(7311), 480–484. https://doi.org/10.1136/bmj.323.7311.480

Bordin, E. S. (1979). The generalizability of the psychodynamic concept of the working alliance. *Psychotherapy, 16*(3), 252–260. https://doi.org/10.1037/h0085885

Borkovec, T. D., Alcaine, O. M., & Behar, E. (2004). Avoidance theory of worry and generalized anxiety disorder. In R. G. Heimberg, C. L. Turk, & D. S. Mennin (Eds.), *Generalized anxiety disorder: Advances in research and practice* (pp. 77–108). Guilford Press.

Brown, T. A., & Barlow, D. H. (2009). A proposal for a dimensional classification system based on the shared features of the *DSM-IV* anxiety and mood disorders: Implications for assessment and treatment. *Psychological Assessment, 21*(3), 256–271. https://doi.org/10.1037/a0016608

Brown, T. A., Campbell, L. A., Lehman, C. L., Grisham, J. R., & Mancill, R. B. (2001). Current and lifetime comorbidity of the *DSM-IV* anxiety and mood disorders in a large clinical sample. *Journal of Abnormal Psychology, 110*(4), 585–599. https://doi.org/10.1037/0021-843X.110.4.585

Brown, T. A., Di Nardo, P. A., Lehman, C. L., & Campbell, L. A. (2001). Reliability of *DSM-IV* anxiety and mood disorders: Implications for the classification of emotional disorders. *Journal of Abnormal Psychology, 110*(1), 49–58. https://doi.org/10.1037/0021-843X.110.1.49

Bullis, J. R., Boettcher, H., Sauer-Zavala, S., Farchione, T. J., & Barlow, D. H. (2019). What is an emotional disorder? A transdiagnostic mechanistic definition with implications for assessment, treatment, and prevention. *Clinical Psychology: Science and Practice, 26*(2), Article e12278. https://doi.org/10.1111/cpsp.12278

Cacioppo, J. T., & Patrick, W. (2008). *Loneliness: Human nature and the need for social connection.* W. W. Norton & Company.

Carryer, J. R., & Greenberg, L. S. (2010). Optimal levels of emotional arousal in experiential therapy of depression. *Journal of Consulting and Clinical Psychology, 78*(2), 190–199. https://doi.org/10.1037/a0018401

Caspi, A., Houts, R. M., Belsky, D. W., Goldman-Mellor, S. J., Harrington, H., Israel, S., Meier, M. H., Ramrakha, S., Shalev, I., Poulton, R., & Moffitt, T. E. (2014). The p factor: One general psychopathology factor in the structure of psychiatric disorders? *Clinical Psychological Science, 2*(2), 119–137. https://doi.org/10.1177/2167702613497473

Caspi, A., McClay, J., Moffitt, T. E., Mill, J., Martin, J., Craig, I. W., Taylor, A., & Poulton, R. (2002). Role of genotype in the cycle of violence in maltreated children. *Science, 297*(5582), 851–854. https://doi.org/10.1126/science.1072290

Caspi, A., & Moffitt, T. E. (2018). All for one and one for all: Mental disorders in one dimension. *American Journal of Psychiatry, 175*(9), 831–844. https://doi.org/10.1176/appi.ajp.2018.17121383

Chambless, D. L., & Hollon, S. D. (1998). Defining empirically supported therapies. *Journal of Consulting and Clinical Psychology, 66*(1), 7–18. https://doi.org/10.1037/0022-006X.66.1.7

Chen, Z., & Williams, K. D. (2011). Social pain is easily relived and prelived, but physical pain is not. In G. MacDonald & L. A. Jensen-Campbell (Eds.), *Social pain: Neuropsychological and health implications of loss and exclusion* (pp. 161–177). American Psychological Association. https://doi.org/10.1037/12351-007

Clarke, K. M. (1989). Creation of meaning: An emotional processing task in psychotherapy. *Psychotherapy, 26*(2), 139–148. https://doi.org/10.1037/h0085412

Coan, J. A., Schaefer, H. S., & Davidson, R. J. (2006). Lending a hand: Social regulation of the neural response to threat. *Psychological Science, 17*(12), 1032–1039. https://doi.org/10.1111/j.1467-9280.2006.01832.x

Cohen, R. A., Grieve, S., Hoth, K. F., Paul, R. H., Sweet, L., Tate, D., Gunstad, J., Stroud, L., McCaffery, J., Hitsman, B., Niaura, R., Clark, C. R., McFarlane, A., Bryant, R., Gordon, E., & Williams, L. M. (2006). Early life stress and morphometry of the adult anterior cingulate cortex and caudate nuclei. *Biological Psychiatry, 59*(10), 975–982. https://doi.org/10.1016/j.biopsych.2005.12.016

Connolly-Zubot, A., Timulak, L., Hession, N., & Coleman, N. (2020). Emotion-focused therapy for anxiety and depression in women with breast cancer.

Journal of Contemporary Psychotherapy, 50, 113–122. https://doi.org/10.1007/s10879-019-09439-2

Côté, S. M., Boivin, M., Liu, X., Nagin, D. S., Zoccolillo, M., & Tremblay, R. E. (2009). Depression and anxiety symptoms: Onset, developmental course and risk factors during early childhood. *Journal of Child Psychology and Psychiatry, 50*(10), 1201–1208. https://doi.org/10.1111/j.1469-7610.2009.02099.x

Courtois, C. A., & Ford, J. D. (Eds.). (2009). *Treating complex traumatic stress disorders: An evidence-based guide.* Guilford Press.

Davidson, L. M., & Demaray, M. K. (2007). Social support as a moderator between victimization and internalizing-externalizing distress from bullying. *School Psychology Review, 36*(3), 383–405. https://doi.org/10.1080/02796015.2007.12087930

De Bellis, M. D., Hooper, S. R., Spratt, E. G., & Woolley, D. P. (2009). Neuropsychological findings in childhood neglect and their relationships to pediatric PTSD. *Journal of the International Neuropsychological Society, 15*(6), 868–878. https://doi.org/10.1017/S1355617709990464

Denton, W. H., Wittenborn, A. K., & Golden, R. N. (2012). Augmenting antidepressant medication treatment of depressed women with emotionally focused therapy for couples: A randomized pilot study. *Journal of Marital and Family Therapy, 38*(Suppl. 1), 23–38. https://doi.org/10.1111/j.1752-0606.2012.00291.x

Dessaulles, A., Johnson, S. M., & Denton, W. H. (2003). Emotion-focused therapy for couples in the treatment of depression: A pilot study. *American Journal of Family Therapy, 31*(5), 345–353. https://doi.org/10.1080/01926180390232266

DeWall, C. N., & Baumeister, R. F. (2006). Alone but feeling no pain: Effects of social exclusion on physical pain tolerance and pain threshold, affective forecasting, and interpersonal empathy. *Journal of Personality and Social Psychology, 91*(1), 1–15. https://doi.org/10.1037/0022-3514.91.1.1

DeWall, C. N., & Bushman, B. J. (2011). Social acceptance and rejection: The sweet and the bitter. *Current Directions in Psychological Science, 20*(4), 256–260. https://doi.org/10.1177/0963721411417545

DeWall, C. N., Pond, R. S., & Deckam, T. (2011). Acetaminophen dulls psychological pain. In G. MacDonald & L. A. Jensen-Campbell (Eds.), *Social pain: Neuropsychological and health implications of loss and exclusion* (pp. 123–140). American Psychological Association. https://doi.org/10.1037/12351-005

Dickerson, S. S. (2011). Physiological responses to experiences of social pain. In G. MacDonald & L. A. Jensen-Campbell (Eds.), *Social pain: Neuropsychological and health implications of loss and exclusion* (pp. 79–94). American Psychological Association. https://doi.org/10.1037/12351-003

Dickerson, S. S., & Zoccola, P. M. (2013). Cortisol responses to social exclusion. In C. N. DeWall (Ed.), *The Oxford handbook of social exclusion* (pp. 143–151). Oxford University Press.

Dillon, A., Timulak, L., & Greenberg, L. S. (2018). Transforming core emotional pain in a course of emotion-focused therapy for depression: A case study.

Psychotherapy Research, 28(3), 406–422. https://doi.org/10.1080/10503307.2016.1233364

DiNardo, P. A., Barlow, D. H., & Brown, T. A. (1994). *Anxiety Disorders Interview Schedule for DSM-IV: Client Interview Schedule, lifetime version*. Oxford University Press.

Egan, S. J., van Noort, E., Chee, A., Kane, R. T., Hoiles, K. J., Shafran, R., & Wade, T. D. (2014). A randomised controlled trial of face to face versus pure online self-help cognitive behavioural treatment for perfectionism. *Behaviour Research and Therapy, 63*, 107–113. https://doi.org/10.1016/j.brat.2014.09.009

Egan, S. J., Wade, T. D., & Shafran, R. (2011). Perfectionism as a transdiagnostic process: A clinical review. *Clinical Psychology Review, 31*(2), 203–212. https://doi.org/10.1016/j.cpr.2010.04.009

Eisenberger, N. I. (2011). The neural basis of social pain: Findings and implication. In G. MacDonald & L. A. Jensen-Campbell (Eds.), *Social pain: Neuropsychological and health implications of loss and exclusion* (pp. 53–78). American Psychological Association. https://doi.org/10.1037/12351-002

Eisenberger, N. I. (2015). Social pain and the brain: Controversies, questions, and where to go from here. *Annual Review of Psychology, 66*(1), 601–629. https://doi.org/10.1146/annurev-psych-010213-115146

Elliott, R. (2013). Person-centered/experiential psychotherapy for anxiety difficulties: Theory, research and practice. *Person-Centered & Experiential Psychotherapies, 12*(1), 16–32. https://doi.org/10.1080/14779757.2013.767750

Elliott, R., Greenberg, L. S., Watson, J. C., Timulak, L., & Freire, E. (2013). Research on humanistic–experiential psychotherapies. In M. J. Lambert (Ed.), *Bergin & Garfield's handbook of psychotherapy and behavior change* (5th ed., pp. 495–538). John Wiley & Sons.

Elliott, R., & Macdonald, J. (2020). Relational dialogue in emotion-focused therapy. *Journal of Clinical Psychology, 77*(2), 414–428. https://doi.org/10.1002/jclp.23069

Elliott, R., & Shahar, B. (2017). Emotion-focused therapy for social anxiety (EFT-SA). *Person-Centered & Experiential Psychotherapies, 16*(2), 140–158. https://doi.org/10.1080/14779757.2017.1330701

Elliott, R., Watson, J. C., Goldman, R. N., & Greenberg, L. S. (2004). *Learning emotion-focused therapy: The process-experiential approach to change*. American Psychological Association. https://doi.org/10.1037/10725-000

Elliott, R., Watson, J. C., Timulak, L., & Sharbanee, J. (2021). Research on humanistic–experiential psychotherapies. In M. Barkham, W. Lutz, & L. Castonguay (Eds.), *Bergin & Garfield's handbook of psychotherapy and behavior change* (6th ed.). John Wiley & Sons.

Fairburn, C. G., Cooper, Z., Shafran, R., & Wilson, G. T. (2008). Eating disorders: A transdiagnostic protocol. In D. H. Barlow (Ed.), *Clinical handbook of psychological disorders: A step-by-step treatment manual* (pp. 578–614). Guilford Press.

First, M. B., Williams, J. B. W., Karg, R. S., & Spitzer, R. L. (2015). *Structured Clinical Interview for DSM-5—Research version.* American Psychiatric Association.

Forgas, J. P. (1995). Mood and judgment: The affect infusion model (AIM). *Psychological Bulletin, 117*(1), 39–66. https://doi.org/10.1037/0033-2909.117.1.39

Fox, S. D., Griffin, R. H., & Pachankis, J. E. (2020). Minority stress, social integration, and the mental health needs of LGBTQ asylum seekers in North America. *Social Science & Medicine, 246,* Article 112727. https://doi.org/10.1016/j.socscimed.2019.112727

Geller, S. M., & Greenberg, L. S. (2012). *Therapeutic presence: A mindful approach to effective therapy.* American Psychological Association. https://doi.org/10.1037/13485-000

Gendlin, E. T. (1981). *Focusing* (2nd ed.). Bantam Books.

Gendlin, E. T. (1996). *Focusing-oriented psychotherapy: A manual of the experiential method.* Guilford Press.

Goldman, R., & Greenberg, L. S. (1997). Case formulation in process-experiential therapy. In T. D. Eells (Ed.), *Handbook of psychotherapy case formulation* (pp. 402–429). Guilford Press.

Goldman, R. N., & Greenberg, L. S. (2015). *Case formulation in emotion-focused therapy: Co-creating clinical maps for change.* American Psychological Association. https://doi.org/10.1037/14523-000

Goldman, R. N., Greenberg, L. S., & Angus, L. (2006). The effects of adding emotion-focused interventions to the therapeutic relationship in the treatment of depression. *Psychotherapy Research, 16*(5), 537–549. https://doi.org/10.1080/10503300600589456

Grafanaki, S., & McLeod, J. (1999). Narrative processes in the construction of helpful and hindering events in experiential psychotherapy. *Psychotherapy Research, 9*(3), 289–303. https://doi.org/10.1080/10503309912331332771

Greenberg, L., & Watson, J. (1998). Experiential therapy of depression: Differential effects of client-centered relationship conditions and process experiential interventions. *Psychotherapy Research, 8*(2), 210–224. https://doi.org/10.1080/10503309812331332317

Greenberg, L. S. (1979). Resolving splits: Use of the two chair technique. *Psychotherapy, 16*(3), 316–324. https://doi.org/10.1037/h0085895

Greenberg, L. S. (1980). The intensive analysis of recurring events from the practice of gestalt therapy. *Psychotherapy, 17*(2), 143–152. https://doi.org/10.1037/h0085904

Greenberg, L. S. (1983). Toward a task analysis of conflict resolution in gestalt therapy. *Psychotherapy, 20*(2), 190–201. https://doi.org/10.1037/h0088490

Greenberg, L. S. (2002). *Emotion-focused therapy: Coaching clients to work through their feelings.* American Psychological Association. https://doi.org/10.1037/10447-000

Greenberg, L. S. (2004). Emotion-focused therapy. *Clinical Psychology & Psychotherapy, 11*(1), 3–16. https://doi.org/10.1002/cpp.388

Greenberg, L. S. (2006). Emotion-focused therapy: A synopsis. *Journal of Contemporary Psychotherapy, 36*(2), 87–93. https://doi.org/10.1007/s10879-006-9011-3

Greenberg, L. S. (2007a). *Emotion-focused therapy over time* [training DVD]. American Psychological Association.

Greenberg, L. S. (2007b). A guide to conducting a task analysis of psychotherapeutic change. *Psychotherapy Research, 17*(1), 15–30. https://doi.org/10.1080/10503300600720390

Greenberg, L. S. (2011). *Theories of psychotherapy: Emotion-focused therapy.* American Psychological Association.

Greenberg, L. S. (2015). *Emotion-focused therapy: Coaching clients through their feelings* (2nd ed.). American Psychological Association. https://doi.org/10.1037/14692-000

Greenberg, L. S. (2017). *Emotion-focused therapy* (Rev. ed.). American Psychological Association.

Greenberg, L. S. (2019). Theory of functioning. In L. S. Greenberg & R. N. Goldman (Eds.), *Clinical handbook of emotion-focused therapy* (pp. 37–59). American Psychological Association. https://doi.org/10.1037/0000112-002

Greenberg, L. S., Auszra, L., & Herrmann, I. R. (2007). The relationship among emotional productivity, emotional arousal and outcome in experiential therapy of depression. *Psychotherapy Research, 17*(4), 482–493. https://doi.org/10.1080/10503300600977800

Greenberg, L. S. (Guest Expert), & Carlson, J. (Host). (2007). *Emotion-focused therapy for depression* [Film; educational DVD]. American Psychological Association.

Greenberg, L. S., & Dompierre, L. M. (1981). Specific effects of gestalt two-chair dialogue on intrapsychic conflict in counseling. *Journal of Counseling Psychology, 28*(4), 288–294. https://doi.org/10.1037/0022-0167.28.4.288

Greenberg, L. S., & Elliott, R. (2012). Corrective experience from a humanistic–experiential perspective. In L. G. Castonguay & C. E. Hill (Eds.), *Transformation in psychotherapy: Corrective experiences across cognitive behavioral, humanistic, and psychodynamic approaches* (pp. 85–101). American Psychological Association. https://doi.org/10.1037/13747-006

Greenberg, L. S., & Foerster, F. S. (1996). Task analysis exemplified: The process of resolving unfinished business. *Journal of Consulting and Clinical Psychology, 64*(3), 439–446. https://doi.org/10.1037/0022-006X.64.3.439

Greenberg, L. S., & Goldman, R. N. (2007). Case formulation in emotion-focused therapy. In T. D. Eells (Ed.), *Handbook of psychotherapy case formulation* (2nd ed., pp. 379–411). Guilford Press.

Greenberg, L. S., & Goldman, R. N. (2008). *Emotion-focused couples therapy: The dynamics of emotion, love, and power.* American Psychological Association. https://doi.org/10.1037/11750-000

Greenberg, L. S., & Goldman, R. N. (Eds.). (2019). *Clinical handbook of emotion-focused therapy.* American Psychological Association. https://doi.org/10.1037/0000112-000

Greenberg, L. S., & Higgins, H. M. (1980). Effects of two-chair dialogue and focusing on conflict resolution. *Journal of Counseling Psychology, 27*(3), 221–224. https://doi.org/10.1037/0022-0167.27.3.221

Greenberg, L. S., & Johnson, S. M. (1988). *Emotionally focused therapy for couples.* Guilford Press.

Greenberg, L. S., & Malcolm, W. (2002). Resolving unfinished business: Relating process to outcome. *Journal of Consulting and Clinical Psychology, 70*(2), 406–416. https://doi.org/10.1037/0022-006X.70.2.406

Greenberg, L. S., Rice, L. N., & Elliott, R. (1993). *Facilitating emotional change: The moment-by-moment process.* Guilford Press.

Greenberg, L. S., & Safran, J. D. (1987). *Emotion in psychotherapy: Affect, cognition, and the process of change.* Guilford Press.

Greenberg, L. S., & Safran, J. D. (1989). Emotion in psychotherapy. *American Psychologist, 44*(1), 19–29. https://doi.org/10.1037/0003-066X.44.1.19

Greenberg, L. S., & Warwar, S. H. (2006). Homework in an emotion-focused approach to experiential therapy. *Journal of Psychotherapy Integration, 16*(2), 178–200. https://doi.org/10.1037/1053-0479.16.2.178

Greenberg, L. S., & Watson, J. C. (2006). *Emotion-focused therapy for depression.* American Psychological Association. https://doi.org/10.1037/11286-000

Greenberg, L. S., & Webster, M. C. (1982). Resolving decisional conflict by gestalt two-chair dialogue: Relating process to outcome. *Journal of Counseling Psychology, 29*(5), 468–477. https://doi.org/10.1037/0022-0167.29.5.468

Gunnar, M. R., Sebanc, A. M., Tout, K., Donzella, B., & van Dulmen, M. M. (2003). Peer rejection, temperament, and cortisol activity in preschoolers. *Developmental Psychobiology, 43*(4), 346–368. https://doi.org/10.1002/dev.10144

Harvey, A., Watkins, E., Mansell, W., & Shafran, R. (2004). *Cognitive behavioural processes across psychological disorders.* Oxford University Press. https://doi.org/10.1093/med:psych/9780198528883.001.0001

Harvey, S. B., Modini, M., Joyce, S., Milligan-Saville, J. S., Tan, L., Mykletun, A., Bryant, R. A., Christensen, H., & Mitchell, P. B. (2017). Can work make you mentally ill? A systematic meta-review of work-related risk factors for common mental health problems. *Occupational and Environmental Medicine, 74*(4), 301–310. https://doi.org/10.1136/oemed-2016-104015

Hawkley, L. C., Burleson, M. H., Berntson, G. G., & Cacioppo, J. T. (2003). Loneliness in everyday life: Cardiovascular activity, psychosocial context, and health behaviors. *Journal of Personality and Social Psychology, 85*(1), 105–120. https://doi.org/10.1037/0022-3514.85.1.105

Hermans, D., Craske, M. G., Mineka, S., & Lovibond, P. F. (2006). Extinction in human fear conditioning. *Biological Psychiatry, 60*(4), 361–368. https://doi.org/10.1016/j.biopsych.2005.10.006

Herrmann, I. R., & Auszra, L. (2019). Facilitating optimal emotional processing. In L. S. Greenberg & R. N. Goldman (Eds.), *Clinical handbook of emotion-focused therapy* (pp. 193–216). American Psychological Association. https://doi.org/10.1037/0000112-009

Hissa, J., Connolly-Zubot, A., Timulak, L., & Hession, N. (2020). Emotion-focused perspective on breast cancer patients' experiences of comorbid anxiety and depression: A qualitative case analysis of three clients' in-session presentations. *Person-Centered & Experiential Psychotherapies, 19*(2), 134–153. https://doi.org/10.1080/14779757.2020.1717988

Holt-Lunstad, J., Birmingham, W., & Jones, B. Q. (2008). Is there something unique about marriage? The relative impact of marital status, relationship quality, and network social support on ambulatory blood pressure and mental health. *Annals of Behavioral Medicine, 35*(2), 239–244. https://doi.org/10.1007/s12160-008-9018-y

Hughes, S., Timulak, L., & McElvaney, J. (2014, June 25–28). *Resolving emotional injury with a significant other through empty chair dialogue in clients with generalised anxiety disorder (GAD)* [Paper presentation]. Society for Psychotherapy Research, 45th International Annual Meeting, Copenhagen, Denmark.

Johnson, S. M. (2004). *Creating connection: The practice of emotionally focused couple therapy* (2nd ed.). Brunner-Routledge.

Jones, W. H., Freemon, J. E., & Goswick, R. A. (1981). The persistence of loneliness: Self and other determinants. *Journal of Personality, 49*(1), 27–48. https://doi.org/10.1111/j.1467-6494.1981.tb00844.x

Kennedy, K. A., & Barlow, D. H. (2018). The Unified Protocol for Transdiagnostic Treatment of Emotional Disorders: An introduction. In D. H. Barlow & T. J. Farchione (Eds.), *Application of the Unified Protocol for Transdiagnostic Treatment of Emotional Disorders* (pp. 1–16). Oxford University Press.

Kessler, R. C., Berglund, P., Demler, O., Jin, R., Merikangas, K. R., & Walters, E. E. (2005). Lifetime prevalence and age-of-onset distributions of *DSM-IV* disorders in the National Comorbidity Survey Replication. *Archives of General Psychiatry, 62*(6), 593–602. https://doi.org/10.1001/archpsyc.62.6.593

Kessler, R. C., Chiu, W. T., Demler, O., Merikangas, K. R., & Walters, E. E. (2005). Prevalence, severity, and comorbidity of 12-month *DSM-IV* disorders in the National Comorbidity Survey Replication. *Archives of General Psychiatry, 62*(6), 617–627. https://doi.org/10.1001/archpsyc.62.6.617

Kiecolt-Glaser, J. K., & Newton, T. L. (2001). Marriage and health: His and hers. *Psychological Bulletin, 127*(4), 472–503. https://doi.org/10.1037/0033-2909.127.4.472

Kite, M. E., & Whitley, B. E., Jr. (2016). *Psychology of prejudice and discrimination* (3rd ed.). Routledge. https://doi.org/10.4324/9781315623849

Klein, M. H., Mathieu, P. L., Gendlin, E. T., & Kiesler, D. J. (1969). *The Experiencing Scale: Vol. 1. A research and training manual.* Wisconsin Psychiatric Institute.

Kwatra, A., Timulak, L., Lu Huixian, S., Joyce, C., & Creaner, M. (in press). *Transforming emotional pain: Client workbook.* Routledge.

Lafrance Robinson, A., McCague, E. A., & Whissell, C. (2014). "That chair work thing was great": A pilot study of group-based emotion-focused therapy for anxiety and depression. *Person-Centered & Experiential Psychotherapies, 13*(4), 263–277. https://doi.org/10.1080/14779757.2014.910131

Lahey, B. B., Applegate, B., Hakes, J. K., Zald, D. H., Hariri, A. R., & Rathouz, P. J. (2012). Is there a general factor of prevalent psychopathology during adulthood? *Journal of Abnormal Psychology, 121*(4), 971–977. https://doi.org/10.1037/a0028355

Lahey, B. B., Krueger, R. F., Rathouz, P. J., Waldman, I. D., & Zald, D. H. (2017). A hierarchical causal taxonomy of psychopathology across the life span. *Psychological Bulletin, 143*(2), 142–186. https://doi.org/10.1037/bul0000069

Lane, R. D., Ryan, L., Nadel, L., & Greenberg, L. (2015). Memory reconsolidation, emotional arousal, and the process of change in psychotherapy: New insights from brain science. *Behavioral and Brain Sciences, 38,* Article E1. https://doi.org/10.1017/S0140525X14000041

Leary, M. R., Twenge, J. M., & Quinlivan, E. (2006). Interpersonal rejection as a determinant of anger and aggression. *Personality and Social Psychology Review, 10*(2), 111–132. https://doi.org/10.1207/s15327957pspr1002_2

Leijssen, M. (1998). Focusing microprocesses. In L. S. Greenberg, J. C. Watson, & G. Lietaer (Eds.), *Handbook of experiential psychotherapy* (pp. 121–154). Guilford Press.

Lenzenweger, M. F., Lane, M. C., Loranger, A. W., & Kessler, R. C. (2007). *DSM-IV* personality disorders in the National Comorbidity Survey Replication. *Biological Psychiatry, 62*(6), 553–564. https://doi.org/10.1016/j.biopsych.2006.09.019

Levitt, H. M., Whelton, W. J., & Iwakabe, S. (2019). Integrating feminist-multicultural perspectives into emotion-focused therapy. In L. S. Greenberg & R. N. Goldman (Eds.), *Clinical handbook of emotion-focused therapy* (pp. 425–444). American Psychological Association. https://doi.org/10.1037/0000112-019

Lieberman, M. D., Eisenberger, N. I., Crockett, M. J., Tom, S. M., Pfeifer, J. H., & Way, B. M. (2007). Putting feelings into words: Affect labeling disrupts amygdala activity in response to affective stimuli. *Psychological Science, 18*(5), 421–428. https://doi.org/10.1111/j.1467-9280.2007.01916.x

Lietaer, G. (1993). Authenticity, congruence and transparency. In D. Brazier (Ed.), *Beyond Carl Rogers* (pp. 17–46). Constable and Company.

Luecken, L. J. (1998). Childhood attachment and loss experiences affect adult cardiovascular and cortisol function. *Psychosomatic Medicine, 60*(6), 765–772. https://doi.org/10.1097/00006842-199811000-00021

Luecken, L. J. (2008). Long-term consequences of parental death in childhood: Psychological and physiological manifestations. In M. S. Stroebe, R. O. Hansson, H. Schut, & W. Stroebe (Eds.), *Handbook of bereavement research and practice: Advances in theory and intervention* (pp. 397–416). American Psychological Association. https://doi.org/10.1037/14498-019

MacDonald, G., Borsook, T. K., & Spielmann, S. S. (2011). Defensive avoidance of social pain via perceptions of social threat and reward. In G. MacDonald & L. A. Jensen-Campbell (Eds.), *Social pain: Neuropsychological and health implications of loss and exclusion* (pp. 141–160). American Psychological Association. https://doi.org/10.1037/12351-006

MacLeod, R., Elliott, R., & Rodgers, B. (2012). Process-experiential/emotion-focused therapy for social anxiety: A hermeneutic single-case efficacy design study. *Psychotherapy Research, 22*(1), 67–81. https://doi.org/10.1080/10503307.2011.626805

Mansell, W., Harvey, A., Watkins, E. R., & Shafran, R. (2008). Cognitive behavioral processes across psychological disorders: A review of the utility and validity of the transdiagnostic approach. *International Journal of Cognitive Therapy, 1*(3), 181–191. https://doi.org/10.1521/ijct.2008.1.3.181

Master, S. L., Eisenberger, N. I., Taylor, S. E., Naliboff, B. D., Shirinyan, D., & Lieberman, M. D. (2009). A picture's worth: Partner photographs reduce experimentally induced pain. *Psychological Science, 20*(11), 1316–1318. https://doi.org/10.1111/j.1467-9280.2009.02444.x

Mayer, J. D., & Hanson, E. (1995). Mood-congruent judgment over time. *Personality and Social Psychology Bulletin, 21*(3), 237–244. https://doi.org/10.1177/0146167295213005

McCranie, E. W., & Bass, J. D. (1984). Childhood family antecedents of dependency and self-criticism: Implications for depression. *Journal of Abnormal Psychology, 93*(1), 3–8. https://doi.org/10.1037/0021-843X.93.1.3

McMahon, S. D., Grant, K. E., Compas, B. E., Thurm, A. E., & Ey, S. (2003). Stress and psychopathology in children and adolescents: Is there evidence of specificity? *Journal of Child Psychology and Psychiatry, 44*(1), 107–133. https://doi.org/10.1111/1469-7610.00105

McNally, S., Timulak, L., & Greenberg, L. S. (2014). Transforming emotion schemes in emotion focused therapy: A case study investigation. *Person-Centered & Experiential Psychotherapies, 13*(2), 128–149. https://doi.org/10.1080/14779757.2013.871573

Middeldorp, C. M., Cath, D. C., Van Dyck, R., & Boomsma, D. I. (2005). The co-morbidity of anxiety and depression in the perspective of genetic epidemiology. A review of twin and family studies. *Psychological Medicine, 35*(5), 611–624. https://doi.org/10.1017/S003329170400412X

Moffitt, T. E., Caspi, A., Harrington, H., Milne, B. J., Melchior, M., Goldberg, D., & Poulton, R. (2007). Generalized anxiety disorder and depression: Childhood risk factors in a birth cohort followed to age 32. *Psychological Medicine, 37*(3), 441–452. https://doi.org/10.1017/S0033291706009640

Murphy, J., Rowell, L., McQuaid, A., Timulak, L., O'Flynn, R., & McElvaney, J. (2017). Developing a model of working with worry in emotion-focused therapy: A discovery-phase task analytic study. *Counselling & Psychotherapy Research, 17*(1), 56–70. https://doi.org/10.1002/capr.12089

Navarrete, V., & Jenkins, S. R. (2011). Cultural homelessness, multiminority status, ethnic identity development, and self-esteem. *International Journal of Intercultural Relations, 35*(6), 791–804. https://doi.org/10.1016/j.ijintrel.2011.04.006

Nemeroff, C. B. (2016). Paradise lost: The neurobiological and clinical consequences of child abuse and neglect. *Neuron, 89*(5), 892–909. https://doi.org/10.1016/j.neuron.2016.01.019

Newby, J. M., McKinnon, A., Kuyken, W., Gilbody, S., & Dalgleish, T. (2015). Systematic review and meta-analysis of transdiagnostic psychological treatments for anxiety and depressive disorders in adulthood. *Clinical Psychology Review, 40*, 91–110. https://doi.org/10.1016/j.cpr.2015.06.002

Newman, M. G., & Llera, S. J. (2011). A novel theory of experiential avoidance in generalized anxiety disorder: A review and synthesis of research supporting a contrast avoidance model of worry. *Clinical Psychology Review, 31*(3), 371–382. https://doi.org/10.1016/j.cpr.2011.01.008

Nicolson, N. A. (2004). Childhood parental loss and cortisol levels in adult men. *Psychoneuroendocrinology, 29*(8), 1012–1018. https://doi.org/10.1016/j.psyneuen.2003.09.005

Norton, P. J. (2012). *Group cognitive–behavioral therapy of anxiety: A transdiagnostic treatment manual.* Guilford Press.

O'Brien, K., O'Keeffe, N., Cullen, H., Durcan, A., Timulak, L., & McElvaney, J. (2017). Emotion-focused perspective on generalized anxiety disorder: A qualitative analysis of clients' in-session presentations. *Psychotherapy Research, 29*(4), 524–540. https://doi.org/10.1080/10503307.2017.1373206

O'Brien, K., O'Keeffe, N., Cullen, H., Durcan, A., Timulak, L., & McElvaney, J. (2019). Emotion-focused perspective on generalized anxiety disorder: A qualitative analysis of clients' in-session presentations. *Psychotherapy Research, 29*(4), 524–540. https://doi.org/10.1080/10503307.2017.1373206

O'Connell Kent, J. A., Jackson, A., Robinson, M., Rashleigh, C., & Timulak, L. (2021). Emotion-focused therapy for symptoms of generalized anxiety in a student population: An exploratory study. *Counselling & Psychotherapy Research, 21*(2), 260–268. https://doi.org/10.1002/capr.12346

Öhman, A., & Rück, C. (2007). Four principles of fear and their implications for phobias. In J. Rottenberg & S. L. Johnson (Eds.), *Emotion and psychopathology: Bridging affective and clinical science* (pp. 167–189). American Psychological Association. https://doi.org/10.1037/11562-008

Öhman, A., & Soares, J. J. (1994). "Unconscious anxiety": Phobic responses to masked stimuli. *Journal of Abnormal Psychology, 103*(2), 231–240. https://doi.org/10.1037/0021-843X.103.2.231

Paivio, S. C., & Nieuwenhuis, J. A. (2001). Efficacy of emotion-focused therapy for adult survivors of child sexual abuse: A preliminary study. *Journal of Traumatic Stress, 14*(1), 115–133. https://doi.org/10.1023/A:1007891716593

Paivio, S. C., & Pascual-Leone, A. (2010). *Emotion-focused therapy for complex trauma: An integrative approach.* American Psychological Association. https://doi.org/10.1037/12077-000

Parker, J. G., Rubin, K. H., Erath, S. A., Wojslawowicz, J. C., & Buskirk, A. A. (2006). Peer relationships, child development, and adjustment: A developmental psychopathology perspective. In D. Cicchetti & D. J. Cohen (Eds.),

Developmental psychopathology: Theory and method (pp. 419–493). John Wiley & Sons.

Pascual-Leone, A. (2009). Dynamic emotional processing cycles in experiential therapy: Two steps forward, one step back. *Journal of Consulting and Clinical Psychology, 77*(1), 113–126. https://doi.org/10.1037/a0014488

Pascual-Leone, A. (2018). How clients "change emotion with emotion": A programme of research on emotional processing. *Psychotherapy Research, 28*(2), 165–182. https://doi.org/10.1080/10503307.2017.1349350

Pascual-Leone, A., & Greenberg, L. S. (2007a). Emotional processing in experiential therapy: Why "the only way out is through." *Journal of Consulting and Clinical Psychology, 75*(6), 875–887. https://doi.org/10.1037/0022-006X.75.6.875

Pascual-Leone, A., & Greenberg, L. S. (2007b). Insight and awareness in experiential therapy. In L. G. Castonguay & C. Hill (Eds.), *Insight in psychotherapy* (pp. 31–56). American Psychological Association. https://doi.org/10.1037/11532-002

Pascual-Leone, A., Yeryomenko, N., Sawashima, T., & Warwar, S. (2019). Building emotional resilience over 14 sessions of emotion focused therapy: Microlongitudinal analyses of productive emotional patterns. *Psychotherapy Research, 29*(2), 171–185. https://doi.org/10.1080/10503307.2017.1315779

Pascual-Leone, J. (1991). Emotions, development and psychotherapy: A dialectical constructivist perspective. In J. Safran & L. Greenberg (Eds.), *Emotion, psychotherapy and change* (pp. 302–335). Guilford Press.

Pearl, S. B., & Norton, P. J. (2017). Transdiagnostic versus diagnosis specific cognitive behavioural therapies for anxiety: A meta-analysis. *Journal of Anxiety Disorders, 46*, 11–24. https://doi.org/10.1016/j.janxdis.2016.07.004

Perls, F., Hefferline, R. F., & Goodman, P. (1994). *Gestalt therapy: Excitement and growth in the human personality*. The Gestalt Journal Press. (Originally published 1951)

Petitte, T., Mallow, J., Barnes, E., Petrone, A., Barr, T., & Theeke, L. (2015). A systematic review of loneliness and common chronic physical conditions in adults. *Open Psychology Journal, 8*(1, Suppl. 2), 113–132. https://doi.org/10.2174/1874350101508010113

Piaget, J. (1954). *The construction of reality in the child*. Basic Books.

Pressman, S. D., Cohen, S., Miller, G. E., Barkin, A., Rabin, B. S., & Treanor, J. J. (2005). Loneliness, social network size, and immune response to influenza vaccination in college freshmen. *Health Psychology, 24*(3), 297–306. https://doi.org/10.1037/0278-6133.24.3.297

Pugh, M., Bell, T., & Dixon, A. (2021). Delivering tele-chairwork: A qualitative survey of expert therapists. *Psychotherapy Research, 31*(7), 843–858. https://doi.org/10.1080/10503307.2020.1854486

Qualter, P., Vanhalst, J., Harris, R., Van Roekel, E., Lodder, G., Bangee, M., Maes, M., & Verhagen, M. (2015). Loneliness across the life span. *Perspectives on Psychological Science, 10*(2), 250–264. https://doi.org/10.1177/1745691615568999

Quirk, G. J. (2007). Prefrontal–amygdala interactions in the regulation of fear. In J. J. Gross (Ed.), *Handbook of emotion regulation* (pp. 27–46). Guilford Press.

Regier, D. A., Narrow, W. E., Clarke, D. E., Kraemer, H. C., Kuramoto, S. J., Kuhl, E. A., & Kupfer, D. J. (2013). *DSM-5* field trials in the United States and Canada, Part II: Test–retest reliability of selected categorical diagnoses. *American Journal of Psychiatry, 170*(1), 59–70. https://doi.org/10.1176/appi.ajp.2012.12070999

Reitz, E., Deković, M., & Meijer, A. M. (2006). Relations between parenting and externalizing and internalizing problem behaviour in early adolescence: Child behaviour as moderator and predictor. *Journal of Adolescence, 29*(3), 419–436. https://doi.org/10.1016/j.adolescence.2005.08.003

Rennie, D. L. (1990). Toward a representation of the client's experience of the psychotherapy hour. In G. Lietaer, J. Rombauts, & R. Van Balen (Eds.), *Client-centered and experiential psychotherapy in the nineties* (pp. 155–172). Leuven University Press.

Rice, L. N., & Greenberg, L. S. (Eds.). (1984). *Patterns of change: Intensive analysis of psychotherapy process*. Guilford Press.

Rice, L. N., Koke, C. J., Greenberg, L. S., & Wagstaff, A. (1979). *Manual for client vocal quality*. York University Counselling and Development Centre.

Rice, L. N., & Saperia, E. P. (1984). Task analysis and the resolution of problematic reactions. In L. N. Rice & L. S. Greenberg (Eds.), *Patterns of change: Intensive analysis of psychotherapeutic process* (pp. 29–66). Guilford Press.

Riley, C., Lee, M., Cooper, Z., Fairburn, C. G., & Shafran, R. (2007). A randomised controlled trial of cognitive–behaviour therapy for clinical perfectionism: A preliminary study. *Behaviour Research and Therapy, 45*(9), 2221–2231. https://doi.org/10.1016/j.brat.2006.12.003

Rogers, C. R. (1951). *Client-centered therapy: Its current practice, implications and theory*. Constable.

Rogers, C. R. (1957). The necessary and sufficient conditions of therapeutic personality change. *Journal of Consulting Psychology, 21*(2), 95–103. https://doi.org/10.1037/h0045357

Rogers, C. R. (1959). A theory of therapy, personality, and interpersonal relationships, as developed in the client-centered framework. In S. Koch (Ed.), *Psychology: A study of a science. Study 1, Vol. 3: Formulations of the person and the social context* (pp. 184–256). McGraw-Hill.

Rogers, C. R. (1961). *On becoming a person*. Houghton Mifflin Company.

Romero-Canyas, R., Downey, G., Berenson, K., Ayduk, O., & Kang, N. J. (2010). Rejection sensitivity and the rejection-hostility link in romantic relationships. *Journal of Personality, 78*(1), 119–148. https://doi.org/10.1111/j.1467-6494.2009.00611.x

Rosellini, A. J., Boettcher, H., Brown, T. A., & Barlow, D. H. (2015). A transdiagnostic temperament-phenotype profile approach to emotional disorder classification: An update. *Journal of Experimental Psychopathology, a2*(1), 110–128. https://doi.org/10.5127/pr.036014

Roy-Byrne, P. (2017). Transdiagnostic cognitive behavioral therapy and the return of the repressed [Editorial]. *JAMA Psychiatry, 74*(9), 867–868. https://doi.org/10.1001/jamapsychiatry.2017.1982

Safran, J. D., & Muran, J. C. (2000). *Negotiating the therapeutic alliance: A relational treatment guide.* Guilford Press.

Sauer-Zavala, S., Gutner, C. A., Farchione, T. J., Boettcher, H. T., Bullis, J. R., & Barlow, D. H. (2017). Current definitions of "transdiagnostic" in treatment development: A search for consensus. *Behavior Therapy, 48*(1), 128–138. https://doi.org/10.1016/j.beth.2016.09.004

Shafran, R., Cooper, Z., & Fairburn, C. G. (2002). Clinical perfectionism: A cognitive–behavioural analysis. *Behaviour Research and Therapy, 40*(7), 773–791. https://doi.org/10.1016/S0005-7967(01)00059-6

Shahar, B., Bar-Kalifa, E., & Alon, E. (2017). Emotion-focused therapy for social anxiety disorder: Results from a multiple-baseline study. *Journal of Consulting and Clinical Psychology, 85*(3), 238–249. https://doi.org/10.1037/ccp0000166

Shahar, B., Carlin, E. R., Engle, D. E., Hegde, J., Szepsenwol, O., & Arkowitz, H. (2012). A pilot investigation of emotion-focused two-chair dialogue intervention for self-criticism. *Clinical Psychology & Psychotherapy, 19*(6), 496–507. https://doi.org/10.1002/cpp.762

Shanahan, L., Copeland, W., Costello, E. J., & Angold, A. (2008). Specificity of putative psychosocial risk factors for psychiatric disorders in children and adolescents. *Journal of Child Psychology and Psychiatry, 49*(1), 34–42. https://doi.org/10.1111/j.1469-7610.2007.01822.x

Slade, T., & Andrews, G. (2001). *DSM-IV* and *ICD-10* generalized anxiety disorder: Discrepant diagnoses and associated disability. *Social Psychiatry and Psychiatric Epidemiology, 36*(1), 45–51. https://doi.org/10.1007/s001270050289

Smoller, J. W., Cerrato, F. E., & Weatherall, S. L. (2015). The genetics of anxiety disorders. In K. J. Ressler, D. S. Pine, & B. O. Rothbaum (Eds.), *Anxiety disorders: Translational perspectives on diagnosis and treatment* (pp. 47–66). Oxford University Press. https://doi.org/10.1093/med/9780199395125.003.0004

Stroebe, M. S., Hansson, R. O., Schut, H., & Stroebe, W. (Eds.). (2008). *Handbook of bereavement research and practice: Advances in theory and intervention.* American Psychological Association. https://doi.org/10.1037/14498-000

Sutton, J. (2007). *Healing the hurt within: Understand self-injury and self-harm, and heal the emotional wounds* (3rd ed.). How To Books.

Syed, S. A., & Nemeroff, C. B. (2017). Early life stress, mood, and anxiety disorders. *Chronic Stress, 1*, Article 2470547017694461. https://doi.org/10.1177/2470547017694461

Thompson, S., & Girz, L. (2018). *Taming your critic: A practical guide to EFT in group settings.* https://docs.wixstatic.com/ugd/581bce_83d6e4227311496da5bee151e2276e24.pdf

Thompson, S., & Girz, L. (2020). Overcoming shame and aloneness: Emotion-focused group therapy for self-criticism. *Person-Centered & Experiential Psychotherapies, 19*(1), 1–11. https://doi.org/10.1080/14779757.2019.1618370

Timulak, L. (2014). Witnessing clients' emotional transformation: An emotion-focused therapist's experience of providing therapy. *Journal of Clinical Psychology, 70*(8), 741–752. https://doi.org/10.1002/jclp.22109

Timulak, L. (2015). *Transforming emotional pain in psychotherapy: An emotion-focused approach*. Routledge. https://doi.org/10.4324/9781315760650

Timulak, L., & Elliott, R. (2003). Empowerment events in process-experiential psychotherapy of depression: An exploratory qualitative analysis. *Psychotherapy Research, 13*(4), 443–460.

Timulak, L., Iwakabe, S., & Elliott, R. (2019). Clinical implications of research on emotion-focused therapy. In L. S. Greenberg & R. N. Goldman (Eds.), *Clinical handbook of emotion-focused therapy* (pp. 93–109). American Psychological Association. https://doi.org/10.1037/0000112-004

Timulak, L., & Keogh, D. (2020). Emotion-focused therapy: A transdiagnostic formulation. *Journal of Contemporary Psychotherapy, 50*, 1–13. https://doi.org/10.1007/s10879-019-09426-7

Timulak, L., Keogh, D., Chigwedere, C., Wilson, C., Ward, F., Hevey, D., Griffin, P., Jacobs, L., & Irwin, B. (2018). A comparison of emotion-focused therapy and cognitive–behavioural therapy in the treatment of generalised anxiety disorder: Study protocol for a randomised controlled trial. *Trials, 19,* Article 506. https://doi.org/10.1186/s13063-018-2892-0

Timulak, L., Keogh, D., McElvaney, J., Schmitt, S., Hession, N., Timulakova, K., Jennings, C., & Ward, F. (2020). Emotion-focused therapy as a transdiagnostic treatment for depression, anxiety and related disorders: Protocol for an initial feasibility randomised control trial. *HRB Open Research, 3*, Article 7. https://doi.org/10.12688/hrbopenres.12993.1

Timulak, L., & McElvaney, J. (2016). Emotion-focused therapy for generalized anxiety disorder: An overview of the model. *Journal of Contemporary Psychotherapy, 46*, 41–52. https://doi.org/10.1007/s10879-015-9310-7

Timulak, L., & McElvaney, J. (2018). *Transforming generalized anxiety: An emotion-focused approach*. Routledge.

Timulak, L., McElvaney, J., Keogh, D., Martin, E., Clare, P., Chepukova, E., & Greenberg, L. S. (2017). Emotion-focused therapy for generalized anxiety disorder: An exploratory study. *Psychotherapy, 54*(4), 361–366. https://doi.org/10.1037/pst0000128

Timulak, L., & Pascual-Leone, A. (2015). New developments for case conceptualization in emotion-focused therapy. *Clinical Psychology & Psychotherapy, 22*(6), 619–636. https://doi.org/10.1002/cpp.1922

Toolan, R., Devereux, M., Timulak, L., & Keogh, D. (2019). Relationship between self-worrying and self-critical messages in clients with generalised anxiety engaging in emotion-focused worry dialogues. *Counselling & Psychotherapy Research, 19*(3), 294–300. https://doi.org/10.1002/capr.12229

Tronick, E. (2005). Why is connection with others so critical? The formation of dyadic states of consciousness and the expansion of individuals' states of consciousness: Coherence governed selection and the co-creation of meaning out of messy meaning making. In J. Nadel & D. Muir (Eds.), *Emotional development: Recent research advances* (pp. 293–315). Oxford University Press.

Umberson, D., Williams, K., Powers, D. A., Liu, H., & Needham, B. (2006). You make me sick: Marital quality and health over the life course. *Journal of Health and Social Behavior, 47*(1), 1–16. https://doi.org/10.1177/002214650604700101

Warwar, S. (2015, October). *Consolidating EFT chair work using in-session teaching and homework* [Paper presentation]. International Society for Emotion Focused Therapy Conference, Veldhoven, Netherlands.

Warwar, S., & Greenberg, L. S. (1999). *Client Emotional Arousal Scale–III* [Unpublished manuscript]. Department of Psychology, York University.

Warwar, S. H., & Ellison, J. (2019). Emotion coaching in action: Experiential teaching, homework, and consolidating change. In L. S. Greenberg & R. N. Goldman (Eds.), *Clinical handbook of emotion-focused therapy* (pp. 261–289). American Psychological Association. https://doi.org/10.1037/0000112-012

Watkins, E. R. (2018). *Rumination-focused cognitive-behavioral therapy for depression*. Guilford Press.

Watson, J. C. (2010). Case formulation in EFT. *Journal of Psychotherapy Integration, 20*(1), 89–100. https://doi.org/10.1037/a0018890

Watson, J. C., Goldman, R., & Vanaerschot, G. (1998). Empathic: A postmodern way of being? In L. S. Greenberg, J. C. Watson, & G. Lietaer (Eds.), *Handbook of experiential psychotherapy* (pp. 61–81). Guilford Press.

Watson, J. C., Gordon, L. B., Stermac, L., Kalogerakos, F., & Steckley, P. (2003). Comparing the effectiveness of process-experiential with cognitive–behavioral psychotherapy in the treatment of depression. *Journal of Consulting and Clinical Psychology, 71*(4), 773–781. https://doi.org/10.1037/0022-006X.71.4.773

Watson, J. C., & Greenberg, L. S. (2017). *Emotion-focused therapy for generalized anxiety*. American Psychological Association. https://doi.org/10.1037/0000018-000

Watson, J., Timulak, L., & Greenberg, L. S. (2019). Emotion-focused therapy for generalized anxiety disorder. In L. S. Greenberg & R. N. Goldman (Eds.), *Clinical handbook of emotion-focused therapy* (pp. 315–336). American Psychological Association. https://doi.org/10.1037/0000112-014

Way, B. M., & Taylor, S. E. (2011). Genetic factors in social pain. In G. MacDonald & L. A. Jensen-Campbell (Eds.), *Social pain: Neuropsychological and health implications of loss and exclusion* (pp. 95–119). American Psychological Association. https://doi.org/10.1037/12351-004

Weissman, N., Batten, S. V., Rheem, K. D., Wiebe, S. A., Pasillas, R. M., Potts, W., Barone, M., Brown, C. H., & Dixon, L. B. (2018). The effectiveness of emotionally focused couples therapy with veterans with PTSD: A pilot study. *Journal of Couple & Relationship Therapy, 17*(1), 25–41. https://doi.org/10.1080/15332691.2017.1285261

Whelton, W. J., & Greenberg, L. S. (2005). Emotion in self-criticism. *Personality and Individual Differences, 38*(7), 1583–1595. https://doi.org/10.1016/j.paid.2004.09.024

Wiebe, S. A., & Johnson, S. M. (2016). A review of the research in emotionally focused therapy for couples. *Family Process, 55*(3), 390–407. https://doi.org/10.1111/famp.12229

Wittenborn, A. K., Liu, T., Ridenour, T. A., Lachmar, E. M., Mitchell, E. A., & Seedall, R. B. (2019). Randomized controlled trial of emotionally focused couple therapy compared to treatment as usual for depression: Outcomes and mechanisms of change. *Journal of Marital and Family Therapy, 45*(3), 395–409. https://doi.org/10.1111/jmft.12350

Wnuk, S. M., Greenberg, L., & Dolhanty, J. (2015). Emotion-focused group therapy for women with symptoms of bulimia nervosa. *Eating Disorders, 23*(3), 253–261. https://doi.org/10.1080/10640266.2014.964612

Woldarsky Meneses, C., & McKinnon, J. M. (2019). Emotion-focused therapy for couples. In L. S. Greenberg & R. N. Goldman (Eds.), *Clinical handbook of emotion-focused therapy* (pp. 447–469). American Psychological Association. https://doi.org/10.1037/0000112-020

Index

Recognition, 27–28, 226–227
Reflection
  on critic dialogue, 214–216
  on emotion, 40
  empathic, 89
  evocative, 89
  in long-term therapy, 252
  on self-interruption dialogue, 151, 152
  on unfinished business task, 240, 241
  on worry dialogue, 168, 169
  on worry dialogue with intrusive object
    and self-compulsion, 179–181
  on worry dialogue with intrusive/
    phobic object, 173, 174
Refocusing, empathic, 48
Rejection, 22, 25–28, 202
Relational difficulties, EFT-C for treating,
  262–263
Relational qualities, of therapist, 87–89
Remote treatment delivery, 262
Resignation, 22, 69
Responsive Other, in unfinished business
  task, 230–232
Restricted emotional expressivity, 255
Retelling of traumatic emotional
  experiences task, 52, 154, 191–192
Rogers, C. R., 34, 38, 87, 103
Rumination
  as avoidance, 72
  enactment of, 190
  as problematic self-treatment, 67
  as symptomatic process, 153
  two-chair dialogue for self-rumination,
    154, 190–191
  worrying vs., 157, 190
Ruminator Chair, self-rumination dialogue,
  190, 191
Rupture repair, 51, 97–99, 245

S

Sadness. *See also* Loneliness
  adaptive, 237
  as chronic painful emotion, 20
  in EFT-T, 21–25
  fear with, 28, 29
  as instrumental emotion, 46
  as primary adaptive emotion, 43–44
  primary maladaptive experiences
    related to, 44, 76–77
  secondary emotions related to, 45
  shame and, 25
  unmet needs associated with, 79

Safety, 31, 226–227
Salgado, João, 42
Sauer-Zavala, S., 16–18
Secondary emotions
  in case conceptualization, 50, 68–71
  defined, 44–45, 73, 74
  diagnosis-specific patterns in, 108
  emotional regulation of, 122
  productivity of, 47
Self-awareness, 63–64, 88
Self-blame, 65–66
Self Chair, in unfinished business task,
  219–222, 224–227, 233–239
Self-compassion
  bathing in experience of, 213–214,
    236–237
  in corrective interpersonal-emotional
    experience, 95
  experience of offering, 229
  generating, as symptom-level task, 83
  to transform core emotional pain, 80, 81
Self-contempt, 65, 198–199
Self-criticism
  in critic dialogue, 196–197
  enactment of, 199–200
  experiential task associated with, 50
  function of, 195–196, 206–207
  marker of, 198–199
  and perfectionism, 18, 19
  as problematic self-treatment, 64–66
  in unfinished business task, 237–238
  worry as part of, 157
Self-defining judgment, 196
Self-disclosure, by therapist, 96
Self-evaluative conflict split, 50, 52–53.
    See also Self-self two-chair dialogue
    for problematic (self-evaluative)
    self-treatment
Self-exploratory mode, 105
Self-harm, 72, 196
Self-interruption, 141–151
  as avoidance, 141–151
  behavioral, 144, 145
  boundary-setting for, 142, 150–151
  in case conceptualization, 104
  as challenge in therapy process, 255
  emotional, 50, 67–68, 72
  enactment of, 145–146
  impact of, 142, 147–149
  markers of, 141–145, 147–149, 218
  two-chair dialogue for, 52–53, 144–151
  worrying and, 159

About the Authors

Ladislav Timulak, PhD, is course director of the Doctorate in Counselling Psychology at Trinity College Dublin, Ireland. In addition, Ladislav ("Laco"— read "Latso") is involved in various psychotherapy trainings in Ireland and internationally. Laco is both an academic and practitioner. His main research interest is psychotherapy research, particularly the development of emotion-focused therapy (EFT). He currently is developing this form of therapy as a transdiagnostic treatment for depression, anxiety, and related disorders. He has written or cowritten seven books, more than 90 peer-reviewed papers, and various chapters in both his native language, Slovak, and in English. His most recent books include *Transforming Emotional Pain in Psychotherapy: An Emotion-Focused Approach* (2015); *Transforming Generalized Anxiety: An Emotion-Focused Approach* (with James McElvaney; 2018); and *Essentials of Descriptive-Interpretive Qualitative Research: A Generic Approach* (with coauthor Robert Elliott), published by the American Psychological Association (2021). He serves on various editorial boards and, in the past, coedited *Counselling Psychology Quarterly*. He maintains a part-time private practice.

Daragh Keogh, DCounsPsych, is an assistant professor in the School of Psychology, Trinity College Dublin, Ireland. He is a counseling psychologist, a certified emotion-focused therapy (EFT) therapist, and a psychotherapy researcher with a particular interest in EFT and emotional change processes. He has been trial manager on three trials investigating the efficacy of EFT. He is a director at the Institute of Emotion-Focused Therapy Ireland, where he maintains a private practice working with children, adolescents, and adults.